Yang Shu'an

LAO ZI

Translated by Liu Shicong

Panda Books

Panda Books

First Edition 1997

Copyright © 1997 by CHINESE LITERATURE PRESS

ISBN 7 − 5071 − 0352 − 8

ISBN 0 − 8351 − 3186 − 6

Published by CHINESE LITERATURE PRESS

Beijing 100037, China

Distributed by China International Book Trading Corporation

35 Chegongzhuang Xilu, Beijing 100044, China

P.O. Box 399, Beijing, China

Printed in the People's Republic of China

Introduction

Teng Yun

In China, literary-style writings about historical events and prehistoric legends preceded fictional narrative and still today historical literature is the field which most clearly displays the strength of Chinese writers.

Chinese historical literature has an ancient origin and thus developed over a long period of time. It occupies a special place in the larger literary picture. Yet there is one aspect about it which stirs some regret. The history of Chinese civilisation is much longer than that of China as a country. Nevertheless it is with political and social history that Chinese historical literature is mainly concerned. For the most part it concerns evaluations of the successes and failures of state affairs, of emperors, princes, generals and ministers, and records the rise and fall of governments.

In Chinese historical literature, little — certainly not enough — has been written about civilisation and culture. In particular, over the last two thousand years, little has been written about our great scholars and philosophers, except in a cursory way. Having ploughed for some time in the fertile but constricted field of the historical novel as a genre, Yang Shu'an became keenly aware of the extensive areas lying fallow, still waiting to be dug over. He produced a number of historical novels featuring ancient thinkers and philosophers such as Confucius, Lao Zi and Sun Zi, for example. Confucius was the first great teacher of what was subsequently called the Confucianist School. Lao Zi was the progenitor of Taoism, and Sun Zi the master of military strategy. In ancient China, military science included not only tactics, strategies and military theories but, like Confucianism and Taoism, it constituted one of the origins of Chinese culture, ideology and learning. One would like to anticipate future biographies of other ancient thinkers and philosophers, or novels about the development of Chinese civilisation. So far as the three aforementioned novels are concerned, their publication has already begun to fulfill this need. Yang Shu'an's efforts in opening up a new literary landscape are creditable.

Novels based on the lives of ancient thinkers pose greater difficulties than those based on peasant uprisings, emperors, princes, generals and ministers; furthermore, they call for more sensitive aesthetic attributes and deeper analysis. Generally speaking, historical novels tend to be emotional, historical writings tend to be rational. Historical novels concerning ancient thinkers and philosophers fall somewhere between the emotional and the rational, or combine them both. Ancient thinkers were indeed both emotional and rational, but their emotions were generally under the control of their rational mind, their wisdom and philosophical thought. The writing of history, including that related to the history of thought, when devoted to biographies of thinkers, is usually confined to the thinkers' ideas and theories. Historical novels, however, centre on the spirit, behaviour and the state of mind of the protagonist, thus in order to create a lifelike image. But novels about ancient philosophers present further challenges. Like ordinary people, their psychologies and personalities are manifested in their everyday activities and social behaviour. On the other hand, unlike ordinary people, their psychologies and personalities give insight to their wisdom, philosophical thoughts, views and theories. The novelist simultaneously writes of the philosopher's physical and metaphysical being. Through the description of his physical being, the novelist reveals his metaphysical being and, by the same token, through the revelation of his metaphysical being, the novelist reveals his physical being. Thus the literary image of the thinker is created in the interweaving of the metaphysical and physical, the noumenonal and phenomenal. This is why it is a more difficult undertaking than the writing of historical works or historical novels in general, and this is where its unique aesthetic attribute lies.

The characterization of Lao Zi, as compared to that of Confucius and Sun Zi, is probably more complex, partly because historical and even legendary sources are sparse, and partly because the "indescribability and unnamability" of his Tao make it difficult not only to portray him as an individual but also to illustrate his thoughts and theories in a fictional approach.

However, complexities notwithstanding, the creation of a novel based on Lao Zi's life is too tantalising to resist, for, as the originator of one of China's ancient philosophies, he has had a strong and lasting impact on Chinese thinking. In his observations concerning opposites, either natural or human, he invariably adopts an unconventional viewpoint. For instance, between existence and non-existence, restlessness and tranquillity, intelligence and ignorance, brilliance and obscurity, high and low, long and short, thick and thin, in front and behind, straight and crooked, male and female, glory and humility, gain and loss, he always prefers the weak (the latter), rejecting the strong (the former). How unconventional!

More unusual is his concept of "non-action" (or non-interference). This by no means proposes detachment from the world; Lao Zi is deeply attached to it, actively involved in it. All his teachings are focused on how to get the world on the right track and how to cultivate man's virtue. This is what his *Dao De Jing* (the Book of Tao and Te) teaches. Throughout his life he was concerned about the operation of the world and the cultivation of man. He proposes to "get all things done" by "taking no action". He advocates abandoning intellectual pursuits and maintaining humility, but he exercises his great wisdom to pursue Tao and prove its existence. He links up thousands of natural and human phenomena with Tao and he finds Tao in everything he sees. He holds the view of keeping to the female "yin", eloquently and convincingly defending his belief; he keeps a low profile and makes himself deliberately obscure, but he endeavours to bring Tao into the spotlight; he advocates tranquillity and simplicity, but he spends a lifetime on the pursuit of his theory; he is content and he is most discontent at the same time; he would rather retreat one foot than advance one inch; he is passive and does not contend, but in fact, he is most active and persevering in his pursuit. Could any novelist resist the temptation to write about such an extraordinary thinker and philosopher?

Not only is Lao Zi a philosopher of wide erudition, he is also a philosopher with a poet's temperament. Of all the pre-Qin thinkers, Lao Zi and Zhuang Zi both had the poet's sensitivity and the philosopher's mind for intellectual enquiry. This can be seen in Lao Zi's description of Tao:

"Tao, as an existence, is impalpable and imperceptible"; "Heaven's net is wide spread; though its meshes are large, nothing slips through it"; "Bellows maybe empty but they are inexhaustible. When set in motion, they produces more wind"; "the gate of the mysterious female", "the mother of all creatures"; the "baby" who is ignorant but full of vitality; the "valley" to which all streams flow and the "sea" that collects water from all rivers... Lao Zi finds Tao in the frozen river and the melting ice; in winds that do not last for the whole morning and rains that do not last for a whole day; in grass which is soft when alive and withered when dead; in man who is soft when alive and stiff when dead; in water which is softer and weaker than everything in the world, yet has the power to break all things; he finds Tao when he sees the baby grip his fists tight though he is weak; that his small penis becomes erect because he is full of vitality, though he is not conscious of the unity of man and woman; that he does not cry himself hoarse though he cries all day, because he is in a harmonious state of mind. He even finds Tao in government from the way fish is cooked...

How would we describe Lao Zi? Is he philosopher or poet? Are his philosophical sparks kindled by his poetic insights or by his profound philosophical thinking? When poetic sensitivity and philosophical enquiries are combined in the one person of Lao Zi, does it not invite literary creation?

In writing *Lao Zi*, Yang Shu'an has found his way by combining illustrations of the difficult and the easy aspects of Lao Zi and describing their interaction. What he has written is a biographical novel based on the founder of one of the pre-Qin philosophical schools, not the ideological or academic biography of Lao Zi as a philosopher. In writing *Lao Zi*, his aim is not to evaluate Taoist culture in critical or complimentary terms, nor is it to illustrate his status in the history of Chinese thought. His aim is only to provide the reader with a vivid description of Lao Zi as a philosopher, his spirit, behaviour, activities, thoughts and personality. However, the author cannot help involving his own feelings and understanding in his descriptions. The conclusion remains to be drawn by the reader. I think his fictionalisation of Lao Zi is basically in compliance with the historical facts of Lao Zi. From the viewpoint of artistic creation the author has made Lao Zi into a believable character; even when viewed from the academic perspective, his portrayal of Lao Zi is not wide of the mark. Though experts in the field of philosophy and historical research have not yet finished their studies of the philosopher, Yang Shu'an's characterization provides a good understanding of Lao Zi, and readers of the translated version may develop a perspective by means of which they will be able to see the early forces at work in the formation of ancient Chinese culture and decipher some of the cultural origins of China's ancient history.

Yang Shu'an is a prolific novelist on historical subjects. Since 1981 he has published *September Chrysanthemums*, *The First Emperor to Unite China*, *The Tragedy of Chang'an*, *Emperor Sui*

Yang Di, The Talented and Romantic Madame Wu, The Short Romantic Life of the Emperor, Confucius, Lao Zi, and *Sun Zi.* His works move from the Sui and Tang dynasties back to the Qin and the pre-Qin period, his historical characters ranging from leaders of peasant uprisings and emperors to ancient philosophers. His writings are based on historical events, combined with his own perceptions that have evolved through his own temperament and interests, as well as by digging deep into the human nature of ancient figures. Most of his works emanate a distinctive poetic appeal. They respect the historical consciousness of the nation and its aesthetic traditions; yet in his cognition of history and his mode of narration, the author brings into play a modern approach. In his works fascinating stories are set against interesting historical backgrounds. Yang Shu'an's language is refined and elegant and his novels are appreciated by both specialised and popular tastes.

1

At last the high city wall of Luoyang came in sight. He was coming from a far-off small state, and arriving in the capital of the Son of Heaven, he felt apprehensive. Would he be able to find a suitable job to earn his living in this strange place?

The vast plain had a desolate look. The city wall appeared formidably high and thick, forming a long semi-circle in the distance. It was now visible from a dozen *li* away.

For years the country had been plagued by wars among the states, the strong bullying the weak, the majority dominated by the minority. In such a big country one could hardly find an area free of shrilling war cries and clashing arms. However, around this capital, there were no military fortifications; everything seemed to be progressing at an orderly pace. A peaceful place indeed!

Luoyang was less than one thousand *li* from Xiangyi County (later called Ku County and now Luyi County in Henan Province). Government officials, riding in horse-drawn carriages along the straight, broad courrier route, would cover it in no more than two or three days, but Li Er, travelling on foot and, in the meanwhile, having to earn his food by polishing bronze mirrors, had taken nearly two months.

> Every inch of the land under Heaven
> Is the King's land;
> Everyone on the land
> Is the King's subject.
> ....

This was the song officials and scholars used to sing to describe the absolute sway of the Zhou Empire when it was in its
prime. Today, however, the emperor had little authority beyond
the two hundred-*li* boundaries of the capital, let alone over "every
inch of the land".

Only the city wall, constructed under the personal supervision
of Duke Zhou, still bore the magnificence of the old by-gone
days of grandeur — none of the small states had city walls that
could compare with it.

Approaching the East Gate, Li Er saw two huge characters
— Tripod Gate — etched high on the tower above.

The gate tower commanded three arched entrances through
which three fifty-metre-wide boulevards shot out, straight and
parallel.

Li Er approached an old man sunning himself by the gate.
"Good day, sir, may I ask why this is called 'Tripod
Gate'?"

The old man sized him up: "This must be your first visit to
Luoyang, I suppose?"

"That's right. This is my very first visit here."

"Where did the name 'Tripod Gate' come from? Thereby
hangs a tale," the old man continued. "When Yu was emper-
or of the Xia Dynasty, he reshuffled the twelve states of his
realm into nine, then issued a decree commanding all nine states
to present their best bronze, to be cast into tripods, as tribute to
the empire. Nine tripods were cast, each representing a state.
Cast on the surface of each was various kinds of information:
a geographical map of the state, its landscape and vegetation, its
indigenous birds and animals, local legends about spirits and
monsters and the amount of tribute the state had paid. When the
Xia Empire fell, it lost the nine tripods to the Shang Dynasty.
When the Shang was overthrown by the Zhou Dynasty, the
tripods, as a symbol of state power, were transferred from Chaoge
(near Qixian County of Henan Province today) to Luoyang.
They were moved into the city through this gate, which, for that

reason, came to be called the Tripod Gate.

"These bronze tripods," continued the old man, "were transported in huge carriages specially built for the purpose. Along their journey of over several hundred *li*, they were accompanied by lively fanfare, with singing and dancing to musical instruments all the way. It was a thrilling spectacle, so I have been told." He sighed: "But that was in the days gone by. What about now? You'll see for yourself. The capital has become quite a miserable place...." Another sigh.

"There's no need to sigh about it," said Li Er sympathetically. "Prosperity is always followed by depression. It's the way things are in the world. Sometimes the prosperity lasts longer, at other times, not so long, that's all."

"Young man, you must've come from the State of Chu."

"Correct, but not completely correct."

"What do you mean?"

"You must've guessed by the way I'm dressed. You're right in one sense: the area I come from has become part of Chu. Regardless of that, we still call it Chen, its former name, not Chu."

"I see," said the old man. "However, I did not detect the Chu characteristic in you by the way you are dressed, but by the way you talk. That is, by your attitude toward the world. To me, it seems slightly indifferent."

Scholars coming to Luoyang from various states in the midland were saddened by the miserable appearance of the capital. They chanted the ode "Millet Grows Dense in Rows" to release the pent-up grief in their hearts.

> Millet's growing row on row
> And sorghum seedlings start,
> Wandering on the country road,
> Great sorrow fills my heart.
> Friends all say that I'm upset;
> Others ask me what I want;

Oh, righteous Heaven! Tell me!
Who has messed up our country?

Millet's growing row on row
The sorghum ears reach high,
Wandering on the country road,
I'm confused and wish to die,
Friends all say that I'm upset
Others ask me what I want.
Oh, righteous Heaven! Tell me!
Who has messed up our country?

Millet's growing row on row
The sorghum ears are ripe,
Wandering on the country path
I feel choked and breathless,
Friends all say that I'm upset
Others ask me what I want.
Oh, righteous Heaven! Tell me!
Who has messed up our country?

This highly emotional poem rich as mellow wine with love of country, and fraught with despair could not have been written by anyone other than a descendant of the royal house of the Ji's who felt heartbroken at the decline of the old capital.

"When the Quanrong tribes from the west took the capital Haojing, they killed Emperor You. Then Emperor Ping moved the capital east to Luoyang. Later when court ministers revisited Haojing and saw millet and sorghum growing in the ruins of the old shrines and palace halls, they were overcome with grief. Oh, Heavens above! Who brought the country to this tragic fate? Wasn't it Emperor You, by plunging the princes into perpetual wars?

"Today people chant this same poem in despair over the decadence of the eastern capital, Luoyang. 'Oh, righteous Heaven!

Who has messed up our country?' If Emperor You was to blame then, who is to blame now? One can easily see that the country is going downhill, but it's not easy to pinpoint exactly who is responsible.''

The old man's eyes filled with tears and he wiped them off on his sleeve. With a forced smile, he went on: "You see, I am being cynical again.''

"Life is short — as short as a wink of the eye,'' said Li Er. "Why burden yourself with so many worries, sir?''

"You're right,'' agreed the old man. "When the sky falls, it will be propped up by tall people. Why should I worry? Since this is your first visit to Luoyang, I assume you've no relatives or friends to stay with. You are welcome to come and stay with me at my humble place.''

"Thank you for your generous offer, but first I'd like to pay Minister Wangsun Yi a visit.''

"I see. Minister Wangsun Yi treats scholars with great hospitality. You really must go to see him first. If he kindly asks you to stay, you will have no worries about a roof over your head or where your next meal is coming from. Besides, you have a chance to be recommended for some office. If, for any reason, he is not prepared to entertain you, you're always welcome to come back to me.'' The old man pointed to a mansion not far from the gate, nestled in trees, the picture of tranquillity.

The capital was built in a square ten-*li* by ten-*li*, the metropolis of the midland. The southern part of the city was occupied by royal palaces, ancestral temples and residential areas for families of the nobility, while located in the northern part were the markets, handicraft cottages, pottery kilns, masonry worksites and bone-processing workshops. In those days, this sort of arrangement was known as a "south for the court, north for the market" layout. The space in between was taken up by living quarters for ordinary people. The desolate appearance of this area formed a strong contrast to the magnificent palaces to the south and the thriving market place to the north.

Entering the gate, Li Er turned left and soon arrived at a large residential complex. It was enclosed in high walls covered with large fancy tiles serving both as reinforcement and adornment. Even compared to the fine houses of the nobles, it appeared magnificent.

Minister Wangsun Yi's original surname, Ji, was the same as that of the emperor, indicating that his ancestors were related to the Son of Heaven. In those days, the descendants of royal families, five generations removed, gave up the surname of their clan and adopted the given name of the fifth generation, or the name of their fief, as their surname. So a family five generations from the royal house branched out into several dozen or several hundred families all with different surnames.

The Wangsuns had been holding ministerial positions in the Zhou government for decades. Two or three generations back, there had been a clan member named Wangsun Man, a minister celebrated for his profound learning and compelling eloquence. Once Prince Zhuang of the State of Chu blatantly demanded entrance to Luoyang to see the nine tripods, it was Wangsun Man who, with skilful diplomatic parlance, talked the prince into dropping his demand, thus ensuring the safety of the empire and retaining the dignity of the emperor.

The Son of Heaven, out of gratitude to Wangsun Man for his meritorious performance, lavished him with gifts and copious funds to extend his mansion.

The ministerial post and the great estate of the Wangsuns eventually passed on to Wangsun Yi, a bold, expansive man by nature, generous and hospitable to scholars. He was interested in entertaining persons with some special faculty or outstanding attainment, regardless of their social status or personal relationship with him. He wanted to serve the Royal House like his ancestor Wangsun Man.

When Li Er came to Wangsun Yi's house, he was surprised to find that it was not heavily guarded, as were those of other noblemen, except for two doorkeepers stationed either side of the gate. His visitors included elegantly dressed noblemen, riding in and out in highly adorned horsedrawn carriages, and common people in ordinary garb, who came and went on foot, often shabbily shod.

"Please inform Minister Wangsun that a young person from the south is here to see him," Li Er said to the doorkeepers.

Scrutinising him thoroughly, one of them asked: "Your name, please?"

"Li Er; literary name, Dan."

"Do you have any special faculty or outstanding attainment?"

"No. None."

"None?" the doorkeeper was at a loss. "What shall I tell him about you?"

"Just tell him what I told you."

"If the minister refuses to see you then don't blame me."

"It won't be your fault."

The doorkeeper turned to go inside, musing to himself: I have heard that southerners are extremely crafty, but this one seems quite honest. Minister Wangsun takes no one without some sort of speciality. Any visitor would say he was good at something, true or not. But him? He says he is not good at anything. This must mean he has come hoping to be put up as a retainer.

Listening to the doorkeeper's introduction, Wangsun Yi decided there was something interesting about the new arrival.

Over the years a good number of people have come to me, he mulled, some saying they are resourceful and eloquent, others that they are strong and good at martial arts; some even saying that they are skilful at thievery; but all have been received with courtesy. They are put up at the hostels, fed good meals and clothed in fine apparel. They have all been treated like honourable guests.

All in all, they are a mixed batch, he concluded. Some are as good as their words, others are not. Those who fail to live up to their words feel embarrassed and leave of their own accord.

But so far, I have not received anyone who simply comes and tells me that he is not good at anything!

"Bring him in and let me see what kind of person he is."

Wangsun Yi was sitting on a reed mat on the floor, in a long gown with loose sleeves and a flat-topped hat — an informal garment for the occasion. But the jade ornaments on his girdle and the sword hanging at his side for self-defence were symbolic of his social status. He was hearty and robust, looking young for his age; he was no more than forty.

Doubling himself up in a courteous bow, Li Er offered a few preliminary remarks of respect for the minister and introduced himself. Then he stepped back, his arms hanging down at full length by his sides.

What a queer name, Wangsun Yi thought. Why is his name related to "ear" (the character "er" means ear in Chinese)?

He glanced at Li Er's ears, and noticed the lobes were unusually long, conspicuously longer than normal.

Wangsun Yi motioned him to sit on a mat next to him.

"At a time of social turmoil like this, young scholars like you are in great demand," he began. To the east there are the states of Qi and Lu, to the south, Chu, and to the west, there is Jin. In fact an enterprising young man your age has a choice of many places. Why did you choose to come to a place like Luoyang which is showing signs of drastic decline? You wouldn't expect to find exceptional opportunities here, would you?"

"The world has too many troubles for me to worry about. I'm looking for a quiet place to get away from it, that's all. As for expecting a great opportunity for advancement, that notion has never crossed my mind. That's not what I came for."

"Ha! Ha! I guess this is how you southerners manage to keep aloof from the world, is that it?"

Leaving no time for Li Er to cut in, Wangsun Yi went on: "The unconventional attitude adopted by you southerners has been interpreted in different ways. Some say it's lofty and expansive; others say it's decadent and cynical; still others say the attitude is evoked by contempt which the midland holds for 'the outside'. That is, 'since the world is not mine, why should I worry about it?' There is another theory. It says the unconventional attitude of the south has to do with its lovely landscape, which has fostered flights of imagination and uninhibited yearnings in their character. There is a variety of conjectures about this. I have no idea which to follow."

Bypassing the question Li Er continued on the same train of thought:

"Northerners take a serious, involved attitude toward the world; this has been interpreted in different ways. Some say it is the result of their conceitedness. As they do not know how big the world is, they think of their country as the centre of the world, of their nation as the most civilised and orthodox, and of other peoples as barbarous tribes. They believe the midland is the world, and therefore abominable, take it upon themselves to get the world on track. It sounds as if, without the midland, the sky would fall and the world would become a sinister place.

"Others say their seriousness, their sense of involvement and their down-to-earth outlook are attributable to their poor land resources and harsh living conditions. Because the land is barren, crops do not grow well; because crops do not grow well, their life is hard. Every day they face problems of life and death. So they cannot be lackadaisical, they have to take life seriously; they have to cling to life, not distance themselves from it; they have to be practical, not aloof.

"There have been dozens of interpretations and I also am not sure which to follow. That's why I've come out to see the world."

Wangsun Yi had received many learned and eloquent scholars in this hall, but not one of them had come up with such original and insightful ideas.

Though the people of the midland are inclined to throw out random comments, he cogitated, and they never leave themselves open to comment. This young man, however, with the eloquence of a southerner, is so bold as to criticise the northerners for their seriousness and conceitedness — something they have inherited from their remote ancestors and worshipped as absolutely correct. Wangsun Yi was shocked to the marrow at the boldness of this young guest.

There was one thing that had puzzled Wangsun Yi for many years. The State of Qin to the west and the State of Chu to the south were becoming strong and prosperous with each passing day. But consider the Zhou Empire; it was the sole orthodox monarchy after the Xia and Shang dynasties, ruled by the Son of Heaven; it had established the rules of propriety and the music for ceremonial rituals. So why was the Zhou Empire declining so obviously? He had long tried in vain to find the answer.

This young man had a sharp and penetrating mind. Perhaps he would be able to find the answer.

"Young man, I find what you are saying very interesting," said Wangsun Yi. "If you wish to make a study of the world, you may stay with me and I'll do what I can to help you."

"Government ministers and officials in the north, like you, receive and entertain people for practical purposes. People coming here are either counsellors or professional politicians, swordsmen or supermen or even pickpockets; in any case, they are useful in practical matters. You have your eyes on what is immediately profitable, or of some use. But I differ from those people. I am interested in thinking about spiritual things only. In fact I am of no use to you at all in practical terms. Would you still want me to stay?"

"Do not suppose that only you southerners are interested in spiritual things and that we northerners are not. The nine tripods, which my ancestor debated in defence of, can also provoke profound thinking. Don't you agree?"

The unexpected question found Li Er somewhat tongue-tied.

Wangsun Yi burst into hearty laughter.

The historic debate over the nine tripods had evoked great mental concussions and the ripples caused by the concussions had not subsided in the mind of either Wangsun Yi or Li Er.

2

The thriving city of Ying (Jiangling County, present-day Hubei Province), capital of the State of Chu, basked sprawlingly on the southern bank of the Yangtse River. Historically a new-comer, it was by now well developed and second to none of the big cities in the midland, where the Empire of Zhou was located, and which had prospered for two or three millennia. Its streets, lined with shops and stores, were packed with jostling customers.

Recently Ying was abuzz with sensational news: The recently-enthroned Prince Zhuang of Chu had cast a set of magnificent bronze bells for use as chimes. There were several dozen in all, the nine largest were bigger and heavier than the nine tripods arrayed before the court palace in Luoyang.

The people of Chu were perplexed.

The Son of Heaven and the other states in the midland had been accusing Chu of disobedience and disloyalty to the empire. This was made an excuse for crossing the Yangtse River to launch punitive attacks on Chu. Admonitions to the prince, both open and discreet, private and official, were raised: Since you have now cast bells even bigger and heavier than the nine tripods, the Son of Heaven and the other states in the north will consider that you are over-ambitious. You have given them another excuse to attack. This is simply inviting trouble.

The State of Chu had been developed on what was originally virgin land wild with shrubs and brambles.

The forefathers of the Chu people, poorly dressed and inadequately equipped, toiled under harsh conditions to reclaim the land and develop it. After conquering several dozen small states and extending its power across an uncreasingly well-developed area, the now prosperous state of Chu covered several thousand square *li* south of the Yangtse River.

But this realm founded by the ancestors under arduous conditions seemed destined for certain ruin, for the new prince spent his days in sensual pleasures to the neglect of state affairs.

In spite of all admonitions, Prince Zhuang went ahead with his decision to hold a grand opening ceremony for the newly-cast chimes.

The Chu palace was magnificent, its towering roof resting on tall wooden pillars set on solid bases. The hall was so spacious that the foremost archer of the day found it impossible to shoot an arrow out from one wall to hit the wall opposite.

Adorning the palace walls were colourful paintings arranged in sets, illustrating old legends, which also served as inspiration for the songs and dances performed at rites, ceremonies, and also at sacrifices to please the gods. Differing in style from those of the north, the songs had a pronounced rhythm to which the dancers paced and whirled in unrestrained and energetic movements.

At sacrifices, young men and women approached each other to choose a member of the opposite sex for companionship, which more often than not led to the singing of love songs.

Following a few favourites from the legendary repertoire, the women would sing love songs for Prince Zhuang:

Tall trees cover the South Mountain but I
cannot rest in their shades
There's a maid strolling by the Han River but I
cannot approach her
So wide is the Han River I cannot swim across
So long is the Yangtse River I cannot skirt its shores.

This was a melancholy air about a young man who failed in his efforts to win the young woman he was in love with. The song was collected by the musicians of the Zhou Dynasty and categorised as a folk song. To suit the melody of the midland, the four lines were broken down:

> Tall trees cover the South Mountain,
> But I cannot rest in their shade.
> There's maid strolling by the Han River,
> But I cannot approach her.
> So wide is the Han River,
> I cannot swim across.
> So long is the Yangtse River,
> I cannot skirt its shores.

Though the Chu dialect and accent were maintained, the song was sung in a rhythm the local people were accustomed to.

The newly-cast musical bells hung in three rows from a huge wooden rock. The horizontal beams of the middle and lower rows were each supported by either the hands or heads of three bronze figures with swords hanging from their waists. The bronze figures propping up the lower beam, from which the nine gigantic bells hung, stood on large, ornate bronze bases. The nine bells, each weighing over ten thousand *jin* were clearly intended to outshine the nine tripods in Luoyang.

The musicians, colourfully costumed, set the ringing with T-shaped wooden hammers and long sticks. The high-pitched bells gave forth ringing, melodious chimes while the bass ones emitted deep, resonant sounds that came in waves. The nine thick, heavy bells especially, discharged a harmonious melody that re-sounded far and wide like thunder enveloping the universe.

However, the grand opening ceremony shocked some ministers loyal to the prince.

Wu Can, an elderly, high-ranking minister, sought an audi-ence with the prince at the risk of his head.

Prince Zhuang was sitting in his magnificent palace hall, his left hand resting on his concubine from the State of Zheng, his right hand on a beautiful palace maid from the State of Yue. Be-fore them was a long table laden with rich food and wine. The prince was enthralled by the palace maids dancing to the accompaniment of the bells.

Wu Can approached the prince with a low bow.

The prince cast a glance at him in haste and asked:

"Are you here to see the bells? Big, aren't they? The biggest ones are even bigger than the nine tripods the Empire of Zhou boasts about so much."

"In the beginning we were not very sure if we would be able to cast them," the prince said, "because we had never cast such huge ones before. When the bells came out of the moulds black and rough they looked capable of only a bang or a clang, nothing more. As it turned out, our worries were absolutely unnecessary. Listen to this beautiful melody! It's amazing that awkward-looking bells like these can work such wonders!"

"I am not here to see the bells, Your Majesty," Wu Can said.

"What are you here for, then?"

"I came here with a riddle that I can't puzzle out. So I must beg Your Majesty's help."

"A riddle? What riddle?"

"A riddle that I hope will add to Your Majesty's amusement."

"Fine, fine! Let me hear it."

"There is a bird on the top of the mountain," Wu Can began. "It has perched there for three years but it has never made an attempt to fly or shown any inclination to sing. I wonder what bird it is?"

The prince who had been on the throne for exactly three years realised instantly to what the riddle alluded. With a smile, he offered his interpretation:

"For three years the bird has made no attempt to fly, but once it starts flying, it will soar up into the sky; for three years it has shown no inclination to sing, but once it bursts into song, it will startle the world. I can assure you, this is an extraordinary bird." The prince's interpretation astonished Wu

Can. This shows Prince Zhuang is an ambitious man, he thought, rather than a fatuous, incorrigible ruler smothered in sensual pleasures.

"I am a wiser man now, Your Majesty." With that he took his leave with grave ceremony.

Prince Zhuang had deliberately put aside state affairs for three years. He ascended the throne when still young and needed time to toughen his resolve and prepare himself for wielding power. He lay low during those years, learning how to grasp and handle the affairs of state. He sat back and observed, trying to determine who was loyal to him and who was not. In the meantime a long-term strategy took shape in his mind that would stand him in good stead in the coming years.

Now the three years had passed and the fully-fledged prince was ready to fly. Abstaining from sensual pleasures, he now dedicated himself to the welfare of his kingdom. He appointed virtuous and talented people as ministers and officials who would help him in his efforts to straighten out internal affairs. He advocated frugality and took vigorous measures to revive agriculture and productive undertakings. By recalling the hard-working spirit of their ancestors, he encouraged his people to work for the strength and prosperity of the state.

He increased the manufacturing of a new bronze weapon — the halberd — a combination of the conventional battle-ax and spear, both lethal, the former with a chop, the latter with a thrust. Combining the merits of both, the halberd was doubly effective.

He innovated the chariot for practical purposes. The traditional four-horse chariot, which was speedier and was a more effective deterrent on a plain, easily overturned on hilly and bumpy terrain. The new chariot, known as the Chu Chariot, with its smaller cabin fixed on a broader chassis, could be driven over almost any type of terrain.

Soon Chu boasted a prosperous economy and a strong military build-up. With no trouble to worry about in the south, Prince Zhuang's mind now began turning toward the north. In particular, asleep or awake, he dreamt of the fabulous nine tripods in Luoyang.

He had heard about the tripods and longed to see them, but the opportunity had never presented itself. They kept appearing in his mind's eye, now glittering with golden brilliance, now darkened with green discolouration; at one moment they turned into cooking utensils for noble families, at another they loomed large, towering above Mount Jing — the highest mountain in the northwest of Chu.

It was said that they were a symbol of royal authority and its power of suppression, that these nine tripods were behind all the humiliations that Chu had suffered. They were believed to have been cast by Yu — emperor of a unified China — over one thousand years earlier. He had divided China into nine administrative districts, called Ji, Yu, Yong, Yang, Xu, Yan, Liang, Qing and Jing, and issued a decree demanding that the magistrate of each district should present its best possible bronze to the central government.

At the foot of Mount Jing (not the one northwest of Chu, but one west of Luoyang) in the midland, near the Tong Pass, there was a large, old smelting works which were known for casting tripods. In ancient times the Yellow Emperor, after defeating his rivals Chiyou and Emperor Yan, had a gigantic tripod cast here of metal excavated from Mount Shou. It was a memorial to his victory and a symbol of the supreme power which he had established, setting himself up as the ruler of all China.

Legend had it that the Yellow Emperor's tripod was four and one third metres tall, and that engraved on the outside, were images of dragons flying amidst clouds, mythical animals, ghosts, and spirits.

Emperor Yu, cast nine tripods to represent each of the nine districts into which he had divided his territory. Carved on the tripods were birds of prey, fierce beasts, ghosts and monsters, respectively characteristic of the nine districts. The number "nine", according to the *I Ching* (*Book of Change*) also stood for strength and the supreme power of the emperor.

The tripod the Yellow Emperor had cast was placed at the foot of Mount Jing and Emperor Yu's nine tripods were displayed in front of his court palace. Emperor Yu, in his lifetime fight against floods, had travelled all over the country and seen countless birds of prey, fierce beasts, ghosts and monsters. He knew the kind of hardships and dangers travellers were likely to encounter. When they saw the tripods before setting out on their journey, they knew what to guard against. The tripods virtually served them as guide maps.

The nine tripods, in the course of being passed down from Xia to Shang and then to Zhou, gradually lost their intended function as guide maps. They had become treasures that emperors used to enhance their status and impose their authority.

Those in possession of the tripods were considered legitimate; all others were thought of as "outsiders", "barbarians", and so forth, fit only to submit.

The State of Chu, a territory within a circumference of five thousand *li*, was a hub of communication with Sichuan to the west, the salt-producing sea to the east and Dongting Lake to the south. It was an area rich in rice and fish, where the people had never known cold or hunger. The numerous rivers and lakes provided easy transportation on water. Deposits of gold and bronze were abundant; bamboo groves and forests flourished in every part of the land. With armed forces numbering up to a million and a decade's grain reserves, Chu was rival enough for the midland.

What right did the midland have to look down on Chu? What right did it have to call the Chu people "barbaric southern tribes"? What right did it have to infringe upon Chu's territory and exact tribute?

Today the House of Zhou, with its armed forces reduced to less than ten thousand and its influence waning, had little authority beyond its capital Luoyang. Was Chu made its subject state then, simply because it possessed the nine tripods?

I must go and see for myself what the tripods look like and what mysterious power they have, Prince Zhuang thought. This time, however, I am not going to Luoyang to pay respects or tribute. I am going there to demonstrate the strength of Chu and induce the midland to change its contemptuous attitude. This, of course, would be held highly impermissible by the Empire of Zhou and the other states in the north. Nevertheless I need an excuse for going to Luoyang — some sort of reason, he thought.

Suddenly his eyes fell upon the bamboo strip bearing an important message. The inscribed information just delivered to the court a few days earlier concerned the infiltration of Rong tribesmen from Guazhou (in Dunhuang, present-day Gansu Province) to the Yichuan area not far from Luoyang; they had been forced to migrate because of incursions by the states of Qin and Jin in the northwest.

It occurred to Prince Zhuang that the presence of Rong tribesmen in the Yichuan area could provide him with an excellent pretext to launch military manoeuvres morthward. According to reports he had received, the Rong tribesmen had long been driven eastward, out beyond the deserts, and at the same time, kept from impinging on areas near the midland. They had been harassing the states of Qin and Jin along the upper frontiers and brought retaliation upon themselves: The two states jointly drove them back toward the midland, to place them under control of the strong armed forces there, hoping some day the tribes would mingle with and gradually become assimilated by the local people.

But according to the law of the Zhou Empire, Rong tribesmen were forbidden to settle anywhere on its territory. This factor entered into Prince Zhuang's calculations: If I just take one hundred thousand soldiers and move up to Luoyang under the pretext of fighting against the Rong tribesmen, neither the empire nor any of the other states can find valid objections. He decided on a march to the midland.

The prince had recently reorganised his armies into three wings, each with a separate task clearly defined, and at the same time, having the ability to form an integral combat force when need arose. The right wing was to ensure the safety of the Commander-in-Chief and his chariot; the left was in charge of provisions; the forward contingent of the central wing was to gather information about the enemy and lead the three wings with flags, and the rear of the central wing was brought up by a powerful assault brigade; in the centre was the seat of the Commander-in-Chief.

Each chariot, in addition to carrying armoured charioteers, was reinforced with one hundred foot-soldiers, twenty-five more than the number that accompanied a midland chariot. As for foot-soldiers, the Chu forces far outnumbered those of the north.

The day before the armies were to set out, Prince Zhuang treated his generals and soldiers to a sumptuous feast. When all had assembled, the prince addressed the gathering:

"It has been three years since I decided to lie low in order to fly high; I intended to keep quiet in order that we could astonish the world later, some day. Since then I have abstained from sensual pleasures and all entertainment. We have now become a strong and prosperous state. As we are now free from trouble at home, I have decided to venture on an expedition to the midland. Before we set out, let us drink together, to our heart's content. This can serve in advance as part of your reward.

"Drink as much as you like, for tomorrow we set out. Once we are on the march, there will be no more wine until we return in triumph to the capital."

Course after course of food was served with plenty of wine. Music filled the air. The warriors ate and drank heartily. Knowing that for months ahead there would be no wine, and perhaps even a scarcity of water, they kept refilling their cups. It was a marathon banquet. When the sun began to set, they were still in the midst of their revelry.

The prince gave a signal to light torches so the banquet could continue. He was now getting tipsy, and the difference between himself as the prince and the armymen as his subjects grew blurred. He summoned Xu Ji — one of his concubines — to serve the warriors more wine.

Xu Ji was a beautiful young princess from the State of Xu (today in Xuchang, Henan Province). Xu was a small state sandwiched between Chu and the midland. Though Xu had to bow to the formidable Chu, it still observed the proprieties formulated by the midland. Prince Zhuang doted on her and often on formal occasion arranged for her to appear.

The most beautiful woman in the Chu palace, mere mention of her name evoked admiration throughout the state. Hearing that she was to join them, the soldiers all turned toward the entrance, straining to catch a glimpse of her charming presence. Presently the concubine, escorted on both sides by palace maids, appeared at the door and entered into the hall with a graceful flowing gait. She was a gorgeous woman. The soldiers were dazzled, and the hall became more brilliant with her presence.

Xu Ji went from table to table, serving wine with a smile in her eyes which never looked anyone directly in the face. She poured wine slightly below the brim of the bowl to keep it from spilling. Her decorous manner elicited among the warriors a mingling sense of intimacy and respect.

The warm, hospitable atmosphere in the hall brought the lively banquet to a climax. The soldiers were served in turn, and in turn they stood up with big bowls in their hands and downed the wine with a few gulps. Together with heartfelt thanks to Xu Ji, they swore loud oaths of allegiance to the prince. Prince Zhuang, enthralled by the enthusiasm and combat spirit of the warriors, was overcome with happiness.

The soldiers were drinking toasts to each other and the banquet was punctuated with waves of enthusiasm. Suddenly a strange gust of wind swept into the hall, blowing out all the torches, turning the hall into complete darkness.

Taking advantage of the commotion, a shadowy figure stealthily darted over to Xu Ji, plucked at her sleeve, intending to steal a kiss. With a jerk of her left hand, Xu Ji yanked her sleeve out of his grasp and with her right hand, reached out for his hat and broke its tassel. Scared, the man hurried off in a panic.

By the moonlight streaming in through the windows, Xu Ji went up to the prince with half of the tassel in her hand. She told him in a whisper what had happened just then and showed him the broken tassel. She urged the prince to have the torches lit quickly lest the hoodlum should manage to slip away.

Prince Zhuang patted her on the shoulder and asked her to keep quiet about the incident. He reassured her that he knew what was the wise thing to do. He spoke up in the darkness:

"I believe the wine has made most of you feel too warm. I suggest you take off your hats and keep drinking. Please do not stand on ceremony."

The guests all took off their hats and now it was not possible to tell whose hat tassel was broken, who the miscreant was. When the torches were lit up again they took up their bowls and resumed drinking, as if nothing had happened. The banqueting continued late into the night.

Back in the rear quarters, Xu Ji, her face still white with anger, complained to the prince:

"Even ordinary women have the right to demand respect, let alone a concubine of the prince. At your request I went to serve wine to the soldiers. They should have felt honoured and grateful, but this rogue tried to take liberties with me. If you let him off like this, how can you expect to maintain a distinction between men and women to say nothing of the proprieties between Your Majesty and your subjects?"

The prince explained with a smile: "Under normal circumstances when the prince drinks with his ministers and officials he is not supposed to drink more than three bowls of wine and the banquet has to be arranged during the day, not at night. But today's banquet is different. After the banquet the armies will march and the soldiers will not be allowed to drink. Tonight I wanted them to have as much as they wanted before they set out. One sometimes forgets manners when he gets drunk. If I had tried to find the culprit, I could have protected your virtue alright, but the morale of the armies would have been undermined and the expedition would be sure to suffer. Have you thought of this?"

Xu Ji was a righteous and sensible woman. The prince's explanation convinced her and settled her grievance.

The State of Chu and the midland were separated by a series of mountain ranges — Funiu, Tongbo and Dabie — undulating in a direction from northwest to southeast.

At the mouth of the valley between Funiu and Tongbo lay a small state by the name of Shen (now located in Nanyang, Henan Province) — a fief granted by the Zhou Empire.

At the mouth of the valley between Tongbo and Dabie lay another small state by the name of Xi (located in Xinyang, Henan Province today) — a fief granted by the House of Zhou to the descendant of one of the royal families.

The two states were like two gates blocking the passes of the mountain ranges and serving as outposts at which the Zhou Empire had held Chu at bay. It was through these same outposts that the Western Zhou (before it moved its capital to Luoyang) had formerly launched expeditions against Chu.

A few decades earlier, Prince Wen, Prince Zhuang's ancestor, had conquered the two states and set them up as two counties governed by Chu's magistrates. Now the two "gates", no longer obstacles, had become stepping-stones facilitating Chu's northward push.

The Rong tribesmen, now scattered along the Yi River near Luoyang, still retained their nomadic life-style. The shortest route to the territory they occupied led across the Han River, through the County of Shen, and across the Yi River. Luoyang then lay within reach.

The next morning after the banquet the Chu armies of one hundred thousand armoured soldiers with several hundred chariots under the command of the prince, marched off toward the north. On the way they met with little resistance, and in less than one month they arrived at the Yi and Luo rivers.

Being a nomadic tribe, when on the move the Rongs could pack all their belongings on horseback, and drive their sheep alongside. The Yi River bank was not their permanent home and there was no need for them to make a stand against the Chu forces in armed combat. They never engaged in positional warfare. When the Chu chariots lined up in a long row and charged, they sprang on their horses and disappeared with their sheep. So long as they and their sheep were safe, they did not regard it as a disgrace or a defeat to be driven away.

Prince Zhuang deployed his chariots and foot soldiers along the Yi River and, seeing the Rong tribesmen withdraw toward the northwest, he burst out laughing.

It was said that the Rongs from Luhun were the toughest tribe in the northwest. They had been harassing Qin and Jin but, when confronted with the Chu armies, they were like eggs dashed against rocks.

The prince was beside himself with joy when he suddenly saw clouds of dust rising along the northwest horizon where the Rong tribesmen had disappeared only moments earlier. They were retreating toward their homeland and the Chu armies were still after them. Was it possible that the Rongs were reversing their course for a counterattack?

No sooner had he realised what was happening than a contingent of mounted men, several hundred in number, came galloping up to him. These must be Rong horsemen, he decided, for he caught sight of Chu soldiers fleeing on foot or in chariots.

What cunning adversaries! They had feigned a retreat to draw the Chu armies after them, while in the meantime, hundreds of their horsemen outflanked the Chu forces in a roundabout comeback and were dashing toward the prince, now cut off from his armies. He had been completely hoodwinked by the illusion that, having driven the tribesmen away, he was now safe far behind the frontlines.

He had no more than thirty chariots to protect him and the royal guards, thrown into panic by the sudden appearance of the horsemen, dashed off in disarray to meet them, leaving the prince behind, alone and unguarded.

The Rong horsemen, instead of galloping headlong against the charge of the Chu royal guards, dodged them by branching off into two groups. When the royal guards divided themselves into two parts in pursuit, their attackers suddenly turned and cut back toward the prince. The Chu royal chariots, no match for mounted horsemen in manoeuvrability, were soon outdistanced and their prince was in imminent danger.

At this critical moment a contingent of chariots, under the command of a young general in red uniform, came rumbling up from the distance. Instead of making for the horsemen, they spread out in a circle around the prince.

The tribesmen, separated from the Chu prince by the chariots, raced around the circle seeking a loophole. When it became apparent that their efforts were in vain and access to the prince was out of the question, they began to use bows and arrows.

The young general stood up in his chariot and shaking his halberd shouted to his charioteers: "Shoot back and fight to the last man to safeguard His Majesty!"

The Chu bowmen began to shoot but few of their arrows hit the swiftly-moving targets. The stationary chariots, however, were highly vulnerable and many of the Chu soldiers fell. The young general, now seriously wounded, remained in the commander's position and the charioteers held out against the shower of arrows. The Rong horsemen dared not draw near for hand-to-hand combat. The two sides became locked in a stalemate. By now more than half of the Chu soldiers were wounded and the prince was in mortal danger. The young general did not falter, believing that when the royal guards returned, the horsemen would be driven away.

At last the royal guard chariots could be seen approaching swiftly. With their timely return, the Rong horsemen could now be attacked from both sides. But as the number of royal chariots was limited, the horsemen were not overpowered immediately. They stubbornly persisted, hoping to launch a final thrust to capture the prince before they retreated. In the meantime, the main force of the Chu armies in the northwest on comprehending the situation, had reversed its direction. When the chieftain of the Rongs saw the dust rising and blackening the sky, he blew a whistle and his horsemen galloped off with him.

The great danger that had threatened the prince like a nightmare was now over. He called the young general to his chariot. With blood still oozing through his hastily bandaged wounds, the general kowtowed and asked to be pardoned. He explained:

"While in pursuit of the tribesmen, I saw a group of them suddenly veer off. The Rongs are cunning people and I guessed they were going back to capture the prince at the rear. Without asking for orders from the commander at the front, I directed my men to follow the Rongs. I deserve punishment for leaving the front in the middle of the battle."

"You acted under the pressure of circumstances and you certainly don't deserve punishment for that. Furthermore you risked your life to save mine, for which I am going to reward you. What is your name?"

"My name is Tang Jiao. Your Majesty has already rewarded me generously. The little service I've done is but a small way of showing my gratitude. I mustn't expect any further reward."

The prince was confused. "I've never seen you before. When did I give you any reward and for what reason?"

"Does Your Majesty remember what happened at the banquet before we set out on this expedition? When the torch lights were blown out by the wind, a man stole up to Xu Ji and tried to take liberties with her. That man was none other than myself. Your Majesty was so kind and tolerant as to spare my life that I decided then and there to repay your kindness with my life if necessary."

The prince said with a sigh: "If the water is too clear, there are no fish in it; if a man is too strict, he has no followers. I believe there is some truth in this saying."

Prince Zhuang issued a decree on the spot that Tang Jiao be granted a certificate of first-class merit and be promoted to a ranking position in the court on their return to the capital.

Tang Jiao went back to his charioteers and said to them:

"I had committed a crime punishable by death. The prince, instead of putting me to death, hushed it up. For that I was resolved to repay him with my life. Since the secret has now become known, do I deserve to accept the prince's promotion and assume a ranking position in the court?"

That night, when everyone had gone to sleep, the young general slipped away from the camp and no one knew where he had gone.

After the battle against the Rong tribesmen, the Chu armies did not return to their capital; crossing the Yi and Luo rivers, they pitched tent in the vicinity of Luoyang, their encampment extending over a good ten *li*.

Emperor Ding of Zhou was panic-stricken. What did the Chu prince mean bringing his armies all the way to Luoyang? Did he intend to take over the Empire of Zhou?

When Chu was first established in the remote south four hundred years earlier it was but a humble state with a small population. It was, in terms of civilisation, far behind the states in the midland. When the Shang Dynasty was overthrown by Zhou, the emperor of Zhou granted the princes of smaller states titles of rank in the order of duke, marquis, earl, viscount and baron according to size of territory. The State of Chu was ranked in the fourth category and its prince accorded the title of viscount.

For three hundred years the people of Chu dedicated themselves to building up their state. The princes of Chu believed that working hard would bring prosperity. Chu developed fast in economy and culture. By the time Xiong Tong became prince, Chu had annexed some of its neighbours and grown into one of the strongest states in the south. However, Xiong Tong was unhappy about his lowly status and petitioned the Son of Heaven to grant him a higher title.

His request was rejected by Emperor Ping of Zhou, who had just barely survived a siege of internal turbulence and been forced under duress to move his capital from Haojing to Luoyang. The refusal threw Xiong Tong into a towering rage. On his own, he declared himself Emperor Wu, placing himself on a par with the Son of Heaven. Since the founding of the Zhou Dynasty, no prince of any state had ever dared to declare himself emperor. Nevertheless when it happened, neither the Son of Heaven nor the other states in the midland could do anything about it. Now Prince Zhuang, on the pretext of fighting the Rongs, was virtually besieging Luoyang with his armies.

Knowing that it was not wise to resort to force, Emperor Ding sent Minister Wangsun Man, a distinguished diplomat, to visit Prince Zhuang at his army camp, ostensibly as an act of courtesy, but covertly to find out his intentions.

Prince Zhuang received him in his tent and, after the customary salutations, went straight to the point: "I hear that Emperor Yu's tripods have been valued as great treasures since the Xia Dynasty and are now being kept in Luoyang. Could you describe to me what they look like? How big are they and how much does each one weigh? Why are they so highly regarded? Is it true that whoever owns them owns the world?"

This pointed inquiry about the tripods set Wangsun Man wondering if the prince was coveting the Son of Heaven's imperial power. This calls for a special rejoinder which will lead him to abandon any such ideas, the diplomat reflected.

"The nine tripods are divine vessels indeed," he answered. "But possession of the tripods doesn't mean you have the world in your hand. The world is won not with tripods but with virtue. The reason why Emperor Yu won the hearts of the people was because he spent his lifetime fighting floods and building irrigation works for them. That is why the people were willing to present bronze and tin to the emperor for the casting of the tripods. In the Xia Dynasty under the rule of Emperor Jie — infamous for his lack of virtue — the nine tripods passed to the Shang Dynasty which continued for six hundred years. Its last ruler was Dixin, or King Zhou, notorious for his cruelty. He fell from power, and the tripods were inherited by the Zhou Dynasty. When the country is ruled by the hand of a virtuous emperor, the tripods are as heavy as mountains and it is impossible to move them away. When the country falls into the hands of an evil emperor, the tripods are as light as feathers and the slightest change of wind can blow them into the hands of a virtuous man.''

Prince Zhuang said with a smile, ''While the princes were engaged in constant wars with each other, the Rongs, taking advantage of the chaos, captured Haojing. At the time, do you think the emperor was a virtuous man? The State of Chu is now four hundred years old. When it was founded, it first settled south of the Danjiang River, then moved to the north of Mount Jing. The people of Chu had very little to begin with, but they worked diligently under tough conditions and reclaimed the land. Through the years, they opened up five thousand *li* of land. Chu has now grown to become the most powerful and prosperous state in the whole country. It surpasses the north in agriculture and mining. Its people are much better off and its armies are much stronger. It has attracted and trained a tremendous number of talents. The people are cultured, so that they no longer deserve to be called ''wild tribesmen'' by northerners. For a time the folk songs of the north were popular all over the country, but their popularity has been dwindling.

> The gentle southern winds blowing,
> Relieve the people of their care.

The southern winds of early spring,
Nurture crops for the people's welfare.

"The ancient Emperor Shun played southern folk songs on his five-stringed lute. When Emperor Yu of the Xia Dynasty toured the south, his wife Tushan missed him and composed a folk song in the southern style. Southern folk songs are again winning popularity. Though they are sung in the southern dialect, though they all contain Chu themes, they have found their way to the north and are enjoyed by the northern people.

"The Yellow Emperor's wife Leizu was the first woman to raise silk worms, but the best silk is produced in the south today. The Yellow Emperor created the musical scale, but today the largest court orchestra is in Ying, the capital of Chu, and its bells are without compare. With all this in mind, how can you explain that Zhou is virtuous but Chu is not?"

Wangsun Man, hard put to answer, nevertheless tried to maintain his position: "It is true that moral standards of the Zhou Dynasty are declining, but the Mandate of Heaven bestowed upon it is not yet ended. Emperor Cheng placed the nine tripods in Luoyang and during a sacrifice to Heaven and Earth, an oracle prophesied that the Zhou Dynasty would rule the country for thirty generations over seven hundred years. As you know, the span of years is far from over and the heavenly mandate still stands. Therefore it's not appropriate for anyone to have doubts about the tripods at the present time."

Prince Zhuang laughed. "If you think I am leading my armies to Luoyang to sieze the tripods, you are mistaken. We have the Bronze-green Mountain and Daye with tremendous deposits of minerals. Take just a tiny chip from each of the swords and spears of our one million armymen and we wouild have enough metal to cast any number of tripods."

The next day Prince Zhuang, accompanied by a small contingent of soldiers, advanced further north along the Luo River until he reached the Yellow River, which he had long yearned to see.

The yellowish silted waters of the river roll past in torrential waves, evoking a contrasting reaction on viewers accustomed to scenes along the green Yangtse. The river seemed endless, flowing down from heaven in the west and rushing pell-mell to the eastern horizon. It was a spectacular sight, one of inexpressible magnificence.

Legend had it that long, long ago an auspicious animal emerged from the river. It had the body of a horse and was covered with dragon scales. About eight feet and five inches in height, it looked somewhat like a camel but had a pair of wings on its shoulders which enabled it to gallop on the tips of the waves as if on flat ground. Its back bore a mysterious map of dots arranged in rows. In each of four directions there were two rows with a different number of dots in each. Rearward, one row had one dot, the other, six; to the front, two dots and seven dots; on the left, three and eight; on the right, four and nine. In the middle were two rows, one with five, the other with ten dots. It was too strange to be anything but a monster of some kind. The legendary Emperor Fu Xi caught sight of it from the riverbank. Staring at it for a few moments, he exclaimed:

"This symbolises the advent of civilisation!"

With a piece of charcoal, Fu Xi copied the map on a stone tablet and with a piece of pointed bamboo, carved it on a wooden plank. Inspired and enlightened by the layout of the dots, Fu Xi worked out eight diagrams which he called *qian*(乾), *kun* (坤), *zhen*(震), *gen*(艮), *li*(离), *kan* (坎), *xun*(巽) and *dui*(兑). *Qian* consisted of three unbroken lines, a symbol of Heaven; *kun*, of three broken lines (in six dashes), a symbol of earth; *zhen*, of two broken lines above and one unbroken line below, a symbol of thunder; *gen*, of one unbroken line above and two broken lines below, a symbol for mountain; *li*, of one unbroken line above and another below with one broken line in between, a symbol of fire; *kan*, of one unbroken line in the middle with one broken line above and another below, a symbol of water; *xun*, of two unbroken lines above and one broken line below, a symbol of wind; *dui*, of one broken line above and two unbroken lines below, a symbol of lake. In each of the eight diagrams there were three *yaos* (lines), and using variations of the *yaos*, Fu Xi succeeded in developing the eight diagrams into sixty-four hexagrams, each of which symbolises a certain object both in form and in nature. Since many things are similar in form and nature, the meaning of each hexagram was extended to stand for many other things. So the sixty-four hexagrams could represent almost everything between heaven and earth. For example, they were used to record events, and rope-knotting, now made obsolete, was abandoned. Human civilisation had taken a big leap forward.

Many years later, a tortoise crawled out of the Luo River with darkish symbols on its reddish shell. The legendary Cang Ji caught it and studied the markings on its shell from every angle. Drawing on the palm of his left hand with his right hand forefinger, he managed to work out one pictograph after another. This was the first step in creating the Chinese written language — another leap forward in human civilisation.

It was said that the ancient Emperor Yan, progenitor of the Chu people, also grew up in the neighbourhood of the Yellow River and later moved south near to the Yangtse. Seeing is believing and only after Prince Zhuang had seen the river with his own eyes was he convinced that it augured profound mysteries. Two days later he quietly left the banks of the Yellow River with his armies and returned to his capital.

The prince's inquiry about the nine tripods and his military venture to the Yellow River caused a sensation throughout the "world". In the past the mention of the "world" had referred to the midland; now the prince realised that the midland was but half of the "world"; the other half was his own state of Chu in the south.

3

Wangsun's guesthouses fell into three categories.

The third category, called "Transient House", was for guests who came and went time and again. They were put up in rooms each big enough to accommodate several dozens and served vegetarian food with plain water. The rooms provided adequate shelter and the food was sufficient to appease hunger. The guests were mediocrities who roamed about picking up free board and lodging wherever they could. They were of little or no service to the host, who left their comings and goings entirely up to themselves. He did, however, take care not to offend them, for among them there might be dangerous persons associated with adventurers. Any offense toward them on his part could bring trouble upon himself. Besides, if anyone found himself neglected, the others would feel sympathetic and hurt. In that case the host's reputation for hospitality would be impaired.

The second category, called "Lucky House", was better equipped than the third. The guests there were put up in smaller rooms and served meals with fish and meat, occasionally with wine. They were treated better because, being specialised in one thing or another, they rendered some service.

The first category guesthouse, called "Substitute House", was equipped with palace facilities. The guests lived in separate rooms or even in private houses if their talents were highly regarded by the host. They were provided with meat and wine at meals and had their own carriages. The group included distinguished personages and people of great talent and insightful vision. Among the honourable guests, they were the one out of a hundred, of potential, or even crucial importance to the host. Next to the guesthouses, in the rear quarters of Wangsun Yi's residence lived a beautiful concubine by the name of Zheng Ji, a new arrival.

In regard to characteristics of the various states, it was commonly held that the people of Chu had contempt for wealth but respected courage; those of Qin were greedy and ruthless, while the people of Qi and Jin were obsequious, crafty, deceitful and profit-loving. When referring to the people of Zheng, they had one word for them — licentious, principally on account of the folk songs they liked to sing.

Listen, listen, brother,
Don't clamber over the wall
Lest you crush the willows.
I care not for the trees,
But scared of my parents.
I have you in my heart,
Yet my parents would nag,
And that is what I fear.

Listen, listen, brother,
Don't jump into the garden
Lest you crush the sandals.
I care not for the trees,
But of gossip I have fears,
I have you in my heart,
Yet neighbours will gossip,
And that is what I fear.

*

You handsome, crafty boy!
You speak to me no more,
For you and you alone
I've lost my appetite.

You handsome, crafty boy!
Refuse to eat with me,

For you and you alone
I cannot sleep at night.

*

If I have a place in your heart,
Lift your robe, cross the river Zhen!
If in case there is no place,
Someone else will come, I'm sure.
What a silly fellow you are!

If I have a place in your heart,
Lift your robe and cross the river Wei!
If in case there is no place,
Someone else will come, I'm sure.
What a silly fellow you are!

*

What a night of wind and rain,
Roosters crow once and again.
Since I'm already with you here,
Why should I not be pleased, my dear?

What a night of wind and rain,
Roosters crow once and again.
Since I'm already with you here,
Why should we not be near, my dear?

*

It's fun to jump up and down,
On the tower of the town!
One whole day that you're away,
Is like three months we didn't play!

*

Grass creeping in the field,
Its blades gleaming with dew.
A maid of beauty passes by,
With limpid eyes and forehead high.
It's true we meet by chance,
Is this a dream or trance?

Grass creeping in the field,
Its blades gleaming with dew.
A maid of beauty passes by,
With limpid eyes and forehead high.
It's true we meet by chance,
Yet who resists romance?

Zheng Ji liked to sing all these popular love songs. One day someone cautioned her in private: "This is not the state of Zheng; we're in Luoyang. Here the proprieties are respected and observed to the letter. You are not an ordinary woman, but a concubine in Minister Wangsun's house. Here you can not sing love songs so freely or you'll be looked down upon as a loose woman. You'll ruin your reputation."

"Oh, I'm just humming to myself — even that is not allowed?"

"No. No matter how or when you sing, someone is bound to hear you and Minister Wangsun will surely get to know about it."

But Zheng Ji loved singing and had kept it up ever since she was a child. If she did not sing even for one day, she felt suffocated. She always felt like singing, and whenever she opened her mouth, she poured forth a love song. It was said that in Zheng, if love songs were prohibited there would be no songs at all. That was quite true. And soon too, it was reported to Wangsun

Yi that Zheng Ji was singing "licentious" songs in the rear quarters.

What had she been singing that was so "licentious"? Ditties like: "You handsome, crafty boy, if I don't see you one whole day, it's like three months that you're away."

Wangsun Yi was an understanding man. "What's so licentious about them? They are all folk songs. Even the court musician sends people out to collect them."

Wangsun Yi approached Zheng Ji, who was now in a quandary: "I hear you can sing quite a few Zheng folk songs...."

Zheng Ji nodded morosely. "What's all the fuss anyhow? Is there anything wrong in singing folk songs?"

"Would you care to sing one or two for me?"

"Fine," she said. I'd like to see just what he has to say about our folk songs, she mused.

She picked one at random and sang it.

Delighted, Wangsun Yi exclaimed: "Even better than I expected! Could you sing another one for me?"

"Why, you seem to enjoy it!"

"Oh, yes," the minister replied.

"Aren't you afraid they're 'licentious' and will offend your ears?"

"Those who have that opinion are either ignorant or hypocritical. Even the court musician is interested in the songs and has sent people out to collect them."

Zheng Ji was delighted to hear that. She went on singing, one after another, rendering each one with more feeling than the last. Wangsun Yi was fascinated. That night the two of them had a wonderful time together. The Zheng folk songs worked like glue holding them close and fast. They had not had many such nights. It was not that Wangsun Yi did not wish to be with her, but that he was too busy with his guests to spare the time.

When alone, Zheng Ji sang to disperse her loneliness. "One whole day that you're away, is like three months we didn't play'' was the one she tended to sing the most.

When alone in her rooms, she found it hard to get to sleep. At night she tossed in bed for hours — throughout the whole night, so it seemed to her. In the morning, drowsy with sleeplessness, she felt too listless to get up. But recently, early in the morning, she had been disturbed by roosters squawking and dogs barking. She wondered where they came from, as Wangsun Yi did not raise them for meat; meat was supplied by butchers from the market. Had any of the guests, dissatisfied with their food started raising them for meat? That was against the rules, and had to be stopped.

One morning when it was just turning light, she again heard the panicky squawking of roosters and the fierce barking of dogs, as if barnyard fowl were being harassed by dogs. Zheng Ji got out of bed and went to look out of the window. There were no chickens or dogs in sight, but the clamour seemed to be drawing nearer and nearer.

Finally she spotted a man squatting in the middle of the courtyard. So that was where the racket came from! He was amusing himself by imitating roosters and dogs! His ludicrous antics made her giggle. As he needed the quiet of the morning to hear his own renditions, her giggling disturbed him. Straightening up he glanced round and saw a woman by the window, still giggling. His face darkened.

He went straight to the host who had just risen. ''What brings you here so early, sir? Is it a very serious problem?''

''I have a question to ask you, Minister Wangsun.''

''What is it? Go ahead and ask.''

''Some artistic skills are respectable, are they not? And others are humble, am I right?''

''Some skills are high and others are low, but they can scarcely be divided into respectable and humble.''

''That is what you told me the day I arrived and that is why I decided to stay with you, assuming that I would not be eating your food for nothing. But this morning I ran into something that tells me you have changed your views!''

"What do you mean, I have changed my views? Have you any evidence to back up your complaint?''

"Of course I am not making a groundless complaint. I agree with you when you say there is only the difference of high and low, but not of respectable and humble. So every morning I get up early and imitate the squawking of roosters and the barking of dogs while the air is fresh and my throat is well rested. Since I started the practice, I have not been disturbed by anything. But this morning I was laughed at by the woman in your house. Obviously she looks down on my skill. If you have changed your views, I leave here at once! If you have not, behead that woman as an apology to your guests!''

"Could you give me some time to investigate? If what you say is true, I will satisfy your demand.''

Wangsun Yi was going to behead his concubine by way of apology to the guest who had felt ridiculed. His family and his guests were shocked.

Some guests gathered in the courtyard, commenting and casting glances at the small, exquisite dwelling next door.

"What does the woman look like? Is she beautiful?''

"What a question to ask! Not only is she a beauty, she can also sing love songs; she has the sweetest voice, I'm told.''

"People all know about the unconventional behaviour of Zheng. I don't believe the minister loves her.''

"You're mistaken! As a matter of fact he does; he loves her very much. Since she came, he has almost forgotten the other women.''

"If he loves her that much, do you think he would behead her?''

"That's why he is respected as a man of outstanding righteousness. He holds nobodies like us in high esteem but holds women in contempt. When his righteous deed is made known to the public, people will swarm to him like a school of carp and swear allegiance to him."

Wangsun Yi was sitting in the hall, his face like an iron mask. It was already lunch time but he could not bear to eat or drink. He was waiting for the report of Zheng Ji's execution.

His servants stood on both sides, their arms hanging straight, not daring to make the slightest noise or movement. The captain of his bodyguards returned.

The minister's heart tightened and a chill shot through his spine. He trembled slightly. His servants took no notice of his nervousness. An efficient man, this captain, he mused, so quick to carry out any order!

The captain knelt in front of him, trembling with fear: "Sir..."

"Is it done?"

"No, sir..."

The minister's tightening heart eased a bit, but his face turned harder, his voice sterner. "Why not?"

"Many people were weeping in the rear quarters. Some were kneeling by the roadside, entreating me to show mercy. I just couldn't bring myself to do it. Would you please reconsider your decision?"

"There is nothing to reconsider," Wangsun Yi said, with a wave of his hand, "Go and carry out my order at once!"

Hardly had the captain left the hall when a servant appeared to report that a guest from the Substitute House was leaving and had come to say good-bye to the minister.

"Why choose this particular moment?" Wangsun Yi was visibly irritated.

The servant spoke in a whisper, careful not to provoke him further: "It's that young pedant from the south. For all your kindness and generosity, he doesn't seem to be the least bit grateful. If you do not wish to see him, I can tell him you are busy and just let him go his way."

After a long pause, Wangsun Yi said, "Let him in."

The man entered. It was Li Er.

"Li Er, why do you want to leave? If you feel neglected in any way, I should apologise. At the moment I am engaged in punishing a concubine for insulting a guest. As you can see, I am doing my best to improve reception so that I can keep more retainers with me."

"When I got up this morning," Li Er explained, "I saw a large muster of mice moving out. I asked the big one at the head: 'Why are you moving out in such a hurry?' The leader said, 'Minister Wangsun is planning to put up a high rise for his guests because some of them have complained that their buildings are too low. A high rise built of tamped earth is bound to collapse some day. When it does, our homes will be smashed and we'll be crushed to paste. Since the mice are all leaving, there is no excuse for me to stay on either."

"Build a high rise for my guests? Ridiculous! Who has given such an order?"

"No one but the minister himself."

"Me myself? When did I ever order a high rise to be built?" Wangsun Yi, already upset, fell into a quandary.

"Please let's not pretend you don't know about it. You have just issued an order to behead Zheng Ji by way of apologising to your guests. Isn't this equivalent to building a high rise for them? If you did so, it would raise their status considerably, but raised too high, they head for a fall; if set too solid, it will break; if their image is too pure, it is easily tarnished."

Wangsun Yi now began to realise what Li Er was getting at.

"I take it you are opposed to having Zheng Ji beheaded?"

"Yes, I am."

"How do you suggest we handle this matter?"

"Why not place her in confinement for ten days? That's punishment enough."

"If the insulted scholar is not satisfied, what then?"

"As a scholar, he should understand this better. One who knows the strong but keeps to the weak becomes the valley under Heaven, for the valley can hold all the streams. Why should one always think about rising high, but not want to be low? The sea can hold water from all rivers because it is low. He who knows the strength of the male but keeps to the weakness of the female acts as a ravine for all under Heaven; all come to him. He who knows the attraction of white but maintains humility can be a valley for all under Heaven. If he does not understand this, what sort of scholar is he? If he is not a scholar, what does it matter whether he is satisfied or not?"

"Reasonable," said Minister Wangsun. "I'll follow your advice. Still it might be too late now — the captain just left to carry out the execution."

"Don't worry — the captain is outside, waiting for you to cancel the order."

"In that case you will not leave?"

"Since you are not building the high rise, I will stay."

4

Zheng Ji was pardoned. Sighs of relief swept over the rear quarters.

But she had long been an object of jealousy and ill-feeling among other concubines.

The customs of the state of Zheng were unacceptably unconventional according to Zhou standards. Both men and women of the south were fond of singing love songs. Women had little sense of decorum or self-importance. Sometimes they would stand by the window and sing flirtatious love songs to the men passing by. If a man passed by without any response, the woman would sing, "Listen, you handsome fellow, if you don't love me, there are others who will!" It was common for men and women to arrange a secret rendezvous out of town. Some contracted marriages without consulting their parents.

Zheng Ji purposely set herself against other concubines who railed at her out of jealousy. The more they censured the songs, the more encouraged she was to sing them.

"She sings such bawdy songs, and right here inside the minister's house! What a disgrace!" the other concubines would
splutter. However, any time Zheng Ji began to sing, they would
open their windows and listen carefully, though some of them
would run her down later on. But Wangsun Yi never considered
that her songs debased the rear quarters in any way.

No move of hers escaped the other concubines, who commented constantly, with much nudging of elbows and pointing
of fingers: "Look, the minister is taking her away for the night.
All the carriage curtains are raised to show off her face. How
pretty she is! What shiny, sexy eyes and white teeth! Quite a
beauty, isn't she? Nowadays it's really hard to find a decent
man in the world. The minister is competely captivated by this
alluring woman."

"You say the minister is going to behead her? Good! He's
come to his senses at last. An indecent woman like her can
cause a disaster. If the minister doesn't get rid of her, his whole
mansion will be corrupted."

"What! She is to be beheaded, but not because of her promis-
cuity?"

"No! Because she laughed at a guest! The guest took it as
an insult and demanded the minister apologise by beheading
her."

"You mean the minister is going to give her up? That's not
fair!" These women, jealous only a moment before, now became
sympathetic towards Zheng Ji.

"Just like a man! All men are heartless! One day's marriage
has a hundred days' love behind it, but his love is not as reliable as a tramp's. When he loves you today, he adores you;
when he tires of you tomorrow, he kills you. Oh, how meaningless and cheap a woman's life is!"

"Listen, I hear the minister changed his mind after Li Er
called on him. It's not that all guests always speak only for
guests. This man has spoken on behalf of Zheng Ji. He has a

sense of justice."

Then suddenly the women's jealousy took over again.

"Only ten days in confinement? That's altogether too light a punishment. That woman deserves to be locked up for life. Never let her see a man again for the rest of her life, that's my opinion. He's too easy on her! There will be no peace in the rear chambers from now on."

"It's about time we left this place," some guests got together and said. "If the minister doesn't want to keep us, we can go somewhere else. No man can resist the allurement of women, not even a hero. It's natural that he would not sacrifice his concubine to appease a poor guest. This will make the poor scholars feel betrayed. I'm sure."

"We are all with you, but why are you turning soft like this? You haven't said one single word to indicate you are sticking to your demand. Do you think you are man enough? Are you leaving this place or not? Afraid of losing your rice bowl?"

"No, I am not leaving. I'm staying."

"Staying? Do you have the face to stay when things have come to this pass? If you don't care about your face, we care about ours!"

"Say no more about it," the man raised his voice like a rooster crowing. "I am staying in order to meet with that Li Er."

"Yes. And who does that Li Er think he is? He is living off the minister, the same as the rest of us; why is he so nasty? Does he think he has got three heads and six arms to cut the ground from under our feet?"

"I agree! We cannot simply swallow this insult and then leave. But where can we find him?"

"The guesthouse is a small place. If you can't find him on this side, you can find him on the other side. Anyway he is somewhere to be found."

"I hear he's living in Substitute House."

"Really? The house for special guests? I knew it — he's better off than we are. He gets fish and meat at meals and a carriage to ride in."

"What special talents has he got anyway? Is he a hero capable of resisting ten thousand warriors, or some sort of superman strong enough to lift a tripod?"

"He's different from you and me, that's for sure. Not a superman at all, but a pedant with a gift of gab."

"There is another thing that distinguishes him — he has a pair of long, fat ears."

"What, hanging down to his shoulders?"

They burst out laughing.

A carriage drawn by three horses was approaching Wangsun's mansion. It began to slow down about one hundred yeards from the entrance and then came to a halt.

The clopping of hooves and the jingling of bells brought out the doorkeeper, who opened the gate, and seeing that both the carriage and the driver belonged to Minister Wangsun's household, let them in.

Li Er did not have many friends or relatives in Luoyang. When he went out it was to observe life in the capital and to visit places of historical interest.

Again and again he had declined the offer of a carriage, saying he preferred to wander about by himself. He enjoyed the leisure and freedom but the caretaker of Substitute House kept insisting. It was a strict regulation, as well as a matter of propriety. The guests at Transient House and Lucky House were not provided with a carriage even if they asked for one; the guests at Substitute House had to ride in one even if they preferred to walk. Breach of these regulations could bring trouble if the minister happened to look into the matter.

Finally Li Er got into the assigned carriage with a patient, resigned smile.

First of all, he wanted to see the nine tripods. Treasured for over one thousand years they were the oldest historical relics in the capital and in the country as well, for that matter.

Many were the mysterious legends surrounding the nine tripods: They were as big as hills, each weighing nearly one hundred thousand *jin*. They were more than mere treasures — they were custodians of the country's stability; who possessed them possessed the country, who lost them lost the country. To men of virtue they were light as feathers and easily moved, but to men of evil they were as heavy as hills, impossible to move even an inch.

These tales and more were of course familiar enough to Li Er. But when he saw them they looked like the kitchen cooking vessels used by noble families, sizeable and measurable, yes, but not in geographical proportions.

What had led the northerners, practical as they were, to cast these mysterious tripods? Examining them carefully, Li Er saw that each one of them bore nine characters: Ji, Yu, Yong, Yang, Yan, Xu, Liang, Qing and Jing. The ancient Emperor Shun had divided the country into twelve districts; later, Emperor Yu reshuffled them into nine districts, each of which had one of the nine characters representing it cast on a tripod. Closer study revealed information about the district: its principal travel routes, its mountains, rivers, minerals, products, tributes paid to the central government and totems worshipped by its people. Now Li Er understood the practical purposes for which the nine tripods had been cast by Emperor Yu.

For one, they served as maps of the districts, maps not drawn on perishable silk, but cast on tripods. These were the earliest maps on record.

Yu, in his wisdom as ruler of the country, had to familiarise himself with its people, their customs, its geographical features, and indigenous products. He had this information cast in vivid images on the tripods for the edification of all. It was a great model of creative state craft comparable to the Yellow Emperor's invention of the cart and the boat in transportation.

It was not hard to understand why Yu had cast the maps on the tripods. In his fight against floods he had travelled far and wide all over the country. In eight years he passed his home three times without dropping in to see his family. He went from district to district, building a series of projects to bring the rivers under control. He began with those in the district of Ji, where the capital of the country was located, and them the rivers in Yan, Qing, Xun, Yang, Jing, Yu, Liang and Yong, dredging channels for water to flow easily out to sea. As he had travelled over almost every inch of the land, he had the country's landscapes firmly pictured in his mind. But the spirits and monsters cast on the tripods did not exist except in his imagination.

There were totems on the tripods. They were different from real things, say, mountains and rivers. They were things born of "non-being". Things born of "non-being" were usually considered grotesque, absurd or beyond reason. But they were not hard to understand. Until heaven and earth began to take shape, the universe was a chaotic mass, or a "non-being", to be exact. By and by, the clear and limpid went up to become heaven, the muddy and murky settled to become earth. Thus heaven and earth came into being and gave birth to the ten thousand things.

Since "non-being" gave birth to "being", "being" also gave birth to "non-being". The nine tripods and the various objects cast on them were all solid "beings" from which so many mysterious "non-beings" were derived. The "non-beings", for example, included notions that the tripods each weighed one hundred thousand jin, that they had an inherent supernatural power and that he who possessed the tripods possessed the country while he who lost the tripods lost the country.

The mutual relationship between "being" and "non-being" was in everything, according to Li Er. He could cite many everyday phenomena to prove it, but he could not explain its mysterious nature. For instance, the wheels of his carriage demonstrated the relationship between "being" and "non-being".

Each wheel had thirty spokes radiating from the hub (which in Chinese was called *gu*). The interior of the *gu* was empty and that empty interior was "non-being". The spokes — "being" — made it possible for the wheels to sustain the weight of the carriage. As the interior of the *gu* was empty — non-being — the axle could pass through it. Without this "non-being", the wheels could not roll. Therefore, the element of "non-being" was indispensable. When the carriage was seen at the entrance of Wangsun's mansion and the gate thrown open, a wide gap appeared. This was the open gate, also an example of "non-being".

There were doors and windows in the walls of the hall — "non-being" within "being". Without the "non-being", the hall was not a hall, the house not a house any more; they were not liveable. Even the caves lived in by the ancients had doors. Zhou Dynasty houses had double stone walls with an empty space in between and a side door at the end. Wasn't that a natural combination of "being" and "non-being"?

Li Er was lost in the interplay between "being" and "Non-being" when he heard a rude voice call out his name and a loud screech as the carriage drew to a halt.

"Is that Li Er in the carriage? Come out, come out!"

"He's an honoured guest of the minister," the driver said. "What do you want?"

"Want? We want to have a look at him!"

"Why? Because he's a famous man?" The driver, not knowing what to do, turned and lifted the curtain. "Some guests from Transient House would like to see you," he said. "Do you want to see them?"

"Why would they want to see me in the street and not at the guesthouse?" Li Er asked. By nature he was not a ceremonious person. "If they want to see me in the street, all right." Lifting the curtain, he got out of the carriage.

Several men standing by the roadside gazed at him coldly, a message of misgiving in their eyes. This interrupted his concentration on the business of "being" and "non-being". He remembered having seen these men somewhere and searched his memory as to where it was, and what wrong he had inadvertently done them. His memory assured him he had never wronged them in any way.

"Are you the fellow from Chu with the surname Li and given name Er?" one of the men struck up.

How do they know my name? Li Er wondered. Have we met before?

"Do you hear? Why don't you answer? Are you Li the Ear or Li the Mouth?"

"I am Li Er of course."

"You did hear me then! You ought to be Li the Mouth, not Li the Ear!"

"Why?" Li Er had never expected them to be so rude.

"Why? That's just the question we're asking you. Tell me, why are you called Li Er?"

"Because I was born with long ears and my grandfather gave me the name."

"Your ears are certainly long enough. But we think your mouth is even longer, so you ought to change your name to Li the Mouth."

"Why? Is my mouth longer than my ears? How come?" Li Er was truly baffled.

Seeing Li Er so puzzled, they burst into laughter: "Since your mouth is not long, why do you poke it everywhere? You talk too much. Better call yourself Li the Mouth!"

They are making fun of me, Li Er thought. There is no sense in continuing this conversation. "What I am called is not important. The Tao that can be expressed is not the eternal Tao; the name that can be named is not the eternal name." So saying, he turned to get into the carriage again.

They quickly stepped in front of him and barred his way. "Don't try to get away until you tell us what you mean by that!"

"In this world," Li Er commented calmly, "everything follows its own course from birth to death. In other words, everything pursues its own Tao. Tao is hard to explain; it cannot be described in words. If it can be explained, it is not the profound, eternal Tao. Things between Heaven and earth, big or small, you cannot say exactly what they are. Or let me put in this way, you cannot give them names. If you try to give them names, convenient as they may be, the names cannot describe the eternal nature of the thing." Li Er turned once more to get into his carriage, but his way was blocked once again.

"Don't go; you have yet to make yourself clear."

"Haven't I made it clear? But I can't make it any clearer. Besides, I'm not entirely clear myself. In short, it's not important what you call it. Please don't take it so seriously. The name is far and away inadequate for describing the profound eternal thing it stands for. The name that can be named is not the eternal name...."

This only threw the ruffians into a fit of exasperation. "Stop quibbling! Trying to make fools of us? Just tell us whether you are Li the Mouth or not. If you don't give us a definite answer, you can't go!"

At that point they were interrupted by a young man who came up to them and said, "Wait a minute you ruffians; aren't you ashamed to treat a scholar like that?"

Turning they looked the young man up and down. He seemed gentlemanly, self-assured and at ease in his surrounding. What was he? A swordsman, a sophist, a scholar? They were nonplussed and as they numbered several against one, they were ready to stand their ground. "Mind your own business! Don't stick your nose into other people's affairs!"

"I'm afraid I have to stick my nose into this affair because we two come from the same place!"

One of the men swept his gaze around at the others in the group and flashed a signal with his eyes: Come on, let's teach him a lesson to make him behave. They instantly spread out into a circle around him and raised their fists menacingly. Before they got close enough to strike, the young gentleman, with a flashing feint, a moment's move, a quick kick, had knocked them all down.

"There's no need to start a fight. You'll only hurt each other," said Li Er gently, trying to separate them. "Please calm down; we can talk it over."

Li Er's fellow countryman bowed and apologised: "I'm sorry I was rude. Please excuse me. I hope you are not hurt."

Crestfallen, the sprawling men got up and dusted off their clothes. Luckily they were not injured.

"I'm sorry to have caused all this trouble," Li Er said. "I would like to invite you gentlemen for a drink at the Guesthouse as an apology. Please come into the carriage; there are enough seats for all."

Still simmering with anger, one of gang muttered: "Knocked down by that bastard, what face do we have left to hang around here any longer! Let's go!" With that they stalked off.

"Who's a bastard? You foul-mouthed scoundrels!" The gentleman struck out after them, but Li Er stopped him, saying, "Really, there is no need to take people like that so seriously. Thank you very much for getting me out of trouble. May I know your name, sir?"

"My name is Yin Xi."

"You mentioned that we come from the same place. Are you also from Xiangyi?"

"Not necessarily from Xiangyi. In northerners' terms we are both from the South. So we are fellow countrymen."

"I see," Li Er said. "I still cannot understand what they wanted of me. I haven't the slightest idea who they are or what wrong I have done them. Why are they so annoyed?"

"Never mind. Don't take it to heart. It's neither here nor there."

"Do you know them?"

"Yes, but not very well."

"Come along. Let's go back and have a chat at the guesthouse."

"If it hadn't been for you, we might have fallen into serious trouble here," the driver said to the young man gratefully. "They're really very rough people. Even the minister has to make all sorts of allowances for them."

On their return to the guesthouse it was already supper time. A servant, laying the table, remarked, "You must be hungry after a whole day of sight-seeing!"

Li Er asked him to prepare supper for two, saying he would pay the additional expense. The servant informed him that this was not necessary because an extra guest coming only once in a while did not cost much. Presently he brought the food in on a tray. There was a pot of wine, four dishes and a bowl of soup.

The two friends sat at the table drinking and chatting as they partook of the fish and meat.

"Who are those people really?" Li Er asked. "Why did they start to make trouble?"

"Did you tell the minister a parable about mice moving out and a high rise being built?"

"Yes, I did. What was wrong with that?"

"Was it your intention to ingratiate yourself with Zheng Ji and at the same time insult the other guests?"

"No, no! That's not what I was getting at!"

"What did you mean, then?"

"I believe everything between Heaven and earth follows Tao from birth to death."

"Are you now talking about the 'Tao' you so often refer to?"

"We have just become acquainted for the first time; how did you know I often speak of it?"

"I have been a guest here for a couple of years," Yin Xi said with a smile. "I've heard people in my guesthouse commenting on a new arrival at Substitute House who hardly ever opens his mouth without using the word 'Tao' in one way or another. But what exactly is 'Tao'? I haven't the slightest idea! What the others know of it is nothing but hearsay and they can't begin to explain it either. Once someone in the guesthouse mentioning these matters referred to you as the one with the long ears. For you, this may be our first meeting, but for me it's not the first."

Li Er was confused. Here I am, he mused, living a quiet life, reading and meditating. I don't talk about Tao all that often except with a few friends. I thought I was always careful not to disturb others or draw attention to myself.

"I know," said Yin Xi. "When you told the minister the story about mice moving out, you were not trying to gain favour with Zheng Ji, nor did you mean to hurt that barnyard mimic. You just wanted to discuss 'Tao' with the minister."

Li Er slapped his thigh and exclaimed: "Great! You're realy a person who understands me!"

"But the mimic and his friends viewed the matter in a different light. That's why they harassed you right out in the street."

Li Er suddenly saw the point. "I see," he said. "But if that is the case, I have a complaint about you."

"A complaint? Is my martial arts technique below par? Or should I have punished them more severely?"

"Your fighting technique is formidable enough to defend a fortress single-handed," said Li Er, "but you should not have knocked them down like that. We ought to have been more patient and invited them over here for a drink. I could have cleared it up with them and removed the hostility between us."

"Here you are getting pedantic again," Yin Xi said. "If you believe everything can be cleared up, there would be no 'Tao' in the world."

"Why not?"

"The Tao that can be explained is not the eternal Tao. This is what you often say yourself."

"Aha, you caught me that time!" he laughed.

"But those people called out 'bastard'!" Yin Xi said. "That was really offensive! What did they mean by that?"

Li Er was at a loss what to say.

Yin Xi, lost in surmise, pursued the matter no further. It only reflected once more that "the Tao that can be explained is not the eternal Tao."

5

"Polish mirrors! Polish mirrors...."

A hawker was plying his trade at the top of his voice in a distinctive Chu accent, heard throughout the neighbourhood of the Li family. The old man was sitting at his desk, his eyes on a book of bamboo strips, his mind wandering in realms of philosophic thought.

In this area of the capital the Chu accent had never been heard before until recently. A southern accent got laughed at, for people took pride in speaking their own pure midland accent. But now the city streets were frequented by peddlers and craftsmen from the south. The Chu dialect could be heard most anywhere. This was also the case in small remote towns and even more so in Bowl Hill, capital of the State of Chen (today in Huaiyang, Henan Province). To the south of the capital, there stood a small hill of four or five dozen metres high. It was like an inverted bowl, rounded at the top and sloping down. This gave it the name of Bowl Hill. As this was one of the capital's scenic spots, the city itself was named after it.

In the capital, Bowl Hill, there were more peddlers and craftsmen from Chu. Also, a good number of witches had come there from the south to ply their trade on the outskirts. They exorcised spirits and dispensed medicines with great fanfare, attracting people from all parts of the state, their clients brought handsome gifts, hoping that good fortune would come their way.

There was a folk song "Bowl Hill" which was sung in the Chu dialect, satirising the witches:

On top of Bowl Hill you dance,
In a swirl and a trance.
To love you is all that I wish,
Be it but a will-o'-the-wisp.

Down at the foot of Bowl Hill,
The drum booms loud like a mill,
Winters, summers, come and go,
The plume dances high and low.

Clear on the road to Bowl Hill,
Sound the vessel of clay,
Winters, summers, come and go,
The plume waves where it may.

The State of Chen used to be a fief granted to the descendants of the ancient Emperor Shun. When Shun was a commoner, he lived on the banks of the Weishui River (in Shanxi Province) which flows into the Yellow River. When he was appointed an official with Emperor Yao, the latter gave his two daughters, E Huang and Nu Ying, to him in marriage. To set an example of filial piety, Shun sent his two wives back to Weishui to look after his parents. Shun's descendants adopted Gui as their surname. When Shun died, Yu succeeded to the throne and enfeoffed Shun's son as prince. During the several hundred years of the Xia Dynasty, a good number of Shun's descendants were enfeoffed. When Emperor Wu of the Zhou Dynasty overthrew the Shang Dynasty, he began to look for Shun's descendants and eventually found Hugong Gui. To show his loyalty to the three great "Sage Emperors" Yao, Shun and Yu, Emperor Wu married his daughter, Tai Ji, to Hugong Gui and enfeoffed him as the Prince of Chen. This was how the State of Chen came to be established.

Chen was a small, weak state occupying a narrow strip of land adjoining its strong neighbour Chu. As the Zhou Dynasty was now declining and the princes of the states were competing for hegemony, Chen became a subordinate of Chu. Chu had not only provided protection for Chen from the constant wars among the states, it had also introduced new techniques and rich cultural advantages to Chen. The witches from the south brought with them songs, dances and medicines. Their prescriptions were highly effective. Chu had a relatively advanced smelting industry. The iron tools Chu craftsmen brought to Chen had improved its farming and increased its crops.

The bronze mirrors cast in Chu, for example, were much better than the local ones. With fine polishing they shone brightly. The images they reflected were true and clear.

"Polish mirrors! Polish mirrors..." With its long-winded cadence, the polisher's drawl sounded very much like singing.

Opening the door, the old man saw the polisher, a gentleman-like craftsman in his early thirties, wearing an old red gown. As southerners worshipped the sun god and the fire god, they liked to wear red garments. But the commoners of humble and low origin usually wore greenish-coloured clothes. This man had to be different from ordinary hucksters.

The mirror polisher bowed courteously and asked: "Sir, do you have a mirror you want polished?"

Some Chu people were arrogant, but this polisher's urbane manner, among other things, appealed to the old man. Yes, he had a mirror that needed polishing; the one in his daughter's room had to be kept shiny. She had been complaining about it for days. The old man invited the polisher in and called to someone in the inner room: "Ruer, bring out the mirror, the polisher is here."

A clear ringing response came from inside and presently a young person with fine features entered with a bronze mirror and handed it to the polisher, who was amazed to see how handsome the lad was. With a little make-up, he could pass as a beautiful girl, he thought.

The lad, being shy, was stared down by the polisher.

"Father, I'm going back in to read."

When the lad had gone, the old man explained that his son was self-conscious in the presence of strangers.

The mirror polisher took a grinding stone from his bag, saying it was a stone from Mount Jing.

The old man said since stone from Mount Jing was hard enough to grind jade, it certainly could give the mirror a bright shine.

The polisher ran the stone back and forth over the mirror, making a soft rasping sound.

The old man took the initiative to pick up a casual conversation with the polisher. "You don't look like a craftsman. What made you take up this trade?" he asked.

"You've got sharp eyes, sir. When you are out travelling, you need money. But a thousand taels of gold in your pocket is not as good as a special skill in your hands."

"So you earn your travel expenses polishing mirrors?"

"A good idea! But wouldn't it be better for a talented young man like you to find a position in the government and serve the country?"

The mirror polisher laughed and said, "This is where northerners and southerners differ. Northerners believe in seeking official positions and serving the country; you always look up to emperors and princes and worry about the future. We southerners set greater store by the spirit within ourselves. The world is inside the spirit, not outside it.

"Although you are a northerner," the young man continued, "I see that you have a southerner's spirit in your bones."

"How do you know?" the old man asked.

"With your knowledge and experience you deserve a ranking position in the court, but you choose to stay in this secluded corner. Isn't that proof enough?"

A bitter smile crept over the old man's face.

"This reminds me of a folk song," the mirror polisher went on, "I wonder if you'd care to hear it?"

A hut of brambles,
Good enough to stay in;
Fresh mud fish and eels,
Good enough to live on.

Feel like having fish?
No need to eat bream;
It's time to marry,
But not a beauty
From the State of Qi.

Feel like having fish?
No need to eat carp;
It's time to marry,
But not a beauty
From the State of Song.

The old man nodded and said, "Live a life of poverty and cultivate a mind of tranquillity as the highest aim in life — in this respect we think alike. You value the cultivation of the mind more than anything else, but I think the mind's mirror needs polishing more than the bronze mirror. Otherwise one gets muddleheaded and bogged down in worldly affairs. The humble son of mine, the lad who brought the mirror a moment ago has just reached the age when his mind's mirror needs polishing. Would you like to stay with me for a year or so and tutor him in reading?"

"You're a learned scholar yourself, so why is it necessary to hire a tutor from outside?"

"All my life," the old man said, "I have been educated by scholars of the northern school. I know the 'ins' of it, but not the 'outs'. So I would prefer my son to be tutored by some scholar from the lively, dynamic southern school."

The conversation continued without altercations, in an amicable atmosphere. Since the old man in good faith invited him to stay, he accepted without hesitation. But he made it clear that he could stay for only six months, or one year at most. The old man agreed to that stipulation for the time being, thinking that by the end of the six months or the year, the tutor might wish to stay on, or better still, he might be persuaded to stay for good.

Six months passed and then another six months. The mirror polisher wanted to leave.

"Your son has keen powers of understanding. In one year he has actually exhausted all I've learned in my whole life. There is no need for me to stay on; I prefer travelling from place to place. It's my greatest joy. If I remain in one area too long, I get restless. So please let me go; I'm anxious to take up the road. So long as I am still on the move, I'll always come back and see you. It's a promise!"

As it had been agreed upon in the beginning, the old man could not but release him.

The mirror polisher made his departure, carrying the same old traveling bag he had arrived with, in which he kept extra clothes and his grinding stone.

Less than one year after he left, something strange happened to the pupil he had tutored, which stirred up waves of gossip in the town of Xiangyi. Not long after the mirror polisher was gone, the old man's son turned into a young woman. The woman, some said, became pregnant after she dreamed that a shooting star had flown into her mouth; others said that she became pregnant after she swallowed a big coloured pearl that fell from Heaven in broad daylight. As it turned out, the birth of the baby was a difficult one. Some said the woman, suffering from severe labour pains, walked around a plum tree in the courtyard. She walked round and round for several days, but the baby would not come. She almost died of exhaustion under the tree. And then, some said, an incision was made in her armpit to deliver the baby; others believed it was a Caesarean birth.

Regardless of the exact details, it was indeed an abnormal birth. It cost the life of the mother, but fortunately the baby survived.

Since the father was unknown, it was against the rules of propriety to have the baby delivered indoors, therefore it had to be delivered out in the courtyard under the plum tree (called "li" in Chinese). So the infant was surnamed Li and because of his extraordinary long ears (the word "ear" is pronounced "er" in Chinese), he was named Li Er.

The fantastic aspects of the infant's birth gave rise to doubts and suspicions throughout the neighbourhood, but most of the neighbours believed whatever they heard. The old man was a learned and honest gentleman who had served in a government post, though not of a high rank. Now retired from his duties, he abided by the law, observed the proprieties and maintained friendly relations with his neighbours. He could not have made up stories to deceive people.

As the infant's mother had died, leaving the old man and his grandson alone, the neighbours grew sympathetic and no one bothered any longer to ponder over how the mother had become pregnant and the circumstances under which the baby was born.

6

When the child was old enough, Grandpa began to consider teaching him to read. But what should he learn from his reading? The first thing that came to mind was the *I Ching* — *The Book of Changes*.

Incidentally the *I Ching* was the very book the mirror polisher from Chu had taught the child's mother.

"The *I Ching* is a book of the northern school," the old man once reminded the mirror polisher. "Are you southerners also familiar with it?"

"Yours is a somewhat one-sided view," the polisher rejoined. "The *I Ching* belongs to the world. It does not fall into the scope of the northern school nor is it limited as an achievement of the southern. If you ask about its origin, I should say it originated in the north but developed in the south.''

"This is new to me," said the old man. "I've never heard this before. What do you mean?''

"The legendary Fu Xi," explained the polisher, "was from the small State of Huaxu in the west. Later he moved to the north and settled in Bowl Hill, now the capital of Chen. When he saw a dragon-horse with markings on its back leaping from the Yellow River, he was inspired, and went on to develop the Eight Trigrams from a copy he made of the markings. Therefore I say the *I Ching* markings originated in the north. Fu Xi's descendents Shennong and Emperor Yan, constantly harassed by Chiyou, moved from Bowl Hill to Qufu. When Chiyou fell, a conflict arose between the Yellow Emperor and the Yan Emperor. Emperor Yan, forced to move to Chu, took the *I Ching* with him and there he continued to promote study of the book.''

"Penetrating and well-grounded," the old man commented agreeably.

The old man had begun teaching the *I Ching* to his daughter early on, but she showed little interest in it. However when the mirror polisher from the State of Chu supervised her studies she was intrigued. This young man teaches better than I do, thought Grandpa. What is the secret? He began to pay more attention to how the tutor explained things. Gradually he realised that the southern school laid a different emphasis on the book's significance from that of the northern school. He had studied the *I Ching* with scholars of the northern school which glorified the *yang*, the masculine, took Heaven as the origin of everything in the world and believed that the *yang* was permanently positive and auspicious. The trigram with the three *yang* signs — three unbroken lines (☰) — named *qian*, was taken as a sign of Heaven, symbolising the purest and most masculine *yang*.

Kun (the earth) indicated by three *yin* signs — three broken lines (☷) — was also believed to be the origin of everything in the world, and an auspicious sign, but as it stood for the *yin*, the feminine, *kun* was not always auspicious. When *kun* preceded the *yang*, it was disadvantageous: things might go astray. Only when *kun* followed *qian*, could the outlook be considered auspicious and beneficial. On the contrary, the young tutor's interpretation of the book, based on the southern view, was quite the reverse. He upheld the *yin*, the feminine, putting more weight on the *yin* than the *yang*.

The old man's daughter, truly puzzled, had once asked her tutor: "Sir, when we eat, don't we depend more on the hard teeth than the soft tongue?"

"When we are old, do the teeth survive or the tongue?" the tutor asked her.

"When we are old, our teeth of course fall out and our tongue will still be there!"

"Exactly," said the tutor, "the soft *yin* survives in the end, and the hard *yang* decays." His pupil was convinced.

The old man, auditing the lesson, nodded to himself. The southern school's interpretation of the book struck him as unique and original, the scholar's lecture, as lively and thought-provoking. No wonder my daughter is becoming interested in the book, he mused, highly satisfied. Nevertheless, the old man thought, the polisher might be well versed in the theory of *yin* and *yang*, but when it comes to sex, he is probably no smarter than a callow youth. Otherwise, how is such a learned scholar unable to distinguish between the *yin* and the *yang* of my daughter? Hopefully he will remain ignorant of the matter, brooded the old man in an effort to set his mind at ease. Otherwise there might well be trouble.

In fact, the tutor was not callow in matters of gender at all; he was just as experienced in this sphere as he was learned in the *I Ching*. The northern school believed in being open, like the sun and the moon in the sky, while the southern school of the *I Ching* believed in reticence, like the dragon under water. He had revealed one side of him and concealed the other. What a scoundrel!

Now, years later, in teaching the *I Ching* to Li Er, the old man unconsciously imbued him with the spirit of the southern school. Whichever the school, one began at the beginning:

Many years ago, a strange animal appeared from the Yellow River. Its body, like that of a horse, was covered with dragon-scales. It measured about eight feet from nose to hindquarters. It was called a dragon-horse, although it bore some resemblance to a camel as well. More astonishing about it was that on its back there was an orderly arrangement of black and white dots. In the rear there was one white dot and six black ones; on the left three white, eight black; on the right, four black and nine white; in the front, two black and seven white, while in the middle, there were five white and ten black dots....

News got around that some monster had leapt out of the Yellow River. When Fu Xi, living in Bowl Hill at the time, got wind of it, he made for the riverbank. A curious diagram on the dragon-horse's back caught his attention; he was inspired by a sudden flash of perspicacity.

"This signifies the dawn of civilisation!" he proclaimed.

For many years after that Fu Xi pondered the event, studying how to invent an appropriate form to represent the diagram, or map; but time passed and he still had not succeeded. Its message, undoubtedly both cryptic and profound, was not easily deciphered.

The young Li Er murmured to himself, as he memorised: In the rear, one-and-six; on the left, three-and-eight; on the right, four-and-nine; in the middle, five-and-ten....What would such a map look like anyway, he wondered. Picking up a piece of charcoal, he traced his ideas on a stone slab, just the way Fu Xi might have done. His first sketch map of dots failed to work out right, so he kept revising it until he was satisfied. "Grandpa, come and see if you think this looks anything like the diagram on the back of the dragon-horse!"

Grandpa came over and examined the diagram in detail.

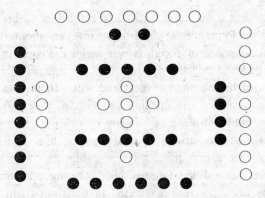

"Oh, certainly, it does! Very much! In every group of dots there are white ones in odd number versus black ones in even number. The odd-numbered white ones stand for the *yang*; the even-numbered black ones stand for the *yin*. Heaven is odd-numbered, standing for the *yang*; earth is even-numbered, standing for the *yin*. When the odd and the even are matched and the *yang* and the *yin* come together, they demonstrate the changes of all things between Heaven and earth. Very probably, Fu Xi had evolved the Eight Trigrams on this hypothesis." His grandson's perspicacity was exceptionally keen; the old man was proud of him.

Li Er loved reading, but found it boring to stay indoors with books all the year round. Each year there were two grand sacrifices to the god of land, the god of grains, and the ancestors — one offered for the Beginning of Spring, the other for the Beginning of Autumn. These occasions provided Li Er with the opportunity to go out and commune with Nature. That gave him inexpressible delight.

At the sacrifice to the god of land and the god of grain, people prayed for a good harvest in the coming autumn; at the sacrifice to the ancestors they reminisced about their clan forbears. The Son of Heaven and the dukes carried out the ritual at their family shrines, but commoners who could not afford to build shrines observed the formalities at the family graveyard mounds.

The worshipping of ancestors was serious. People of the same descent gathered together and, when the sacrificial ritual was over, shared the offerings of meat and wine. In this way they revived their sense of kinship and consolidated their clan relations against possible intrusion of bullying by other clans.

Graveyards were usually located between hills and rivers according to geomantic omens. The worshippers trailed along the Guo River toward the forested hills carrying offerings of meat and wine, their procession reflected in the transparent waters of the river. It was like an outing in spring when the fields were turning green with grass, or an excursion in autumn when the sky was high and the air crisp. These celebrations, however ritualistic, were relaxing and joyous experiences. Walking along between the green hills and the clear river to the sound of drums, the worshippers were accustomed to expressing remorse to think that their ancestors had not lived long enough for them to show their filial piety adequately. On this point, the observance, in return, gave comfort to the living.

According to ancient custom the worshippers chose a living person to appear on the altar as an impersonation of the deceased to eat the meat and drink the wine offered as sacrifice. That person was dubbed the "living ancestor". The worshippers bowed and prostrated themselves before him, expressing the greatest possible reverence, as if he had in fact been resurrected from the dead. The "living ancestor" was chosen from among the young. Young Li Er had been chosen to act as the "living ancestor" several times. Some believed he had auspicious features for this role because, young as he was, he had a pair of long ears, stretching seven inches; others considered him a young man of virtue with profound powers of understanding, for after studying the *I Ching* for only two years, he was able to re-invent Fu Xi's original *He Tu*, or Yellow River Map, as it came to be called.

However, Li Er was not at all proud of his role; he took it as something slightly hilarious, if not fantastic. As he stood on the altar in formal attire, the ritual master declaimed praises of the proprieties, while the senior clan member solemnly raised the cup of sacrificial wine and poured out a libation to the dead. The worshippers then bowed and prostrated themselves before the "living ancestor". In Li Er's mind, the custom was ridiculous, a form of skulduggery. In appearance, these good people were worshipping their ancestors, but in fact the elders of the clan were worshipping the young. Li Er's grandpa was also there, kow-towing to him in earnest. The common people worshipped their ancestors that way, so did the Son of Heaven and the princes. It seemed no one had ever raised any doubts about the practice.

While the elders bowed and prostrated in reverence, young Li Er up on the altar made no response, outwardly receiving their piety as a matter of course. The ceremony over, he sat down, and ate and drank to his heart's content.

As descendants, people believed that, by putting a real live person on the altar, they gave substance to the formless, and sound to the voiceless, spirit of the dead. When they saw him eat and drink their offerings, they felt they were making up for what they had neglected doing, at least doing sufficiently, while their ancestor was alive.

7

In the capital of the Chen State there was only one school run by the government. It was open only to children of ministers and high ranking officials.

The official position and salary of an aristocrat were inherited by his lineal heir. The descendants of his cousins and in-laws, by the fifth generation, were relegated to the commonality and de-prived of the privilege to attend the government school. Most of them became farmers but, with their highly educated origins, some of them had their children educated at private schools.

Those who refused to be reconciled to their lowered status trained their children at home. After mastering the "six arts", they could be appointed to minor positions in the government if chances came their way.

Later, when the Zhou Empire was in decline, the subordinate states rose up and contended for hegemony. They sought the services of learned people to help shore up their positions and expand. Thus opportunities arose for learned commoners to become ministers and high-ranking officials, in some cases, overnight.

These realities expedited the development of private education.

Li Er was educated at home. He spent a good number of years studying the *I Ching* with his grandpa. This book was very simple, and at the same time very complicated. It was simple because it consisted of only sixty-four symbols, each of which was made up of two signs, the sign of the *yang* (——) and the sign of the *yin* (— —) in various combinations. The teacher needed nothing more than a piece of charcoal and a stone tablet while lecturing. By way of illustration, he would draw each of the Eight Trigrams (*qian*[≡≡], *kun*[≡≡≡≡], *zhen*[≡≡≡], *xun*[≡≡], *kan* [≡≡≡], *li*[≡≡≡], *gen*[≡≡≡] and *dui*[≡≡≡]), which made up the basic content of the book. The other fiftysix symbols were variations of these trigrams.

It was also a complicated book. With two symbols, or lines, to represent *yang* and *yin*, and Eight Trigrams, or their sixty-four variations, it could explain all things between Heaven and earth and their changes as well. The book was complicated, for in the hands of one educated in its mysteries, it could deal with countless natural and social phenomena.

The symbol for *yang* is an unbroken line (——) and that for *yin*, a broken line (— —). Simple? Yet each of the two would take months, if not longer, to elucidate. The symbol (——) stands for the hard, the masculine, the monarch, the strong, the odd number and the positive. The symbol (— —) stands for the soft, the feminine, subjects, the weak, the even number and the negative. Everything between heaven and earth has opposite aspects symbolised by *yang* and *yin*, the hard and the soft, the strong and the weak and so on. But *yang* and *yin* are relative and changeable.. Therefore the concept of *yang* and *yin* becomes complicated when it is applied in understanding and explaining specific phenomena.

The hard *yang* and the soft *yin*, opposite and complementary, bring forth endless changes. *Qian* is relatively dynamic, and *kun* static. However, when the dynamic reaches an extreme, it becomes static, and vice-versa. There is static in motion and motion in static. Either the hard *yang* prevails or the soft *yin* does, but which ever prevails, there is always the *yin* within the *yang*, or the *yang* within the *yin*. They are part of each other, complementary to each other.

The Trigram *qian* is formed with three *yang* lines and the trigram *kun* is formed with three *yin* lines. Both trigrams are simple, but they can interpret millions of phenomena and their changes in the universe. One trigram could not be completely explained even in half a year.

Li Er enjoyed reading. So even as for the loneliness and isolation it involved, he could cast them aside as he explored ideas in his fancy and imagination. As he listened to his grandpa, his mind would wander off, Grandpa's voice turning into an indistinct buzz which drifted off into the void, quavering fainter and fainter....

... Before heaven and earth took shape and before *yang* and *yin* became distinct, the universe was a formless mass, endless and boundless, with no beginning and no end. That state is called the Extreme Terminus, or the Grand Terminus, in the *I Ching*. From the Extreme Terminus, or Grand Terminus, came *yin* and *yang* and from *yin* and *yang* came the ten thousand other things.

What did the Extreme Terminus, or the Grand Terminus, look like? Li Er wondered. Was it misty clouds or fog or air that flowed everywhere, the light and clearness of which ascended to become heaven, with that which was heavy and muddy subsiding to become earth and the rest becoming the ten thousand things in between?

......

"What are you thinking about, Li Er?"

"I'm listening to your lecture on the *I Ching*. Is the *I Ching* always explained in this way, Grandpa?"

"Yes, it is. Your mother learned the *I Ching* from a teacher who travelled from Chu to Chen to continue his own education. Although quite young, the teacher was exceptionally erudite. This is the way the book was explained to your mother."

Li Er had never heard about how his mother was taught the *I Ching* by someone from Chu. "Was the teacher a man or a woman? Where is the teacher now?" Li Er asked.

Grandpa's face fell. "All this happened some time ago. Don't get distracted; let's get back to our lesson."

Li Er could not concentrate on the lesson. He kept wondering: Was the teacher a woman? But I have never seen or heard of a woman teacher before. Was a woman allowed to go out and teach? Or was the teacher a man? But was a man allowed to teach a woman in her room? Never heard of that either.

"You have not told me whether the teacher was a man or a woman and you don't let me ask questions. What's wrong?"

......

The mirror polisher used a piece of charcoal and a stone tablet to explain the *I Ching* to his student. They stayed in the wingroom discussing the book from morning till noon and would not stop for lunch until the old man reminded them of the time.

Worried that his daughter might get bored sitting so long for one session, the old man tiptoed to the window and listened.

The teacher was in the midst of an explanation:

"...Why is *yang* a continuous line and *yin* a broken one? When Fu Xi invented them, what did he intend them to mean?

Since ancient times there have been numerous interpretations. I believe when Fu Xi saw the dragon-horse by the Yellow River, there must have been a male and a female. When the dragon-horses climbed out of the water, Fu Xi was fascinated by the strange maps on their backs. But when he saw that the male was ready to go in and the female opened, Fu Xi must have been excited and inspired. It was a sacred scene — the unity of *yang* and *yin* that gave birth to the ten thousand things in the world.

"Enlightened by the way the male went in and the female yielded, Fu Xi invented the sign *yang* (——) and the sign *yin* (— —). By combining *yang* and *yin* in variations, he worked out the Eight Trigrams which were further developed into sixty-four hexagrams. Is that clear? Do you understand?"

"Enlightened by the way the male went in and the female yielded, he invented the sign *yang* and the sign *yin*?" the girl recited easily, but could not suppress a giggle at the end.

The eavesdropper at the window stepped back with a start.

"What is there to giggle about?" the mirror polisher asked sternly. "We are discussing the way of Heaven and earth. This is nothing to be frivolous about. In ancient times it was believed that some sort of Heavenly God was the creator of everything, including man. Legend has it that, when Fu Xi's mother lived by the Wei River, she happened to tread on the foot-prints of a giant. Instantly, a rainbow encircled her and she became pregnant. From the unity of the dragon-horses Fu Xi surmised that the joining together of *yang* and *yin* gave birth to everything, including man. This was an extraordinary discovery. After that man began to view the world from an entirely new perspective: it was not created by a Heavenly God; it was the outcome of *yang* and *yin* coming together. Heaven is not God. Heaven was formed of the light and clear elements that arose from the formless mass."

The old man listened, convinced that the argument was correct and indisputable. I'm teaching the *I Ching* with the charcoal and tablet because the mirror polisher taught this way, he reflected to himself, but it would be improper to say any more about him to Li Er.

Year in and year out, Li Er bent over the *I Ching*. Eventually there came a time when he began to weary of it. "Grandpa, is there only one book in the world? Could you teach me from some other books?"

"Of course there are others. For example, *Sanfen*, *Wudian*, collections of folk songs through which the court learns about the lives of ordinary people. Also there are records compiled by court historians, regulations concerning proprieties and ceremonies, official documents and proclamations and the like. But they are all kept in the Imperial Archives of the court. You have no access to them outside the court. You need a lot of information to write a book. The text must be carved character by character on bamboo strips. This requires a lot of time and labour. Ordinary people like us cannot afford it."

"The *I Ching* is easy to teach because it has only sixty-four hexagrams," Grandpa went on. "Even if you don't have a copy you can write them from memory and then explain them one by one.

"For one thing, the diagrams in it are fewer in number and simpler in form than those in other books. That's partly why it is so popular. For another thing, the *I Ching* covers a far broader range of subjects, all of which are dealt with in depth. It provides rich food for thought that one can chew over again and again, and it never tastes insipid. It is the foundation of all learning and an inexhaustible source of knowledge. It deserves deepgoing study. That's why people use it as a textbook to educate their children."

"I see," said Li Er, thinking to himself: I hope some day I'll be able to go to the Imperial Archives and read some other books too; I want to read all the books there.

One day after his lessons, Li Er said, "Grandpa, I want to

travel and see the world."

"Travel? But you've never left home even on a small trip by yourself before."

"Don't worry about that. I am already grown up."

"You're a teenager — how can you say you're grown up? Well of course, a young person can have a grown-up's ambition. Where were you thinking of going?"

"Luoyang, Luoyang — the capital of the Zhou Empire! You once said the court of Zhou had the greatest archives with the largest collection in the country. Luoyang is not too far from here, why couldn't I go there and see what it's like?"

What! Go abroad? Leave the country? Outrageous! The old man himself had never in his life thought of doing such a thing. The idea of visiting the Imperial Archives was too far-fetched. No ordinary person could get anywhere near there. However, he did not want to dampen the boy's enthusiasm, and affected a moderate stance: "True, Luoyang is not too far away, but it is not an easy trip at all. You have to pass through the State of Xu and the State of Zheng to get there. Anyhow, travel expenses are way beyond our means."

"I can support myself by polishing mirrors along the way."

Support oneself by polishing mirrors? This only called forth the grief in his heart that had taken years to allay. When the mirror polisher had been asked to stay as tutor to his daughter, he had continued to polish their mirrors and the old man had learned the skill from him. After the tutor left, he polished the family mirrors himself. When Li Er was around seven or eight years old, he couldn't sit still and just watch any longer.

"Grandpa, let me do it."

"Do you know how to do it?"

"Let me have a try."

Not only did he know how to do it, he left the mirror smooth, shiny and without a blemish, having watched the procedure for three or four years. After that Li Er did all the polishing.

"How is it Li Er also thought of raising travel expenses by

polishing mirrors along the way, though he had never set eyes on the young tutor from Chu?'' The old man was bewildered.

"There's no hurry about it,'' said Grandpa. "Let's think it over some more.''

Li Er was determined. Once he had made up his mind, he would not change it. Finally he wheedled the old man into consenting.

"By teaching me the *I Ching* you've led me to the gate of a great, mysterious world, but how about the key to open it? You haven't got it, and neither have I. I must go and find this key!''

In the end the old man reluctantly yielded to his persistent enjoinments and agreed to let him go. "My dear lad, if you are determined to go and search for the key, go then. You have my blessing.''

However, the moment he obtained his grandpa's consent, Li Er relented.

"Grandpa, maybe I shouldn't go after all, and leave you behind like this. You're getting on in years. I should stay home and take care of you.''

"No one can help getting old. You're still a young man and you have a long life ahead of you. I must not keep you here with me year after year; it would only spoil your future. Heaven and earth gave humans a form bursting with life and spirit. When a person gets old and dies, the body goes back whence it came.''

"'Spirit' also means 'to spirit away'. Everyone must go. When one goes, the spirit ascends to Heaven and the form descends to earth. This is unalterable. When my time is up, I will go back to Heaven and earth whether you stay with me or not. Nothing can keep me from going. I understand this and I'm prepared for it. You just go ahead and don't worry about me.''

This drove the point home. Li Er was left with nothing more to say. It would have been strange if Grandpa, who had studied the *I Ching* all his life, had missed one of the most essential points of the book.

Li Er packed a few extra clothes into a travelling bag and took along a grindstone.

Grandpa had prepared some hard-boiled eggs to send along with him.

"Grandpa, we have only one chicken and I would like you to keep the eggs for yourself. With this grindstone, I can earn enough to eat while I'm on the road."

"It's not the eggs that I'm giving you, but the message in them. The Great Round is above and the sun is round. Being round means being moderate and being moderate means success. I wish you success!" Seeing the point, Li Er took the eggs without further ado and put them in his bag.

8

One day Yin Xi invited Li Er to go with him to a blind musician's street performance.

Li Er looked up from his book of bamboo strips. "You know that I don't especially enjoy listening to music...."

"But this man is not an ordinary performer. He is not just an ordinary blind man playing an instrument. Really, you mustn't miss him."

"What do you mean he is not ordinary?"

"That's a long, long story," said Yin Xi. "His name is Shi Kuang. He is from the State of Jin and came to Luoyang on a diplomatic mission. He has been in Luoyang for two months waiting to see Crown Prince Jin of Zhou, but has been given no word; but it is still uncertain when the prince will receive him or even whether he will receive him at all. He has voluntarily to come to Luoyang, and is determined to stay until he has an audience with the prince."

Six months ago Prince Ping of Jin sent Minister Shu Xiang to negotiate with Zhou about two border towns in dispute. Shu Xiang had been Prince Ping's teacher when he was young.

Later when he ascended the throne, he appointed Shu Xiang his counsellor. This Shu Xiang is a learned man, very articulate and ever so quick to turn circumstances to good account. He was well prepared with five 'unanswerable' arguments for annexing the two towns as Jin's territory. But he was hardly through with the first three arguments when he was thoroughly refuted by the Prince of Zhou. He was left tongue-tied, unable to bring out the other two arguments.

He returned to Jin, thoroughly crushed. He reported to the prince: "Although Prince Jin of Zhou is only fifteen years old, I am no match for him in negotiations. We had better give up the two towns, otherwise when he succeeds to the throne, he will form an alliance with the other states and launch a punitive expedition against us."

Prince Ping of Jin, thoroughly frightened, prepared to give up his claim to the two border towns. When Shi Kuang learned of this, he petitioned the prince to send him to Luoyang to consult with Prince Jin of Zhou. "If he can talk me round," he said, "it will not be too late to cede the two towns on my return."

One day a member of his entourage came in to report that the millet they had brought from the State of Jin was running short; what little money they had left had to be put aside for their return trip. He asked Shi Kuang what to do.

Shi Kuang was the official in charge of music at the Jin court. Envoys sent by various states to Luoyang were usually entertained at the government hostel for three or five days, or ten days at most. If for any reason they had to stay longer, they were expected to pay for their food out of their own pocket. By now Shi Kuang had lived at the hostel for two months. This had given rise to unfavourable gossip. Some said he would be evicted before too long. He suspected that Prince Jin of Zhou had adopted delaying tactics to deal with him. That is, when he ran out of grain he would have to leave of his own accord.

Minutes passed. The attendant asked again: "Sir, we have

nothing left for tomorrow. What shall we do?"

"Don't worry." Shi Kuang stood up. "I have my instrument with me. We can go to the streets and earn our food playing music."

"Work for our food by performing in the streets?" The attendant was surprised. "Surely that would not be appropriate since you are the Director of Music at the Jin Court, not an ordinary musician!"

"But don't forget I was a blind street musician before I received my appointment at court. Why is it so inappropriate for me to play out in the streets again?"

"And that is why he has started singing and performing in the streets again," Yin Xi explained. "That way he has managed to get along fine, actually. Besides, I believe by playing in the streets he is sending a message to the Prince of Zhou — that is, he is determined to stay in Luoyang until he is received. He's quite extraordinary, isn't he?"

"A blind musician, and at the same time so dedicated to state affairs?" Li Er was amazed.

"Yes, he is. He is not only a talented musician, but also takes a keen interest in politics. In the State of Jin many strange stories circulate about him."

"Really?"

"When he plays his instrument, he often attracts rare birds. White magpies, black cranes, and many other kinds of birds come flocking around him."

"He must have planted many rare trees at his home," Li Er suggested.

"Once when Shi Kuang was playing his instrument," Yin Xi went on, "a pair of black cranes descended from Heaven. Fluttering their wings they danced round him, each holding a big pearl in its beak. They were so intrigued by the melody that one of them began to sing along with him. The moment it opened its mouth, the pearl fell out. The crane found the pearl on the ground, picked it up again and flew off as if embarrassed. Of course Shi Kuang could not see what was happening around him, but sensing all the subtle details, he smiled."

The story brought a smile to the lips of Li Er also.

"If you think this is fantastic, let me tell you something even more incredible."

Once Prince Ping of Jin had a set of huge musical bells cast and he asked some court musicians to assess their temperaments. After testing the bells, they all said the temperaments were in harmony. When Shi Kuang was asked to check them, he said they were not, and the bells had to be recast.

"Strange, all the other musicians say they harmonise," insisted the prince. "Some day," Shi Kuang replied, "a real musician will tell you the bells are not in harmony. I'm sorry, but I feel this is a disgrace to the court."

Two years later, Prince Ling of Wei visited Jin with his court musician Shi Juan. When they arrived at the Pu River, it was late and they put up there for the night. In the middle of the night, Prince Ling heard a pleasant melody drifting in from the distance. When he asked his entourage if they had heard it, they all said they had heard nothing. He summoned Shi Juan: "I heard music a moment ago, a very pleasant melody. But the others all say they did not hear it. Was it music from the spirit world that I heard?" He asked Shi Juan to listen carefully and to write down what he heard.

Shi Juan went back to his room, set up his instrument and started playing the melody as he heard it. The next morning he told the prince that he had written down the music but needed more time to familiarise himself with it. He asked for permission to stay there for another day. To this, the prince agreed.

On the third day, they continued their trip to Jin. Prince Ping of Jin treated Prince Ling to a banquet in the Shiyi Tower. While the festivities were in progress, Prince Ling, standing up, proposed a toast to Prince Ping and offered to play some music they had picked up on their way to Jin. Prince Ping was pleased.

Shi Juan, the court musician of Wei, set up his instrument

and began playing. Shi Kuang was sitting next to him. When the Wei musician was only half way through the melody, Shi Kuang stopped him abruptly, saying the music was that of a conquered state and must be stopped before the end.

Prince Ping, however, was enthralled by the music. He asked Shi Kuang why he considered it the music of a conquered state.

Shi Kuang said it was composed by Shi Yan, court musician of the Shang Dynasty at the time of Emperor Zhou. His principal duty was composing evil and licentious music for the emperor. When Emperor Zhou was defeated by King Wu of the Zhou Dynasty, Shi Yan slipped away and fled toward the east. When he reached the Pu River, he drowned himself. Shi Juan must have picked up this melody by the river.

Shi Kuang's speculation was correct. Prince Ling and Shi Juan had to admit it. They wondered whether it had been Shi Yan's spirit playing music that night or whether he had once taught it to someone living by the river who had passed it down over the years.

"I only care about the melody," Prince Ping said. "I don't care who composed it or for whom. Let him finish it!"

When Shi Juan was through with the melody, Prince Ping asked Shi Kuang what its mode was. Shi Kuang said it was "Qing Shang" played at a high pitch, with fast plucking of the strings.

"Is it a sad mode?" Prince Ping asked.

Shi Kuang replied that it was not as sad as "Qing Zheng", which had a higher pitch and was played with even faster plucking of the strings.

The prince asked him to play "Qing Zheng" for him. Shi Kuang said that only a king of virtue could appreciate such a piece; as Prince Ping was lacking in virtue, he could not stand the sadness of its tune.

The prince replied that at the moment, he was interested in hearing the melody only, not anything else.

Shi Kuang could not but obey; he began. The moment his

fingers touched the strings, sixteen black cranes came flying in from the south and alighted on the beams of the tower. When he began to play it the second time, the cranes descended from the beams in single file. When he began to play it the third time, all sixteen cranes spread their wings to dance and raised their necks to sing. Their singing, harmonious with the melody, echoed up to Heaven.

It was fantastic! None of them had ever witnessed such a majestic spectacle before. Prince Ping was amazed, as were all the others. Standing up, he proposed a toast in honour of the musician. Sitting down again, the prince said, "I doubt that there is anything sadder than 'Qing Zheng', am I right?"

"But 'Qing Zheng' is not as sad as 'Qing Jiao'," answered Shi Kuang.

"Can you play 'Qing Jiao' for me?" the Prince inquired.

"I'm afraid I cannot," Shi Kuang answered. "It was the melody played for the Yellow Emperor when he worshiped the Ghost and the Spirit on top of Mount Tai. Since you are not to be compared with the Yellow Emperor in virtue, you cannot listen to 'Qing Jiao'. It is too sad for you. If you listen to it, you will only bring trouble on yourself."

"My days are numbered," said the Prince. "What trouble is there to be afraid of? I only care for the music. I don't care what it brings on me. Go ahead and play it. Let me hear what it sounds like."

Again Shi Kuang had to obey. The moment he began to play, black clouds rose in the northwest. When he went on to play it a second time, his fingers worked on the strings like flying wheels, producing a high pitch like howling winds sweeping through a forest. Suddenly a storm broke out. Heavy rain beat down, while high winds dashed rocks and tiles against the doors and windows, tearing up curtains and damaging the walls.

The guests panicked and fled for their lives. Prince Ping, frightened to death, fell prostrate on the floor, unable to move.

Afterwards the State of Jin was struck by continuing drought.

For three years in a row, there were no crops.

Prince Ping lay paralysed in bed.

If a ruler neglects state affairs, people complained, and seeks sensual pleasures, this is what happens to him. Too much enjoyment can only end in disaster. He deserves it.

Shi Juan was asked to test the bells. He said their temperaments were not in harmony and the bells had to be recast. He backed up Shi Kuang's evaluation.

"He's really an extraordinary musician, don't you think so?" Yin Xi asked Li Er.

"Yes, quite extraordinary!" said Li Er. "Since through his music he can commune with divine spirits, why doesn't he just forget about politics and devote himself to music? He could become a sage musician."

"But I hear he is just as enthusiastic about politics as music," said Yin Xi. "Once when he was with Prince Ping in his chamber, the prince said to him, 'You have been blind since birth and your life is full of darkness. Don't you feel miserable?'

"As the story goes, Shi Kuang said, 'There are five kinds of blindness in the world. I suffer from just one of them. I am not too miserable.'

"The prince asked him to explain what he meant by the five kinds of blindness.

'While ministers and officials bribe their way into office,' Shi Kuang began, 'and the people who are ill-treated have no place to go to have their grievances redressed, the ruler, though he has got eyes, does not see it. This is the first kind.

'While loyal ministers are not trusted, trusted ministers are not loyal; while mediocrities hold ranking positions and worthless people are regarded as talents, the ruler, though he has eyes, does not see it. This is the second form of blindness.

'While crafty and evil ministers practise deceit and the national treasury is exhausted; dreadful deeds are covered up with petty tricks; virtuous people are exiled and traitors seize power, the ruler, though he has eyes, does not see it. This is the third kind of blindness.

'While the state is poverty-stricken and the people are exhausted; wars are constantly waged and selfish desires run rampant; villains fabricate cases against the upright, the ruler, though he has eyes, does not see it. This is the fourth type of blindness.

'While right and wrong are not distinguished; laws are not enacted; officials are made up of the dishonest and the people are not ensured of security, the ruler, though he has eyes, does not see it. This is the fifth kind of blindness.

'Any state that suffers from these five types of blindness is sure to fall. My blindness is but a minor one. What harm does it do to the state?'''

"Shi Kuang must have been hurt when the prince called him 'blind','' Li Er said, "so he used satire to get back at him. I think he listed the five forms of blindness just to play down his own real physical disability. It's not necessarily proof of his devotion to politics.''

"If he answered Prince Ping with the five kinds of blindness because he took his remark as a personal insult,'' said Yin Xi, "there are two more instances to prove that Shi Kuang really does concern himself with politics. For example, once Prince Ping said to Shi Kuang, 'I am already seventy years old. Isn't it too late for me to learn?' 'If it is too late,' said Shi Kuang, 'why not light a torch?' Prince Ping's face fell, 'I've never heard of a minister who made fun of his prince,' he said.

'How dare I make fun of Your Majesty?' said Shi Kuang. 'But I hear when a child is interested in learning, he has the brightness of the morning sun; when a middle-aged person is interested in learning, he has the brightness of the mid-day sun; when an old man is interested in learning, he has the light of a torch. When you travel at night, do you prefer travelling with a torch or groping about in the dark?' Prince Ping said nothing.

He was convinced by Shi Kuang's arguments."

"As a matter of fact," said Li Er, "he was talking about learning, rather than admonishing the prince."

Yin Xi went on with the other story. "Once Prince Ping asked Shi Kuang how to be a good ruler. Shi Kuang said, 'Remain tranquil and take no action; love the people and use the worthy; keep your eyes and mind open; don't drift after the tide and don't let your hands be tied by your subordinates; stand high and be farsighted; strengthen administration and keep your ministers and officials under control. These qualities, I believe, make up the moral integrity of a good ruler.'"

"This is pure politics," said Li Er.

"Wait a minute," put in Yin Xi. "He has advised his prince in more drastic ways. Once Prince Ping treated his ministers and ranking officials to a banquet. In the middle of the banquet Prince Ping stood up and announced with pride: 'The prince is the happiest man in the world because he is never disobeyed.' Just then Shi Kuang happened to be playing music for the banquet. On hearing what the prince said he picked up his instrument and dashed toward him. The prince dodged quickly causing him to bump into the wall, and smashing his instrument. 'Who are you trying to hit?' Prince Ping asked. The prince thought the musician might have been irritated by someone and had tried to strike him but had dashed at the prince by mistake.

"'I aimed at the mean person sitting next to you,' Shi Kuang explained. 'I heard him say the prince is the happiest man in the world because he is never disobeyed.' 'There must be some misunderstanding,' said the prince. 'It was I who said that, not someone else.' 'But it is not appropriate for the prince of a state to say this sort of thing,' said Shi Kuang. After the banquet, this trusted ministers urged the prince to get rid of Shi Kuang, but the Prince disagreed: 'Say no more about it. I should learn a lesson from this.'"

Li Er said, "What a lot of information you've collected

about Shi Kuang. All right, let me go with you and see what kind of a musician he is!''

9

The mansion of Minister Wangsun was in the south of the capital next to the court palace. The market and cottages were in the north.

Li Er and Yin Xi crossed the residential area in between on their way to the market. This area was divided into units of ten households each. The dwellings of each unit were laid out in a square with a well in the centre. Most of them were thatched huts with doors made of branches and brambles. Those with adobe walls and tiled roofs were rare. According to the system of the Zhou Dynasty, each group of households, called *yi*, had ten measures of land to cultivate, each measure covering one hundred *mu*. Each year only half of the allocated land was cultivated, the other half allowed to lay fallow for use the next year.

Each household of the *yi* had its own private land but it was obliged to help cultivate the state land with its own tools and seeds. The state land, all of which belonged to the Son of Heaven, was given priority over private land and the grain harvested from it filled up the state granaries.

The area, inhabited mostly by farmers, looked bleak and inhospitable by comparison with the luxurious court palace in the south and the thriving market place in the north.

As Li Er and Yin Xi neared their destination, they began to hear the strident cacophony of the marketplace the clanging of metals, the whistling of belows, the insistent hawking of craftsmen and peddlers.

There were stone-grinding cottages, pottery kilns and workshops handicrafting bone articles, carriage fixings and whatnot. There were wheel-barrow makers, blacksmiths and leather-tanning shops. All these cottage enterprises used to be run by the government, catering to the needs of the court and ministers, but during the past few years privately-run workshops had sprung up with various tradesmen and craftsmen making specialised articles and products in exchange for what they needed.

A new trend had arisen in the capital. Some of the officials were resigning from their posts and taking up more profitable trades and business dealings outside the government.

Li Er and Yin Xi rarely visited the market. They were not the least interested in the colourful goods displayed in the stalls and shops. They searched right and left, listening for the blind musician. In the distance, not far ahead in the middle of the street, they caught sight of a clump of people standing about in a loosely-formed circle, not exactly loitering, but not transfixed either. When the two got closer, they heard a man singing. He was none other than the blind musician.

His fair complexion was lined with a thin mustache. His eyes looked sunken and inert. As they learned later, it was not the result of an eye disease; he had been born without eyes.

Sitting on the ground, he sang and played his instrument in accompaniment. His face was set with a serious expression, his husky voice carried a tinge of sorrow as his dexterous fingers flew back and forth over this instrument:

> Ah, the never-ceasing rains
> Are ruining my crops.

These first two lines were repeated at a high pitch as if he were voicing an appeal to Heaven for mercy.

There was not a single cloud in the sky, to say nothing of rain. His listeners were perplexed.

As he went on, the theme of the song gradually emerged.

> Oh, great blue Heaven!
> Lacking in virtue,
> Brings calamity,
> Tortures the living.
> Heaven is fearful

> The ruler lacks justice.
> Criminals run rampant
> The innocent are blamed.
> ......
> A clumsy tongue in my head,
> My song is not clear.
> The clumsy tongue in my head
> Speaks unheard, tells of trials.
> He with a sweet tongue in his mouth
> Is raised to an honoured post.
> ......

The words of the song were too pessimistic, the music not appealing enough. Although the musician sang from his heart, the listeners were inattentive and began to slip away unobtrusively.

"He is an official from Jin; he's not asking for money! Why are you leaving?" someone in the crowd shouted.

"Even if he does ask for money," the last one on his way out remarked, "who wants to listen? He's not singing, he's giving us a lecture!"

There were no black cranes or white magpies flying about, nor did any animals come prancing around. Obviously the blind musician had failed to move the Divinity, least of all to hold the attention of his listeners on earth.

Is this the much-vaunted "sage" musician of the day? His singing is not a far cry from the performance of an ordinary village yodeller, Li Er thought.

"If you listen carefully," Yin Xi said, "you can sense its rhythm and flavour. His virtuosity is really terrific. The melody is highly refined. The more refined a melody is the less it can be appreciated. Few listeners can really understand it."

"I hear," Yin Xi continued, "he has composed three other melodies: 'The Sunny Spring', 'White Snow' and 'Xuanmo'. 'Sunny Spring' is conceived with the idea of spring rejuvenating all things as the gentle breezes blow, 'White Snow' was inspired by the coldness and whiteness of the crystal snow and the clear, crisp sounds produced by the rustling of bamboos. 'Xuanmo' makes you feel that Heaven and earth have suddenly closed in and you have become one with Nature, away from the human world. In that state, you become unconscious of yourself and the external world, melting completely into the eternal universe. The joy you draw from it is beyond words..." With a faraway look in his eyes Yin Xi could not go on.

In response to Yin Xi's mystical and infectious description, Li Er smiled: "Only those who can commune with his music can achieve that state. Is there anyone among the listeners who can commune with his music? Not one. Some stand uncomprehending like fools, others, completely inattentive, are talking and laughing among themselves."

Suddenly Shi Kuang stopped playing and spoke up above the murmuring of the crowd:

"I'm really fortunate to have appreciative listeners nearby!"

Li Er and Yin Xi looked at each other, astonished. What sensitive ears he must have to hear what we are whispering at such a distance.

"Won't you two gentlemen draw near so we may chat?" Shi Kuang said, motioning toward them as if he had seen them.

They had hoped to come unnoticed and to leave in the same way, but now they felt obliged to approach him.

Mutual introductions were not necessary, they had long heard of each other. Yin Xi asked, "Why didn't you play some of your masterpieces, like 'Sunny Spring' and 'White Snow'?"

"You must have seen how few listeners there were...."

The blind musician put aside his instrument. The crowd dispersed in search of other amusement, leaving only Li Er and Yin Xi engaged in conversation with Shi Kuang.

"They like listening to supernatural, romantic stories, as well as popular folk songs," the musician explained. "They wouldn't understand 'Sunny Spring' or 'White Snow'. Why should they? As you were saying a moment ago, the more refined the music is, the fewer there are who can appreciate it. Not many people can understand my music."

"Since you've come out into the street, why don't you play music that people can understand and enjoy? Don't you like to draw a large crowd of listeners?"

"I have to disagree with you partly," Shi Kuang said with a serious expression on his face. "As an artist, naturally I enjoy playing for an appreciative audience; the larger the better. If the audience is small, say, one hundred, ten, even five or three, I still enjoy playing so long as they understand and appreciate it. Music plays an important role in setting the trend and civilising the people. As literature can convey truth, music can do the same. It cultivates fine virtues and spreads them far and wide. When you add music to a poem, the poem becomes a song; when proprieties are formulated, they are matched with music. Music is played on certain occasions and proprieties are observed with certain ceremonies. Music can hold people together and draws people from far and wide. If I cater to vulgar tastes by playing decadent music, it corrupts the moral fiber of the people and leads the country astray. As an official court musician, don't I have to be careful?"

His attendant, finding his words irrelevant and boring, now approached him with a tray in his hands. He picked up two small knife-coins from the tray and dropped them again with a clatter.

"Sir, this is your reward for half a day's efforts. Two coins," remarked the attendant.

"Two are better than nothing," said Shi Kuang. "Money was not my purpose in coming here."

"It's all very well to say money is not what you came for, but our rice pot is empty and you want to stay on in Luoyang until you are received by Prince Jin. Without money, how can we eat? I am afraid we'll be thrown out of the hostel."

Yin Xi was surprised to hear that Shi Kuang was in such straits.

"As an official envoy," Shi Kuang said with a smile, "I am

prepared to sacrifice even my life to fulfill the mission. What's a shortage of rice in the pot?''

Li Er kept quiet. He had heard that Shi Kuang had blinded himself with burning smoke to avoid being lured by the sensual pleasures of the external world so that he could dedicate himself to music. Now that he was blind, Li Er thought, he was still not free from day to day worldly anxieties.

What a pity! Li Er mused: The soul and the spirit must not become slaves of the outer world or part from each other. If the soul wants to remain quiet, but the spirit wants to break away, how can one's vigour last? One cannot endure unless his soul and spirit are one. Only when the soul is dependent on the spirit, the spirit on the soul, can one live forever.

Can you stay as innocent and docile as an infant and keep your soul clean? Can you keep your eyes unveiled and your mind unbiased so that you can see the world as it is? Can you follow the natural course, live amongst the people and govern the country by taking no action?

Yin Xi produced a string of coins and placed it on the tray the attendant was holding. Though it was not a large sum, it was all he had in his pocket.

Li Er felt in his pockets for quite a while but found no money. He seldom took money along when he went out.

Shi Kuang said he was sorry he had to take their money. Yin Xi told him they were staying at the Wangsun's, and if there was anything they could do, they would be glad to help.

"Although I'm blind and may miss a lot," Shi Kuang said, "I've heard there's a learned scholar by the name of Li Er in Luoyang. He is dedicated to the studies of such classics as *Sanfen* and *Wudian* in pursuit of tranquillity and simplicity. He advocates the idea of "non action". His learning and thinking are far ahead of our time. His positive remarks are often mistaken as negative comments. How is it he has not said anything today?"

Li Er motioned Yin Xi with his eyes to explain for him.

"This friend of mine is a learned scholar, but he doesn't talk much. When we two are together, usually I do the talking and he does the listening. Once in a while he cuts in, but it is a matter of one or two words. With strangers, he is completely tongue-tied."

"What he says is so," Li Er said. "Please don't take offence."

"Taciturn people," Shi Kuang said, "are usually thoughtful people. I hear Li Er comes from Chu. You must know the famous remarks Prince Zhuang once made, 'For three years it has not made any attempt to fly, but once it starts flying, it will soar up into the sky; for three years it has not shown any inclination to sing, but once it starts singing, it will startle the world!' Are the Chu people all like this?"

"Maybe so," Li Er answered.

Back in their rooms, Yin Xi said, "He has a sharp mind but he has no eyes. What a pity!"

"A man without eyes is not really blind," said Li Er. "It's not such a great pity really."

"Here you go again," said Yin Xi. "You're full of paradoxes. If a man without eyes is not blind, who is blind then?"

"He who does not know himself but insists on trying to do what he is incapable of is blind and most pitiful of all."

"Do you mean to say Shi Kuang is to be pitied not because he is blind, but because he does not know himself, and insists on doing what he is unfit for or incapable of?"

Ignoring Yin Xi's question, Li Er went on as if talking to Yin Xi and himself at the same time:

> He who knows others is clever;
> He who knows himself is enlightened.
> He who conquers others is strong;
> He who conquers himself is powerful.
> He who is content with his lot is rich;
> He who acts with persistence has will.

He who keeps to his root is long-lasting;
He who dies does not perish but endures forever.

10

The carriage arrived at a park-like enclosure in the centre of which stood a building with upturned eaves surrounded by green luxuriant foliage. The driver drew the horses to a halt: "Here we are, sir."

When Li Er had first arrived in Luoyang two years earlier, and seen the imposing city wall, he wondered whether he could find a suitable job in such a place. Though board and lodging were now being provided by the hospitable Minister Wangsun, he was reluctant to go on indefinitely as a guest in someone else's house. Now that he had been offered a position at the Imperial Archives, he was relieved and happy.

"We have arrived, sir," the driver repeated. Lifting the carriage curtain, Li Er saw a small but splendid-looking structure nestling in green trees. The park resembled that surrounding Minister Wangsun's mansion except that here, the atmosphere was more serene and quiet.

"Where are we?" Li Er ventured to ask.

"The Imperial Archives," came the announcement, ringing with importance.

The Imperial Archives? Only two or three big states in the whole country had archives. Small states did not even have court historians, let alone archives. Some middle-sized states had court historians, but no archives. Court historians were usually posted at the ancestral shrine of the prince and, in addition to their main duties, they took charge of sacrificial rites and various other ceremonies. That was the case in Chen, Li Er's home state.

Different states had different names for the keeping of their histories. In the State of Jin it was known as *Cheng*, in Chu as *Tao Wu* and in Lu as *Chun Qiu* (*Spring and Autumn*). Court historians were usually faithful to the historical realities, and when they felt it necessary they even ignored interference from the throne. These states laid great stress on the writing of their histories, but did not keep separate archives. They affiliated their archives with their ancestral shrines.

"The Ancestral Shrine of Zhou is still ahead," said Li Er, "next to the palace. The Archives are most likely located inside the Shrine. We'll have to go on a bit farther, probably."

"This is the Archives," said the driver. "I often drive ministers and officials here. The Shrine and the Archives are not in the same place. We drivers ought to know our way about Luoyang after all."

Leaving the carriage, Li Er walked hesitantly toward the building. When he entered the gate, several people came up to him along the path. They greeted him and introduced themselves. One of them was the chief archivist, the others court historians. By now Li Er's doubts about the location of the Archives had vanished. He was pleased with his job here and grateful to Wangsun Yi for his recommendation. As for the environment, it was particularly enthralling for a nature-lover like himself.

He went to Minister Wangsun's house on invitation later that day. Arriving there, he heard some girls giggling in the hall. Unmarried, Li Er was sensitive to women's voices though these were not loud or noisy. He stopped at the door, feeling it would be impertinent to go in at such a moment.

A maid came out smiling sweetly. "Are you Li Er from Substitute House? Please come in. The minister is waiting for you in his inner chamber."

"Is he with his family?"

"No. Please come in and you'll find out for yourself."

He followed the maid along a zigzag of corridors.

Wangsun Yi and an attractive woman rose to greet him.

Li Er stole a glance at the woman and then quickly dropped his eyes to the floor about one foot from his feet.

a "Don't stand on ceremony, sir," Minister Wangsun said. "I hear in your home state there are few restrictions on behaviour between men and women. They are free to visit each other, talk, laugh and sing together. Thus they are different in some ways from women in Lu, Qi, Jin or Qin, or even here, the capital of Zhou."

"That is true," said Li Er. "Heaven and earth regard all creatures as 'straw dogs'. They exercise no favouritism whatever. The sages regard all people as 'straw dogs'. They are not biased against men or women, the noble or the humble. Why should men and women guard against each other?"

Wangsun Yi had often attended court sacrifices. He knew what straw dogs were. They were dogs fashioned out of straw and placed at the altar as part of the offerings. After the sacrifice they were either burnt or simply discarded.

When Li Er said Heaven and earth regarded all creatures without favouritism, it was true. They treated them like straw dogs, leaving them to live or die on their own. Good kings and princes should treat all people, men and women, the same. They should exercise no favouritism but leave the people to their own likes and dislikes.

Wangsun Yi was impressed by Li Er's profound observations. A little thought to an everyday occurrence enabled him to quickly grasp its essence and bring out a reasonable interpretation.

Wangsun Yi told the woman that this was the gentleman who had saved her life, and therefore deserved her gratitude. The woman lifted her skirt and bowed to him.

Li Er was confused, explaining in haste: "I'm but a humble scholar who wanders from place to place. I myself have to live on the generosity of the minister, how could I have saved anyone?"

"This lady is none other than Zheng Ji," said the Minister, "the one who offended one of my guests by laughing at the wrong time. If it had not been for you, she would have been beheaded. She owes her life to you."

"No need to thank me," put in Li Er. "It was not really a matter of trying to save her life, but of pursuing Tao, the truth; or, you might say, the way things should be. As I was saying a moment ago, whether sages or ordinary people, men or women, they are all straw dogs on the altar. Men are not superior to women. Why should that man take a woman's laugh as a personal insult and insist that she be executed?"

Zheng Ji was open and forthright. Seeing Li Er had no prejudice against women and that Minister Wangsun shared his impartiality, she said, "Sir, just for this one remark, 'men and women are all straw dogs on the altar', I must thank you once more." So saying she made another low bow before him.

"Please don't do this," Li Er hastily tried to stop her. "Let's dispense with formalities, I find them nothing but a bane. Let's just be natural and relaxed."

"I suggest," Minister Wangsun said to Zheng Ji, "you should sing a song to Li Er. Chen and Zheng are neighbouring states and their folk songs are somewhat similar in style. I believe Li Er would enjoy it."

In fact Li Er did not enjoy listening to songs, but could hardly decline the offer. That would have been bad manners on this occasion.

Zheng Ji, who loved singing, needed no persuasion. Gathering her ideas for a second, she began:

> Poplars at the east gate
> Rustling sound their leaves.
> It must be getting late,
> Stars peep through the trees.
>
> Poplars at the east gate
> Still rustle their leaves.
> Stars glitter so ornate,
> In the morning breeze.

It could be a young man singing; usually in affairs of the heart, men seemed more eager than women. A young couple had arranged to meet at the east gate. The youth was first to arrive. After waiting in vain for a long time, he grew anxious and began to sing this melancholy strain.

It could as well be the young woman singing. In Chen and Zheng some women were bolder than men.

Li Er soon regained his composure. He became thoughtful: The reason why the world is scourged by perpetual warfare is because men's material desires are allowed to grow rampant; the five colours blind the eyes, the five tones deafen the ears, the five flavours dull the sense of taste, hunting drives one crazy, and rare treasures cause people to rob and grab. The Sage seeks to satisfy his belly not his eyes. In a troubled world like this, one should be content with a full belly; indulgence in sensual pleasures brings trouble.

"Sir, how did you like this song?" Minister Wangsun asked.

"Music is beyond me," said Li Er. "I'm sorry; I hardly know how to comment. Just a layman."

Wangsun Yi and Zheng Ji were slightly disappointed.

However, Li Er relieved their embarrassment. "It doesn't sound like a Zheng folk song, I might say. It seems rather like a folk song from my home state."

Zheng Ji was excited: "What a layman in music you turned out to be! You can certainly tell folk songs from different places."

"I've had the pleasure of reading some of your writings," said Wangsun Yi. "They are rhythmical and in good rhymes. You must have made a thorough study of poetry."

"Poems and songs are inseparable," Zheng Ji added. "I'm sure you can sing. Could you please sing us a song and give this low-brow woman a chance to hear a piece of your high-brow music?"

Li Er declined, saying that he had no sense of pitch and he could not carry a tune.

"Oh, come on! What do you mean you can't carry a tune?" said Minister Wangsun. "You have a very resonant voice. I'm sure you can sing a melody. Don't be so modest. Sing us one! Just for fun!"

"I really can't sing," Li Er insisted. "But when you say my writings are in rhymes that's true. Let me chant a few lines quoted from the inscription on a bronze basin. How would that be?"

Wangsun Yi and Zheng Ji were both pleased.

Li Er began to chant in a pleasant tone:

> Indulge in water
> Rather than in lust.
> Indulge in water, you can swim;
> Indulge in lust, you are lost.

Li Er chanted the four lines rhythmically and distinctly, in a full, expressive voice. Wangsun Yi and Zheng Ji felt that if only he had developed an interest in music, he could have been an outstanding singer.

Li Er repeated the four lines three times.

"Only four lines?" Zheng Ji wanted to hear more.

"But you cannot judge by the number of lines," Wangsun Yi said thoughtfully. "The four lines carry the weight of forty, or four hundred lines. There is a lot to think about in them."

Zheng Ji was silent.

Wangsun Yi said, "Have the attendant lay the table. Li Er will have lunch with us."

Li Er said he preferred having lunch back at the guesthouse. Wangsun Yi countered that he had something he wanted to discuss with him during the meal. "We have no delicacies to offer," he went on, "but we have dog meat — roasted, baked and stir-fried. This is an all-dog-meat lunch!"

"In the south we don't have anything like this," said Li Er.

"My idea of an all-dog-meat lunch was inspired by your

'straw dogs' concept,'' said Wangsun Yi.

"It was only an offhand remark,'' Li Er said. "Please don't take it too seriously. You are offering me an all-dog-meat lunch today because I mentioned 'straw dogs'. If I talk about cows tomorrow, will you give me an all-beef meal?''

"For your enlightening ideas, I would be more than happy to provide it.''

"Wonderful!'' exclaimed Zheng Ji. "If you speak of dogs to-day, cows tomorrow and then pigs, sheep, deer, bears, wild ducks, wild geese and whatnot, I'll arrange a banquet of each for a long time to come.''

"As you have been here for some time,'' Wangsun Yi said, coming to the point, "I should like to recommend to you a post so that you can have a regular job to do.''

"In difficult times like these,'' said Li Er, "I'm quite satis-fied with my life here. So long as I have enough food to eat, enough books to read and enough time to go around and see things, there is no hurry about a job. I hate to give you trouble.''

"You must not miss the chance,'' said the Minister. "You'll find it to your taste.''

"Really?''

"There is a vacancy at the Imperial Archives and I should like you to fill it. An archivist is not a senior official and has no power. Mind you, I wouldn't want to recommend any of those over-ambitious guests for the job; they only dream of becoming ministers and of taking charge of the whole country as their per-sonal responsibility. I know you are fond of a quiet life and indif-ferent to fame and wealth. It's out of this consideration that I would like to recommend you to this post, insignificant as it is.

"There you can have all the three things you want. There you can earn enough for your food and to spare; you will have all the books you want — the place is packed with books; you have access to all sorts of secret documents and rare books. If I want to read anything, I can only get it through your good offices. Even the Son of Heaven must go to you to borrow books. As for free time, you will have plenty of it. You can go and see historical relics here and antiques there. If anything sensational occurs, you can go straight to the scene, investigate the details and write them down as you see fit. You have all the time in the world for visiting places."

Li Er was moved.

"Take it or leave it," said Wangsun Yi, "it's entirely up to you."

"I'll take it," said Li Er.

"You can leave it if you don't like the position. I can always recommend you to something else, you know. You're not obliged to accept...."

"I like it. I do really."

There were only three or four people, including the chief archivist, at the Archives. The quarters were really too big for such a small staff. One or two rooms set apart in some temple yard would have provided ample space.

But the Imperial Archives of Zhou were different from the others. All the relics and books inherited from previous dynasties were kept there. A spacious building of fine architecture had been created, as deemed necessary for such valuable collections.

On his first day at the archives Li Er was intrigued, especially by the books.

The chief archivist expected the staff to gather materials from all possible channels and encouraged them to study historiography, that is, the methodology of writing history. He often cited historians of the past who had sacrificed their lives to set down truthful records of important contemporary events. One morning, he called the archivists together and declared in an indignant tone that an outrageous event had occurred in the profession.

What could it be, they wondered — as archives were not

disreputable places and archivists not money-grubbers, what unusual event could have happened?

"A family of archivists have sacrificed their lives for justice," the chief archivist went on. "They have died martyrs and done credit to our calling!"

As a matter of fact the event had taken place two years earlier, but the news had taken a long time to reach Luoyang. For one thing, communications were poor; for another, the subordinate states largely ignored the court of Zhou and neglected keeping it informed of the happenings in their states.

In Qi there was a minister named Cui Zhu who had a steward by the name of Dongguo Yan. Dongguo Yan's sister was married to Minister Tang Yi and after the marriage she was called Tang Jiang. The above-mentioned scandal centred round these persons.

One day Dongguo Yan, grief-stricken, asked Minister Cui Zhu for leave, saying his brother-in-law Tang Yi had died and he was obliged to attend the funeral.

Cui Zhu had heard that Dongguo Yan's sister Tang Jiang was a famous beauty in Linzi, the capital of Qi. She was so attractive, it was said, that even the prince's concubines paled in her presence. It happened that Cui Zhu's wife had just died and he was considering remarriage. Minister Tang Yi's death gave him a convenient excuse to visit Tang Jiang. If, with Dongguo Yan's help, he could win her consent, the remarriage would be ideal for both partners.

Cui Zhu suggested to Dongguo Yan: "Minister Tang Yi and I are both court officials. We often met at court sessions. So your sister and I are related in a way. I ought to go and offer my condolences to her at the funeral."

Dongguo Yan was touched. He drove the carriage himself and took Cui Zhu along.

Tang Jiang, a liberal-minded woman, came out of her chamber to receive them in person. She was wearing white and hemp, and appeared without any make-up on. Her natural fair complexion was attractive; her melancholy expression added to her beauty. Cui Zhu was infatuated the moment he saw her.

Cui Zhu tried his best to ingratiate himself with her. When she found out how thoughtful and soft-spoken the middle-aged ranking official was, she made every effort to engage him in pleasant conversation. About one year after the funeral, Dongguo Yan married his sister off to Cui Zhu.

After the marriage, Prince Zhuang of Qi began to pay frequent visits to Cui Zhu.

The prince used to trust Yan Ying and had appointed him prime minister. Cui Zhu considered Yan Ying unqualified for that position on grounds that he received the appointment only because the prince appreciated his eloquence. Cui Zhu, therefore, harboured rancour against Yan Ying and, on this account, was also not on convivial terms with the prince. As now the prince kept visiting him and asking for advice about state affairs, Cui Zhu began to wonder whether the prince had changed his attitude toward him and intended to promote him.

By and by he came to realise that the prince was not paying visits to him but to his wife. He was only being used as a camouflage.

One day the prince came when Cui Zhu was out. Tang Jiang looked worried. Prince Zhuang took her hand in his, asking: "What is the matter with you? Has Minister Cui found out about us? Even if he has, so what? Your ex-husband Minister Tang had found out, but what could he do about it?"

Withdrawing her hand from the prince's, Tang Jiang said that Cui Zhu was not as meek as Tang Yi; he was a very tough adversary. She begged the prince not to come so often, or she would be in trouble.

"Trouble?" the prince said with scornful smile. "What trouble? I am the prince of the state and he is but a minister. His life is in my hands. If I want to get rid of him he cannot save himself, let alone his wife."

He stayed in her bedroom for a long time. On leaving, he

picked up Cui Zhu's hat from the table and took it away with him.

The gatekeeper stopped him on his way out and asked him to leave the hat behind.

"Why do you insist this is Cui Zhu's hat? Do you think only Cui Zhu has a hat? I'm planning to give this away as a gift."

When Cui Zhu learned of the matter, he fell into a towering rage and resolved to kill the prince in revenge for the insult.

In May that year, the head of Qi's vassal state Ju came to Linzi to pay tribute to the prince. The host was delighted and entertained him at a grand banquet near the north gate of the capital. Minister Cui lived nearby but did not attend the banquet on the excuse that he was not feeling well. The prince thought that he must be suffering from some serious ailment.

Pretending to pay a sick call on Cui Zhu, he went there the next day. The doorkeeper said the minister had just taken medicine and was now sleeping in his bedroom. Prince Zhuang laughed up his sleeve.

He met Tang Jiang in the hall. Instead of inquiring after Cui Zhu, he took her hand and said, "It's been such a long time — I've not seen you for several days and I'm dying of thirst!"

"Please wait here and let me fetch some honey soup for you," Tang Jiang said, making a graceful exit from the side door.

Tang Jiang was gone for quite a long time. Prince Zhuang began to get suspicious. He struck up a song, beating out the time on a column in the hall:

I was holding your hand in mine,
But off you went in steps so fine.
There is no point in fetching soup,
And no need to bring me honey.
For my thirst can never be quenched

Except by you my dear sweetheart.
My heart keeps on beating like mad
Oh what, I wonder, does it mean?

Suddenly he was startled to hear the clang of weapons. Sensing imminent danger, he dashed toward the back door only to find it locked. Soldiers were catching up from behind. He scrambled up the wall and just when he neared the top, an arrow hit him in the leg. He dropped back to the ground. Armoured soldiers swarmed up and killed him on the spot.

Prime Minister Yan Ying came and burst out crying over the dead prince. He got up and paced three times in a funeral dancing gait around the corpse to express his condolences. Cui Zhu's subordinates urged him to kill Yan Ying but Cui Zhu said Yan Ying was highly regarded both in the court and outside. It would do credit to Cui to spare his life.

Cui Zhu put Prince Zhuang's son Chu Jiu on the throne with the title of Prince Jing and appointed himself Senior Minister. He ordered Court Historian Bo to put down that "Prince Zhuang died of malaria in the summer of the Year of the Pig." Bo refused. Instead, he wrote, "Cui Zhu assassinated Prince Zhuang of Qi in the summer of the Year of the Pig."

Cui flew into a rage and had Bo killed.

Bo's three brothers were all court historians. His brothers Zhong and Shu recorded the event in exactly the same way as Bo had and they were killed too. Bo's youngest brother Ji, defying death, wrote the same thing: "Cui Zhu assassinated Prince Zhuang of Qi in the summer of the Year of the Pig."

Cui Zhu, holding the bamboo strip in his hand, said to him, "Aren't you afraid to die? Your three brothers were executed because they insisted on this version. Correct it here and now, and I will spare your life."

"It's my duty to tell the truth," said Ji. "I would rather tell the truth and die than tell a lie and live. If I do not write it this way, other historians will. Someone will find out about it, anyway. It's no use trying to cover it up. If you try to, you will be laughed at when people get to know the truth. If you want to kill me, do as you please!"

Cui Zhu said with a sigh, "Prince Zhuang wasted his days in revelry. I had to kill him and I did it for the safety of the state. Even if you record it just as it happened, the people will understand me and overlook it." Throwing the bamboo strips back to Ji, he turned and left.

Ji went to file the bamboo strips in the State Archives and place them under seal. At the gate of the Archives he came across Nan, one of his colleagues. Nan hurried up to him with a blank bamboo strip in his hand. "I hear your three brothers have all been killed for telling the truth," he said. "I'm afraid the summer incident might be hushed up, so I've come to you with this blank bamboo strip...." When Ji showed him what he had written on the strips, Nan went back.

The listeners were deeply moved by the story their chief archivist related to them. He turned to Li Er: "What do you think of this, Li Er?"

Sleepy-eyed, Li Er looked up from his book.

"Did you hear?"

"Well, yes, I did."

"Tell us what you think of it."

"I do not see much in it," he said. "In ancient times virtuous rulers taught without using words. They let the people take their natural course and live their natural lives. They did not take any action for any particular purpose. When the Great Tao was abandoned, people lost their sincerity and simplicity. Those who still retained a smattering of sincerity and simplicity came to be regarded as kind and righteous. When people stay simple, the family and relatives are on good terms. When family and relatives abandon simplicity and are on bad terms, thus arises filial piety. When the ruler takes no action, people will be transformed of their own accord. When the ruler has no desires, the people will become simple themselves. When the world is free from trouble, there are no loyal ministers and officials. Beauty in the extreme means no beauty; good in the extreme means no good. Low ranks in comparison with high, long in comparison with short, and loyal in contrast with treacherous. Only when the state is in trouble are there loyal ministers and officials.''

This fellow is certainly full of complaints, the chief archivist thought. In this matter of upholding faithfulness and righteousness or abandoning them, everyone here is deeply touched by what I said, but he alone is left cool and indifferent. Worse still, he comes out with so many absurd comments. Since he has no sense of faithfulness and righteousness, how can he work here as an archivist? Yet, as he was recommended by Minister Wangsun Yi, the chief archivist could not bring himself to dismiss the newcomer.

Li Er heaved a long sigh. He had expected the Archives to be a really quiet place. Ah, so there were busy-bodies also in quiet places as well....

11

On the third of the third lunar month, the daughters of noble families in Luoyang all went out to the suburbs to enjoy the warm sunshine and fresh air of spring. They bathed in the Luo River to exorcise misfortune and avert ill health, picnicked on its banks with singing and dancing, and had a gay time of it. It was said that the custom dated back three hundred years to the time of Duke Zhou.

When the Zhou Dynasty was first established, Emperor Wu annihilated seven hundred thousand troupes of the Shang Dynasty and then captured its secondary capital Chaoge. There he held a grand sacrifice to Heaven and earth and changed the name of the dynasty from Shang to Zhou. The return of his armies to the capital, Fenghao, in the fourth month of the same year, marked the end of the perpetual wars. The war horses were taken to the south of Mount Hua to rest, the herds of cattle were put out to pasture at Taolin and princes were enfeoffed.

Now Emperor Wu began to contemplate expansion. Under the Shang Dynasty, Zhou was a small tribe in the west. Its chieftains were called Xibo — a name held in wide contempt. Since Shang was finished and Zhou was ordained by Heaven with rule over the country, he could now contemplate the whole vast area from the west leading to the seas in the east.

Fenghao was located far out to the west, but it was not yet time to move the capital to the east. As the ancestral tombs and shrines were all in Fenghao, if, after ascending the throne, he was to move, leaving his ancestors' graves and shrines behind, people would point their fingers and wag their heads behind his back. Besides, the midland had been the base of Shang and its people might not be reconciled to their defeat. It was neither a safe nor auspicious venture to adopt immediately at the beginning of the dynasty.

A feasible solution would be to keep Fenghao as its western capital and eventually build a secondary one in the midland — its eastern capital. Shang had established two capitals — the principal one in Anyang and a secondary one in Chaoge. But where to build the eastern capital? Somewhere between the Yi and Luo rivers seemed an ideal place. It was roughly the geographical centre of the country and at a more or less equal distance from the adjoining states. The area between the two rivers used to be occupied by ancient tribes of the Xia Dynasty. Its natural defenses made it strategically important — easily defended from within and difficult to attack from without. As for mountains, there was the Funiu Range to the south and the Taihang Range to the north. The Yellow River bordered on the north, the Yi and Luo rivers on the south. In its vicinity rose the towering Mount Song.

One day Emperor Wu said to his younger brother Duke Zhou, "I would like to move the nine tripods from Anyang to Luoyang and make Luoyang our eastern capital. This would facilitate administration of the eastern part of our country.''

Duke Zhou agreed. But in the early years of the new dynasty there was so much to attend to that Emperor Wu was unable to carry out his strategic plan before he died. His thirteen-year-old son inherited the throne as Emperor Cheng, and he appointed his uncle, Duke Zhou, prime minister. Other uncles of his were enfeoffed at Guan and Cai (both in present-day Henan Province). Backed by the local people of the former Shang Dynasty, they rose in revolt, determined to pluck the throne out from under the young emperor.

Duke Zhou crushed the rebellion in a punitive expedition. After the victory, he realised how urgent it was to build the eastern capital. He had the site surveyed and took over personal supervision of the work. The huge project was completed at the beginning of the third month. Duke Zhou selected the third of the month, presumably an auspicious day, for the dedication. A grand banquet was laid out by the Luo River and a lively celebration was held with singing, dancing and folk operas. In the warm, fresh breezes of spring, the participants felt joyful and carefree.

Minister Wangsun Yi had come to join in the celebrations with Zheng Ji and her maid Zhen Gu.

It was a rare opportunity for city people to gather in the suburb. Men and women in colourful costumes crowded along the river enjoying the scenery. They were entertained with singing and dancing staged on picture-boats which floated up and down. The lively music of stringed instruments filled the air. The long winter with its piercing north winds was past and the people were happy to emerge from their "hibernation". Now the grey wintry clouds had melted, unveiling the blue sky and the smiling sun; the mild spring breeze was warm, the fields were resplendent with green grass, trees bursting in leaf and blooming flowers. Men and women shed their bulky winter outfits for light spring trappings and took to the outdoors.

Viewing landscapes is a joy but seeing women on an outdoor

excursion is also a pleasant experience. Sometimes one is amazed at the wonders Nature can work.

Wangsun Yi strolled along the river with Zheng Ji toward a temporary lookout pavilion specially put up for them. Their attendants served wine and special delicacies while they watched the passing boats and enjoyed the performances. Not far from the pavilion there was a witch singing and dancing, calling for the return of the souls of sick people. She shouted to the skies: "Come back, soul of Wang San (name of a sick person)!"

The call was answered by a voice from the opposite shore: "Coming back! Coming back!"

After the calls were repeated a few times, the wandering soul would return and re-enter the body of the patient, and the sickness would be cured, it was said.

Zheng Ji noticed one of the attending maids was missing. "Where is Zhen Gu?" she asked.

She was there a moment ago; where had she gone?

The other attendants looking around saw her standing by the river.

She was standing bare-foot on a stone slab, holding her skirt up with her hands. The stone, big and smooth, lay immersed half way in the river. Her white and tender feet, paddling for a time in the clear water, no longer felt the pinch of cold. Altogether, she seemed to be enjoying a rare experience.

She was celebrating the third of the third month, the day to wash off the dirt and diseases of the past year and usher in a new year of health and good fortune.

Standing in the water, Zhen Gu felt so refreshed she began to sing:

> The Luo and the Yi
> Brim high with water.
> Both men and women
> Hold orchids so fresh
> So fragrant and sweet.

Says the girl:
"On the third of the third,
Go and see the rivers."
Says the man :
"The rivers I've seen
On the third of the third."
"Go and see the new things.
The River Luo is clear,
The Yi is glistening.
Songs come like waves,
Crowds form like hills,
Joy and happiness reigns."

Side by side,
In mirth and banter.
The boy and girl,
Laugh, tease and chatter.
The boy hands a peony
To his sweetheart.

This was a folk song from the State of Zheng by Zhen River
where Zhen Gu was born and brought up. Originally the first
line began with mention of the two rivers Zhen and Wei in
Zheng. Inspired by the festive atmosphere, she changed the Zhen
and Wei to the Luo and Yi rivers.

Suddenly Zhen Gu felt water dripping onto her head and
trickling down her face. It could not be rain, with the sky cloud-
less and the sun shining! Turning, she saw a young man with a
smile on his face holding a wet willow branch over her. He was
dipping it in the river then holding it up to let it drip on her
head. Highly annoyed and not all amused, she was about to
lose her temper. Then she thought better of it remembering that
on this day innocent mischief of any kind indicated future blessings.

The young man cast a quick look around and asked "Did

you come by yourself?"

Not knowing what he would ask next, Zhen Gu did not answer. She just tossed him a quick smile.

"Shall we go and have a look over there?"

"What is there to look at?"

"There are lots of exciting things going on there — singing, dancing, operas, witches casting spells, boys and girls singing duets and antiphonal chants and much more..."

"I'm not going. I'm staying right here."

"Will you accept my peony then?"

"I don't want it."

Crestfallen, the young man remarked: "You're quite a good singer, but you're not a brave girl."

"Can you sing?" Zhen Gu asked.

"Who? Me?" The young man was slightly taken aback for a moment. "Yes, sure, I can sing..."

"Will you sing one for me?"

Obligingly he cleared his throat and began at the top of his voice:

"Ah, yi, heho, on the third of the third..."

He suddenly stopped short. Zhen Gu waited for him to go on, but he remained silent. When Zhen Gu urged him to continue, he said that was all. "That's all? You call that a song?"

"Why isn't that a song? Young people in our village all sing this way — Ah, yi, heho! Ah, yi, heho!..."

"What I mean by a song is words with a tune, something like a poem. Like the one I was singing a moment ago. Not your 'Ah, yi, heho!' See what I mean?"

Dumbfounded, the lad was at a loss what to say.

Zhen Gu smiled. She now realised that he was an uneducated farm boy — "a country bumpkin".

"Are you from a big family?" he asked shyly.

At this moment someone from the pavilion called: "Zhen Gu!"

"Yes?"

The answer in her musical voice wafted slowly out only to wane away in the distance.

Wangsun Yi, who could see only Zhen Gu's back, said, "Why is she standing there alone with her feet in the water? What is she doing there?" He sounded slightly annoyed.

"Oh, leave her alone," Zheng Ji felt sympathetic. "On this day why not let her paddle in the water to wash off her misfortunes."

"It looks like a young man is chatting with her out there."

"What's all the fuss? So she's chatting with someone? This is the time to meet and chat with people."

"You sound like a self-appointed guardian of hers," said Wangsun Yi. "She's no longer a child, remember. She has reached precarious age. This doesn't look to me like a casual chat at all. No doubt it's just another case of 'a young man luring an innocent girl who is hungering for love.'"

"If the young man is a gentleman," said Zheng Ji, "what harm is there if he is interested in her? When a girl is grown up and no one takes an interest in her, that would be something to worry about!"

Suddenly Wangsun Yi pointed toward the path and said, "Speak of gentlemen and the gentlemen appear. Look, two are heading toward us."

As they came nearer, Zheng Ji thought that one of them looked familiar, but she could not recall where she had seen him.

"Good morning, Minister Wangsun," the two gentlemen exclaimed. "We are so pleased to meet you here today!" One of the two was Li Er, the other Yin Xi.

Wangsun Yi invited them to come into his pavilion and to be seated. After a while Li Er got up and explained that, as Wangsun Yi had his family with him, they should not interrupt by staying such a long time.

"You have been at the Archives for a really long time, why do you distance yourself from us?" Wangsun Yi said. "Zheng Ji is no longer a stranger to you; she often speaks of you as her great benefactor."

Zheng Ji also enjoined Li Er to stay, reminding him he should not stand on ceremony with friends. Li Er and Yin Xi had no recourse but to sit down again, while attendants brought on more wine and cakes.

"As I understand, Li Er spends every moment of the day reading," Wangsun Yi went on, "so what could have brought you to this bustling place? Yin Xi must have had to drag you away from the Archives."

"Yes, it was my idea," admitted Yin Xi, "but actually Li Er did not need much persuasion this time. He accepted my suggestion readily and has been in a good mood all the way here."

"Really?" Wangsun Yi was slightly amazed.

"This festival boasts a long history," said Li Er. "Born and brought up in the south, I am not very familiar with northern customs. This occasion offers a good chance for me to become acquainted with the culture of the north. I couldn't miss it."

"That's true," said Wangsun Yi. "It's not enough to study our culture through reading only. It's necessary to come out and see the folk customs and the lives of the people. Even the court sends out officials to collect folk songs from all parts of the country."

Zhen Gu had now returned from the river, her cheeks pink with excitement.

"Come and pour wine for our guests," Zheng Ji said to her. "This is the Li Er who saved my life."

Her repeating of "Li Er who saved my life" made him feel ill at ease.

"I can't bear to hear any more about how 'Li Er saved my life'," Li Er complained. "It makes me feel like a stranger among you. If you keep saying that, I shall have to go."

"But I really mean it. You are my benefactor," Zheng Ji explained.

"Only Heaven is worthy of that honour," said Li Er. "But

Heaven would not accept it. Heaven gives birth to all things but does not possess them. Heaven nourishes all things but does not attribute it to his own ability. Heaven raises all things but does not claim mastery over them.''

Wangsun Yi said with a smile: "Is this the 'superior virtue' or 'Tao' you have been studying?"

"Enough, enough! What 'superior virtue' or 'Tao' are you talking about anyway?" Zheng Ji interrupted. "You're simply splitting hairs. I don't understand either one of them. Let's have another drink. Zhen Gu, why are you standing there like an idiot? Come over and pour some more wine for us!"

Zhen Gu began to fill the wine-cups. Suddenly she stopped, the pot still in mid-air, her eyes wide and startled as if she had heard some terrifying noise.

She dropped the pot and began to sing: "Cuckoo, cuckoo." She bit her lower lip with her upper teeth until blood began to drip.

"What's the matter with you?" Yin Xin was shocked to see her lip bleeding.

"I heard a cuckoo call a moment ago," said Zhen Gu. "In spring, the one who first hears a cuckoo is in for some bad luck, a sorrowful leave-taking or something of the kind. However, the bad luck can be exorcised by imitating the cuckoo immediately and shedding blood."

"Zhen Gu had pretty sharp ears," commented Zheng Ji. "Of all the people here, she was the first to hear the cuckoo!"

Zhen Gu told them to listen carefully. In a few moments they seemed to begin hearing the clear, melodious cries of a cuckoo echoing in the blue. Suddenly the sky seemed brighter, the mountains greener, the river more limpid and the spring air more exhilarating.

"This is a custom of our home state," said Zheng Ji. "The first person to hear the cuckoo is doomed to part with his or her people. The way to exorcise the bad luck is to imitate the cuckoo and shed drops of blood to the ground. There is another way to overcome the bad omen. It is not shedding blood, but it looks a bit unbecoming." She stopped.

When she was urged to reveal it, she almost burst out laughing:

"You have to bark like a dog in answer to the cuckoo! I believe Zhen Gu knows this, but I don't think she is willing to do it. She would rather shed blood!"

Zhen Gu smiled shyly to the amusement of all.

"We have this bird in the south," said Li Er. "We call it cuckoo, after the sound of its song. It's similar to your cuckoo whose song is almost the same. In winter they go to the seaside, in spring they return to the north. The first cry of the cuckoo shows it's time to start spring ploughing. Farmers in the south do not take the cry of the cuckoo as bad luck. On the contrary, it's good luck. It marks the beginning of the farming season. So cuckoos are not divided into birds of good luck and bad luck. It's just a matter of how you perceive it. A departing person hears it with sadness, thinking the cuckoo causes the parting. Therefore he takes it as bad luck. But farmers in the south look forward to its return. They are happy to see the bird again because they think their return is a sign of good crops."

Li Er asked Zhen Gu if her lip still hurt. Zhen Gu smiled faintly, saying it was just a skin scratch, nothing to worry about.

Li Er found Zhen Gu's lip cause for concern. He wondered whether it was rouge or blood that made it so red. At least it was not bleeding any more, and at this, he felt relieved.

Li Er's attentiveness did not escape Yin Xi. "Li Er is usually careless about trifles, but why was he so considerate toward Zhen Gu today?"

Li Er hurried to explain that the mouth was one of the seven external openings in the head and, should any one of them bleed, it had to be taken seriously. One could not be too careful.

Zheng Ji teased Zhen Gu: "Whenever I tell Zhen Gu what a kind-hearted gentleman Li Er is she invariably regrets not having had the chance to meet him. Now Li Er is right here today —

tell us what you think of him?''

Zhen Gu said he was a truly kind-hearted gentleman.

"In what sense is he kind-hearted?'' Wangsun Yi inquired.

Abashed, Zhen Gu bent her head, not knowing what to say.

"Let me answer the question for you,'' said Zheng Ji. "He is both learned and considerate. Right?''

Zhen Gu nodded her head in agreement.

Li Er rose and said to Yin Xi: "This is a family gathering. We should not stay too long and disturb them. Don't you think it's time to go?''

Yin Xi broke into a smile, 'If you scold him, he will stay and listen with his ears pricked up; if you praise him, he gets up to go. This is the way he is. He can't help it.''

Li Er explained: "It's such a fine day for the festival! We should go around and try to see a bit of everything. Otherwise we would be wasting a fine opportunity. This holiday comes only once a year!''

With polite good-byes, they went off to stroll along the river.

A cuckoo flew over across the sky. Cuckoo! Cuckoo! Its song sounded faintly.

Wangsun Yi glanced at the bird, then at Zheng Ji and Zhen Gu. "The one who hears the cuckoo's cry first will part company,'' he said. "I have a feeling it's going to happen.''

12

Off and on since the excursion on the third of the third month, the bird's cuckooing seemed to echo in Li Er's ears incessantly.

"Tranquillity overcomes restlessness,'' he mused; for he was now becoming restless because he had something on his mind which was bothering him. Such a state of mind was detrimental to one's health and disruptive to one's word. The best way to overcome restlessness was to compose oneself, to concentrate on reading and meditating. Yet this was not always the remedy. Most of the time tranquillity can overcome restlessness, but not always either. Li Er was unable to concentrate; the cuckoo kept singing in his ear.

He went out into the alley. There was the woman next door holding her baby boy in a sitting posture over the door-step to help him urinate. She whistled softly in imitation of the sound, but nothing came. The baby clenched and cried, unable to rise to the occasion. The mother kept whistling until the baby's small penis became erect and a trickle of water burst forth.

Li Er loved children and was fond of studying them. They were a source of inspirations to him:

How lovely and innocent the baby is! As he is ignorant, he has no desires. As he is weak, docile and not harmful, nothing harms him.

When wasps or scorpions are irritated, they sting. As the baby does not irritate them, they do not sting him. Wolves and hawks are fierce, but they do not eat abandoned babies. Sometimes they protect and nurse them.

He knows nothing of the sexual union between male and female, but his organ is complete though immature, and often erects because his vital force is intact. He cries most of the day without becoming hoarse. He cries with his throat, but his mind is in harmony. A balanced mind is conducive to health. Adults have a lot to learn from a baby. A man of complete virtue resembles a baby.

Any infant is innocent and weak and does not contend. He keeps his vitality intact and his mind in harmony. Harmony is the highest and most normal state of things. To know this is to know the way of the world. A person whose mind is not in a harmony tends to enforce things and "enforcement" goes against Tao. It's like pulling a plant to make it grow, but a plant pulled to enforce growth does not grow.

"You're thinking of babies, aren't you?"

Li Er turned and seeing Yin Xi, asked: "Don't you love babies?"

"I do, of course. I have children at home. You obviously

love babies, but you are not even married yet.''

"Married?'' Li Er queried with a blank smile. "Me? What makes you think of that?''

"It's time you got married,'' said Yin Xi. "There is a go-between office in the court to oversee people's marriages. Newly-born babies are named three months after birth and they get registered at the office with their name, sex, and date of birth. It is stipulated that men should get married by the age of thirty and women by twenty. If a person is found to be single beyond the age limit, the office will take up the matter and offer to arrange for a spouse. This is a stipulation of the Zhou Proprieties. All persons, official or ordinary, are obliged to abide by them. Are you waiting for a go-between to help you?''

"Are you making fun of me? Why should I wait for a go-between to help me get married?'' Li Er protested. "The Zhou Proprieties have all sorts of stipulations. Do you think all of them are being observed? I doubt it. It sounds good to say 'men should get married by the age of thirty and women by twenty'. But do you know how many men and women there are in the country who are not married by the stipulated age? Is the court prepared to help all of them?''

"The court may not be able to assist those living in remote villages,'' said Yin Xi, "but you are a court official, an archivist. The court will certainly take up your case. Do you know how many men of your age in the court are still unmarried? You can count them on the fingers of one hand. If the go-between does not deal with you, who do you suppose he will deal with?''

"Even if he himself is reluctant to take up this matter, his superior will look into it when he learns about it. Do you think the go-between would have the effrontery to shirk his duty? Like it or not, he has to interfere. The Son of Heaven sets great store by the Zhou Proprieties. He regards them as the foundation of the dynasty. So long as they are observed, Zhou will be respected, its legitimacy will be upheld and the Son of Heaven will remain firm on the throne. If they collapse the Zhou Empire will perish. Do you think the go-between will let a court archivist get by with openly flouting the proprieties?''

Li Er gazed at him with curiosity. "So you also worry about the collapse of the proprieties?"

Yin Xi laughed: "I am not about to debate an academic issue with you. I am talking about a practical matter, pure and simple. Let me ask you, do you like the maid or not? Tell me the truth!"

Li Er was caught unawares. Sometimes a question about personal feelings might be more difficult to answer than one about the most mysterious abstruse problem in metaphysics.

"Why, what maid? Who?" Li Er stammered.

"The one named Zhen Gu."

"Zhen Gu? But who is Zhen Gu?"

"Don't pretend you don't know who I'm referring to. On the third day of the third month, in Wangsun Yi's pavilion, remember, there was a beautiful young maid who bit her lip and imitated the cuckoo? Have you forgotten her?"

"I see. You mean her."

"Look me in the eye," said Yin Xi. "You always advocate truthfulness, simplicity, and abhor hypocrisy and craftiness. Tell me the truth — do you like her or not?"

Cornered, Li Er had to be frank: "Yes, she is a lovely girl. Don't you like her too?" Li Er asked Yin Xi.

"Yes, I do. But the way I like her is different from the way you do. I was not the only one to notice how attracted you were to her. Minister Wangsun Yi and Zheng Ji also noticed it."

"But how was it so noticeable?" Li Er was puzzled.

"Don't ask me. You can answer with your own oft-repeated words:

> 'Affection' as an existence
> Is impalpable and imperceptible.
> Though impalpable and imperceptible,

> Yet it has form;
> Imperceptible and impalpable,
> Yet it is substantial.
> Though deep and subtle,
> It has vital force;
> Which is real and reliable."

Hearing this, Li Er couldn't help laughing.

During their discussions, Yin Xi always felt Tao was altogether too mysterious. It was invisible, inaudible and intangible. In short, it was just too impalpable to grasp.

"The greatness of Tao lies in its impalpability," Li Er often said. "It seems to be in existence and, at the same time, it does not. However, if you say it is not in existence, it gives birth to all things between Heaven and earth; if you say it is, you cannot see, hear or touch it. While meeting it, you cannot see its head; while following it you fail to see its back.

"Tao's objective existence is imperceptible. Though it is imperceptible, it has image; though it is imperceptible, it is substantial; though it is deep and subtle, it has vital force and the vital force is real, it can be sensed with intuition. This intuition is not one of the five senses, but it is reliable."

Yin Xi had imitated Li Er's words about Tao to describe his affection for Zhen Gu and the application was appropriate. He said, "Minister Wangsun Yi and Zheng Ji have asked me to serve as the gobetween to bring you two together. Since you love her, why not prepare the six betrothal gifts so that I can present them and propose to her on your behalf?"

"Oh, come on, the mere mention of the six betrothal gifts gives me a headache!" Li Er complained. "I can't stand these tedious ceremonies, let alone the expenditure involved!"

According to the Zhou Proprieties the second month of the year is most propitious for a wedding. People are encouraged to get married in that month. The prospective bridegroom must go through six stages (or offer six betrothal gifts) to achieve an agreement.

The first stage is to propose. The bridegroom's family asks the go-between to go to the bride's family with a tentative proposal. If it is accepted, the bridegroom's family will make the formal proposal and with it a gift of a pair of live wild geese.

The second stage is to inquire about the bride's name and birthday. The go-between goes to the bride's side to ask for her name and the hour and date of her birth and compares them with those of the bridegroom to see if they are compatible. If they match well, the marriage will be a good one. The inquiry rates another pair of live wild geese as a gift.

The third stage is the engagement. The bridegroom's side notifies the bride's family that since the hours and dates of their births are well matched and the marriage will be a good one, he is willing to be engaged. The bridegroom gives the bride still another pair of live wild geese as a gift for the engagement.

The fourth stage is to confirm the engagement. To confirm the engagement the bridegroom gives the bride twenty *zhang* (one *zhang* is roughly ten feet) of silk and a couple of deer-skins.

The fifth stage is to select the wedding day. When the propitious day for the wedding is chosen the bride's side is notified of it and asked to give its approval.

The sixth stage is to welcome the bride. The bridegroom, formally dressed in a wedding costume, escorts the bride home in a wedding carriage.

For each of the six stages, the bridegroom must give the bride gifts. Of the gifts, the twenty *zhang* of silk alone is beyond the means of an ordinary family. The live wild geese are not very expensive, but nowadays, wealthy families, instead of giving live ones, give wild geese made of gold and silver which cost more than the silk.

"Since it is Minister Wangsun Yi and Zheng Ji's idea," Yin Xi went on, "they don't care about the gifts. Besides, the Zhou Proprieties are not very strict about the gifts in cases of men over thirty and women over twenty. The couple do not have to go through all the six stages; they can be spared one or

124

two of them, the idea being to encourage marriages.

"Apart from the gifts for the bride's family, the bridegroom must give the go-between some gifts. But since I am the go-between, we can make an exception. Not only do I not want any gifts, but I will help to procure some for you and take them to the bride's family. What about that?"

Li Er was grateful. "I don't know how I can thank you enough! You are really going to so much trouble on my behalf!"

Yin Xi said it was his great pleasure to help him get married to someone from Wangsun Yi's family.

13

Yin Xi wandered in the market place for two or three hours but only managed to find one live wild goose. He came back carrying the goose upside down by its legs, while it cackled hoarsely all the way.

The vociferous protest of the bird brought Li Er out.

"You've got them?" he asked excitedly.

"I managed to get only one," Yin Xi said.

"This is the best time of the year for hunting wild geese," said Li Er. "Flocks of them pass by here every day on their way south. But why have you got only one? You mean you can't find even two in the market?"

"Yes, I can," Yin Xi answered. "There are plenty of them but, as they were all shot down by arrows, they are either dead or wounded. You wouldn't want to present dead or wounded ones as gifts, would you?"

After a pause Yin Xi said, "Let me take this one to them tomorrow. I can explain that live wild geese are hard to find these days. As Minister Wangsun is a thoughtful man and strongly approves of the marriage, he will not mind if we present only one goose."

"On the other hand," Li Er said, "we must not be too

lackadaisical. The Wangsuns are a highly cultured family."

The armies of Qin, riding in three hundred chariots, were on the move day and night heading east. With lowered banners and muffled drums, it was to all intents and purposes a secret manoeuver. They were now approaching Luoyang. Appraised of the situation early on, the court of Zhou was disturbed.

Military expeditions were to be launched only by order of the Son of Heaven, but the princes of the various states, engaged in perpetual strife, did not take the Son of Heaven or his orders seriously.

Which state was Qin planning to attack?

Emperor Xiang, standing on the tower of the Northern Gate, watched the Qin armies pass by. With him was a child, the son of a minister of royal descent. The three hundred chariots were thundering past, kicking up clouds of dust that darkened the sky. Suddenly the commander caught sight of the yellow canopy on the gate tower and realised it was the Son of Heaven watching. He ordered his charioteers to stop, get down and salute the emperor, their helmets in hand. Presently jumping onto their chariots with great agility they turned and drove off to catch up with the chariots that had pressed ahead.

The child shook his head and said, "This is rude. Passing by the Imperial Gate, they should have taken off their armoured uniforms, put away their weapons, halted the chariots and saluted the Son of Heaven!"

Emperor Xiang knew he was an intelligent lad. He asked: "Wangsun Man, what do you think of all this?"

"They look strong and invincible," said the child readily, "but they are doomed to defeat." He was confident and unassuming.

"How do you know?"

"They were doomed to defeat from the very start. They are imprudent and unrestrained. Being imprudent they cannot look into the future seriously and plan ahead: because they are unrestrained, they are reckless in action. They are sure to be defeated!"

In fact before the Qin armies set out on the expedition, the senior minister Jian Shu had warned Prince Mu not to venture a military attack against the State of Zheng on any account, for it was more than one thousand *li* away.

Prince Mu explained: "Military advisor Qi Zi whom we planted in Zheng has sent a secret message saying he has been entrusted with the key to the Northern Gate of Zheng's capital. If we launch a surprise attack, we can take Zheng easily."

Jian Shu said, "I've never heard of such a military manoeuvre — attacking a state so far away! When your chariots roll thundering along the road, do you think you can keep it a secret? Zheng will get to know about it in no time! By the time you arrive our armies will be at the end of their tether. What will happen when their exhausted ranks are confronted by the fully prepared armies of Zheng?"

Notwithstanding Jian Shu's warning, Prince Mu appointed Meng Ming, Xi Qi and Bai Yi as commanders and ordered the armies to set out.

Standing by the Eastern Gate Jian Shu, with tears in his eyes, warned Meng Ming: "I am seeing the armies off, but I shall not see them return."

Prince Mu flew into a rage. "It's high time you died," he fumed. "By now the tree on your grave should have been the size of one man's embrace! What do you know about warfare?"

The brash Qin armies were ambushed at Mount Xiao by the forces of Jin, a big state lying between Qin and Zheng. Before their puffed-up vanity collapsed, the Qin ranks were annihilated. Generals Meng Ming, Xi Qi and Bai Yi were taken prisoner.

Events proved Wangsun Man's prediction true. The precocious child became widely known in the capital for his familiarity with the proprieties, while his family was even more highly esteemed as a cultured family of wide education.

"I suppose," suggested Yin Xi, "you are afraid of losing Zhen Gu because the number of gifts don't add up — or so it seems. You always say 'take no action'.... 'be free from desires'. But you want to be engaged to Zhen Gu! Isn't this 'desire'? Isn't this 'action'?"

"What are you talking about?" Li Er became flustered. "They are horses of a different colour! When I say 'take no action' or 'be free from desires', I refer to Tao, to human life in the broader sense. How can you mix them up with the basic needs of individuals?" Li Er cudgeled his brain for better terms in which to explain himself, but to no avail. At a loss, he sighed resignedly.

"Don't take me too seriously," Yin Xi said with a burst of laughter. "Can't I tease you once in a while? Don't worry about the other goose, I'll take care of it somehow."

"How? Where will you get it?"

"Catch it ourselves, that's how!" said Yin Xi. "This is just the right season for hunting wild geese. I used to do it at home when I was little."

It was a moonless night when they set out.

They each held a pot in one hand and a stick in the other. Inside the pot they carried a small lighted torch. Approaching the river band outside the capital, they could hear the autumn insects chirping and water gurgling as the river flowed by. The short, muffled cackles of wild geese, as if emitted in drowsy discourse, reached the ears from time to time. They held their breath and tiptoed in the direction of the sound.

They saw in the distance a huge flock of wild geese, perhaps several hundreds, sleeping by the river.

Venturing closer, they took the torches out from their pots, waved them a couple of times and put them back again.

The geese on sentry duty fluttered and sounded the alarm.

Wild geese are well organised and highly disciplined. During migration they stop to rest by rivers and lakes or on islets. The leader of this flock was sleeping in the centre of the islet with sentries stationed on guard.

At the alarm, the leader was the first to awake. Commotion and panic spread among the flock amidst a few screeches. The leading bird fluttered about to see what was happening while the whole flock strained their necks in apprehension. There was nothing wrong. Their cries became soft cuckoos of reassurance: Everything's all right; don't be afraid. Go back to sleep; we have a long journey ahead of us tomorrow.

When the birds had calmed down, the two hunters crept closer stealthily. They took the torches out of the pots, waved them a couple of times and replaced them. Again the sentries signaled the alarm, rousing a hustle and bustle among the flock. The leader rose to look round but perceived no threat. It emitted an angry reprimand, and calm reigned as before.

After this trick was repeated a few more times, the leader became furious. It punished the sentries with a severe peck with its beak for their false alarms.

When the birds settled back to sleep once more, the two men quickly moved toward them. The sentries spotted them but, fearing to bring on further punishment, issued a couple of inaudible cries in their throats as a sign that they were not ignoring their duties.

The two men furtively moved forward, snatched up a sleeping wild goose and thrust it in the bag they had brought along. The move was so swift the bird was not startled. It did not cry out nor did it struggle. Uttering a few soft rumblings in its throat, it went back to sleep in the bag.

On their return, Yin Xi said, "It takes knowing how. Now we've got the two wild geese for your gifts!"

Li Er sighed and said thoughtfully, "This is what we call 'governing the country with honesty, waging battles with trickery.'"

"You also subscribe to 'trickery'?"

"The trickery I mean applies to whatever you do. That is, you must do a thing in a way that brings the maximum effect with the least effort. Sometimes you can even produce miraculous results. Therefore, a good traveller leaves no tracks or foot-prints behind; a good speaker makes no errors in speech; a good calculator needs no tallies; a good guard needs no bolt or key yet no one can open what he has shut; he who is good at binding uses no ropes or knots so that no one can untie what he has bound."

"Let me add one more thing," put in Yin Xi. "A good hunter can catch wild geese without arrows or nets. What about that?"

"That is exactly what I mean," Li Er assented.

"I think that head bird was a bit stupid, don't you?" Yin Xi commented.

"It is not only the leading goose that is stupid," said Li Er. "Don't you think there are many human beings who think of themselves as always correct? I believe the good man is the teacher of the bad, while the bad serves as an example for the good man to guard against. He who does not respect the 'teacher' or he who does not value the 'example' is muddle-headed though he thinks himself wise."

"What lesson would you draw from this?" asked Yin Xi.

Li Er thought for a moment and explained: "He who does not rely on his own eyes sees clearly; he who does not claim to be always in the right is able to tell right from wrong; he who does not boast about himself succeeds; he who is not conceited can lead. That leading bird relies on his own eyes only, so it can not see clearly; it always thinks itself as correct, so it can not distinguish between right and wrong. It is stupid, but thinks it is clever. So such a conceited bird cannot be a good leader."

Yin Xi mused over this for a while and came to believe that what Li Er said was true.

So he who stands on tiptoe does not stand firm; he who takes long strides does not go far; he who relies on his own eyes cannot see clearly; he who claims to be in the right is not distinguished; he who boasts of himself does not succeed. From

Tao's point of view, these are like left-over food and morbid growths. Therefore, they are abhorred by all and not sought after by those in pursuit of Tao.

The captive in the bag had been lying still. Suddenly it set up a dismal cackling as if to complain: It was the conceited leading fowl that brought this disaster on me.

14

Lifting the bridal veil off her head, he gazed at her blooming face, familiar but strange, real but imaginary.

"The bride must wear a veil over her face."

Beautiful things enrapture the soul. Why cover up such a beautiful face? Why not just take off the veil and gaze at it?

In fact, the newly-weds knew each other; the veil was nothing but a formality.

"To tell you the truth," he said, "our meeting on the Luo River was really unforgettable! Since that I have looked forward to this day!"

"So have I," she said to herself with a smile.

"Minister Wangsun's house is only a couple of *li* from here," Li Er said, "but it isn't an easy matter for you to come over. The *Book of Proprieties* says: 'Marriage unites the bride and bridegroom to worship at the ancestral shrine and to continue the clan line. That is why it is valued by virtuous people.' But isn't marriage the concern of the bride and the bridegroom? What does it have to do with families or ancestors? To continue the clan line by producing children is the natural result of marriage, but not its prerequisite. If 'to serve the ancestral shrine and continue the clan line' is regarded as more important than the marriage itself, marriage is not marriage any more, it becomes a religious duty and a social obligation. Isn't it putting the cart before the horse? Is our marriage a cart put before the horse?

"No," he hastened on to explain. "Ours is different. In the

first place we met some time ago, had a chance to become acquainted, and fell in love. But people always say, according to the proprieties, the purpose of marriage is to serve the ancestral shrine and continue the clan line."

Is that the reason why there are the six tedious formalities to hurdle? Proprieties should be in line with Tao. In other words, they should conform to the natural course of things. Instead, the present proprieties are made to fulfill an artificially designed purpose. For example, marriage purports to unite the bride and the bridegroom in order to serve the ancestral shrine and continue the clan lines but is not taken to be the natural outcome of love.

Such proprieties advocated by the authorities and made compulsory by laws are quite strict and too harsh. People are required to abide by them to the letter; otherwise, they are punished as criminals.

Such proprieties are an ill-treatment of loyalty and can only end in disaster.

"You are really a silly bookworm. Do you know what night this is? Do you expect me to listen to your lecture all night long?"

Meanwhile she lifted her hand and stuffed something into his mouth. His lecturing stopped all of a sudden.

"It's sweet. What is it?"

"Guess."

He spat out the hard stone, round in the middle and pointed at both ends, like a spindle.

"Is it a date?"

Opening her hand, she showed him some dates.

On the wedding day everyone was happy and busy. The groom was up before dawn. His friends spent hours helping him get washed and dressed until finally, relaxing their standards a bit, they had to let him go.

Yin Xi waited at the door with a cup of wine in his hand.

According to marriage proprieties, the bridegroom was to drink the wine poured by his father before he set out to fetch the bride. But where was his father? Who was he? He did not know, nor did his grandpa. Only his mother knew who his father was, but the poor woman had passed away when he was born.

His father might have been the mirror polisher from Chu who taught her the *I Ching*. Where was he? Did he know he had committed a sin, leaving a young man fatherless when needed to pour wine at his wedding?

Yin Xi had an embarrassed expression on his face. He was sensitive to the fact that he was playing the role of someone he was not. Li Er, however, received the wine as a matter of routine and poured it down his throat.

Arriving at the Wangsun's, he was welcomed with princely courtesy. "The bridegroom is received outside the gate and entertained at the ancestral shrine," dictated the proprieties. Though Zhen Gu was treated at the Wangsun's as a member of the family, she was not a full-fledged member of the Wangsun clan after all. The banquet accordingly was not arranged at the ancestral shrine. However, Wangsun Yi observed the whole ceremony as if he were, in fact, the bride's father. Therefore, the essence of the reception was of the best.

The bridegroom entered the hall with a pair of wild geese and bowed to Heaven and earth and the Wangsuns. The wild geese were killed as part of the ritual, symbolically exhorting the new couple to remain loyal to each other till their last day.

The ceremony over, the bridegroom retired from the hall, went back to his carriage at the gate and took the driver's seat. He had learned archery and charioteering, therefore for him driving a carriage was easy.

He circled three times round Wangsun's mansion and then halted at the gate to wait for the bride. When she came, escorted by her bridesmaids, her head draped in a veil, he helped her into the carriage. Back home the bride and the bridegroom went through the ceremony of eating a piece of meat together and drinking out of the same gourd. After the whole day's hustle and bustle Li Er was hungry. He ate the first date and asked for more.

The bride took out a silk bag saying, "There are plenty more. Have as many as you like."

The bag held dates, chestnuts and beef chips. The beef chips, cooked with ginger and cassia bark, were delicious.

It was customary to look after the bride and bridegroom solicitously. Having gone through the multifarious ceremonies of the day, they were both hungry and, perhaps, the bride even more so. The bridegroom offered to share the food with her but she said it was prepared for him alone and the bride was not supposed to touch it.

"Go ahead and have some," Li Er urged her. "There is no one around to see us."

"Tomorrow morning," the bride said, "the left-over dates, chestnuts and meat will be placed in bamboo baskets as offerings to the gods. Some of them will be saved for your uncle and aunt when they come."

"There are enough for the gods," said Li Er. "Besides, I have no uncles or aunts. We should save some for Yin Xi. He has done so much to make our wedding possible."

When Li Er put his hand into the silk bag for more dates and chestnuts, his fingers ran into something hard. He took it out, to find it was a small jade sculpture of a dragon. Li Er was surprised.

"Zhen Gu, where does this come from?" he asked. "Wangsun's family cherish the proprieties — how did he make such a mistake?"

"What mistake?"

"When Prince Zhuang married Ai Jiang," Li Er said, "he allowed the wives of his ministers with the same surname as his to present jade and silk gifts. Minister Yu Sun advised him, instead, to allow men to present jade and silk, or animals and birds, according to their positions, and to let women only present things like hazelnuts, dates, chestnuts and dried meat to show their good will and respect."

"But now men and women both have given us the same type of gifts! How, then, do you propose to distinguish between men and women? Distinctions between men and women make up the fundamental law of a county and proprieties should not be violated on your account," explained Li Er.

"Do you also think it violates the proprieties? Do you also think distinctions between men and women are the fundamental law of the country and therefore that they should not give the same gifts?"

"This is not what I mean," said Li Er. "In fact I find it great fun to see the proprieties violated by a household that esteems proprieties above everything."

"If this is what you mean," said Zhen Gu, "let me tell you the truth. This dragon is not carved out of jade at all, but out of a block of salt. I carved it myself as a gift for my dear husband."

"So this is a salt dragon!" Li Er was amazed. "What a thoughtful gift! Oh yes, salt is the source of all other flavours. It's the most common spice in our foods, and at the same time it's the most precious spice. We cannot get along without it. As I understand, salt is presented as a gift on the most formal occasions.

"I read something about this at the Imperial Archives. Once the Son of Heaven sent Duke Yue on a visit to the State of Lu. Prince Xi of Lu entertained him at a banquet. The food served included a dish of finely-ground spiced meat, rice-cakes and black millet cakes and a tiger carved out of a salt block.

"Duke Yue said to Prince Xi, 'When emperors are entertained with richly flavoured foods it is to praise their virtues. When they are presented with salt tigers, it is to symbolise their political and military achievements. I am not worthy of the fine foods or the salt tiger.'

"With the first part of his remark, he was trying to be modest. Spiced meat, rice cakes and black millet cakes were nothing special. He was certainly entitled to them. However, the last part of his remark was true. The salt tiger symbolised great achievements. Only a few people in the world deserve such an honour.

"Now," Li Er went on, "I have eaten the dates, chestnuts and the dried meat. As for the salt dragon I cannot accept it."

"Salt is the mother of all flavours," said Zhen Gu. "It's extracted from the earth. Metal, wood, water, fire and earth are the five fundamental elements of Nature. If salt is not earth, it is a mineral from nature, a very common thing. You must take it!"

"If it is made of salt, I'll accept it," said Li Er.

"But this particular salt dragon does not symbolise great achievements," said Zhen Gu.

"What does it symbolise then, if I may ask?"

"The dragon, like the snake, symbolises the *yin* and the feminine. Madam Wangsun says you are somewhat queer, in a way. Here you are, a man seven feet tall, yet you seem to worship the feminine and the female, the *yin* and the weak."

"Is that what she says?"

"At first, I could hardly believe it. High ranking officials at the court, including Minister Wangsun, all worship the monarch, the masculine, the *yang* and the strong; they despise the feminine, the female, the *yin* and the weak. Madam Wangsun says you once said to Minister Wangsun that you know the strength of the male but you keep to the weakness of the female; you prefer the low ravine to the high mountain. She says Minister Wangsun did not quite agree with you and each of you stuck to your own views. She said, in order to convince him, you even used a vulgar metaphor!"

"A vulgar metaphor?"

"Yes, terrible! Such vulgar words are used only between husband and wife or among close friends, men with men or women with women."

"Did I ever say anything vulgar to Minister Wangsun?" Li

Er was perplexed.

"Maybe it was a slip of the tongue and you don't remember. What you said was: the female can certainly conquer the male because the female has a deep door and everything in the world comes out of that door. You yourself, Minister Wangsun, didn't you come out from that door of your mother?"

"That door of the mysterious female," said Li Er, "is the source of Heaven and earth. It is continuous and inexhaustible."

"Stop it! Stop it!" Zhen Gu flushed and covered her face with her hands. "What a shameful thing to talk about!"

"So this is why you think it's vulgar!" said Li Er with a laugh.

"Madam Wangsun told me she could have been executed but for your chivalrous interference. I was moved by the story," Zhen Gu said. "I doubt if, in this world today, there is another man — a man like you whose words carry weight — who would be willing to speak on behalf of women. With this incident in mind I put this salt dragon in the bag as a gift for you."

Li Er could not help but be moved also.

"In the world today," Li Er said, "it is not the ranking officials of self-proclaimed learned men who understand me, but the humiliated and so-called 'ignorant' women like you and Madam Wangsun."

"If you really think of women the way Madam Wangsun has described, my salt dragon has found its way to the right person."

"When I say the 'deep door'," Li Er continued, "I do not refer only to the birth-giving depths in women."

"There you go again, shaming me to death!" objected Zhen Gu, embarrassed by his persistence in a topic of such delicacy.

"What's so shameful about that?" Li Er said soberly. "That birth-giving thing is a sacred thing. It has given birth to mankind and all creatures in the world. But when I talk about it, I am not referring to any specific object. In fact, I refer to it as the symbol of a spirit, the symbol of Tao."

Zhen Gu looked up uncomprehendingly.

"You women tend to understand things from a very practical even very literal point of view," continued Li Er. "Now let me follow along the line of your argument. The valley is like the thing of the female and the hill is like that of the male. All the ravines in the hill go down to the bottom of the valley. The vast empty valley can hold all the water from the ravines. Doesn't it represent the image of the Tao I have been pursuing all along? That's why I worship the female, the *yin* and the weak. I prefer to be the valley."

"Madam Wangsun told me," said Zhen Gu, "that you never knew your father or in a certain sense, you never really had a father, and that is why you feel such deep affection for your mother." She looked at him with sympathy. "Maybe this is why your conception of women differs from that of all other men in the world. You worship the tranquil, the weak, and prefer to be the valley."

Li Er's heart seemed to stop. The shady plum tree in the yard at home, the pool of blood near the trunk and that poor woman who moaned and bled as she was cut open to bear her child before she died became real again before his eyes. As his mother had been the cause of the anguish buried in his heart, he was afraid to be reminded of her. For the past decades he had been suffering from perplexity and heartache, trying to find out the truth. Was he going to bear this heartache for the rest of his life?

There was a long silence.

"What's the matter?" Zhen Gu asked. "Did I hurt your feelings?"

"Nothing," he pulled himself together. "Why are you asking so many questions on a night like this? Now it's my turn to put a date in your mouth."

He took a date from the silk bag and tried to put it into her mouth. Zhen Gu in an effort to dodge threw herself off balance, landing on the bed. She could only laugh, her eyes filled with warmth and anticipation. Li Er went down with her and held her tight in his arms, his nose instantly inhaling a fresh and fragrant aroma.

"Such a gentle, refined woman as you, prefers to be on the lower side," said Li Er affectionately, "and the masculine strong man has to go along. However, the female conquers the male with lowness, tranquillity and weakness…"

15

Tall, elegant horses galloped along a street in Luoyang, pulling a bright, shiny but not lavishly decorated carriage. There were no guards of honour accompanying it, but only one or two attendants, therefore it did not attract the doorkeeper's attention when it arrived at the Imperial Archives.

One of the attendants approached him and said, "Go in and report to the chief archivist that Prince Jin is here for a look round."

"Which Prince Jin?" asked the doorkeeper.

"How many Prince Jins do you think there are in Luoyang?"

This rebuff threw the doorkeeper into a dilemma. He eyed the curtained carriage with reservations.

The prince is sitting in this carriage with no entourage and no guards of honour? He asked himself in disbelief. Nevertheless, he turned and went inside as the duties of his post required.

The chief archivist was taken aback by the unannounced visit of the prince. Straightening his clothes and adjusting his hat, he scurried out.

The prince had come out of the carriage and was busy scrutinizing the Archives building.

The chief archivist apologised, bowing with intrepidation. "We did not know your Highness was coming. I am terribly sorry for the delay in greeting you! Welcome, welcome! This reception is inadequate..."

"Since you did not know I was coming," said the prince with a genial smile, "you are not to blame. There is no need to apologise."

The chief archivist sent the gatekeeper back to tell the general archivists to come and welcome the royal visitor.

The prince stopped him, saying there was no need for that; he had come just for a look round and he did not wish to disturb anyone. He would like only the chief archivist to accompany him; the others could carry on with their work.

The prince considered the exterior of the Archives attractive and its surroundings clean and quiet. However, as compared with other court establishments, the building was a little shabby and old-looking.

The chief archivist pointed out the poor condition of the Archives now that the opportunity had arisen. He said the building was about one hundred years old; some parts of it were put up back when Duke Zhou undertook to construct the city of Luoyang — as long ago as that. The exterior retained its basic majestic conformation, but the interior walls had started to crumble and the roof leaked. He implied, as strongly as he dared, that it was time the court appropriated funds for repair.

The prince was sixteen or seventeen years old, of good moral calibre and keen intelligence. As everyone knew, Emperor Ling doted on him and entrusted him with state affairs. A mere nod from him would mean money granted. He understood what the chief archivist was getting at, but knew better than many what difficult financial straits the court was in. Times were no longer the same as when Duke Zhou undertook to construct the city of Luoyang or when the capital was first moved from the west. The country had squandered its vitality and the treasury was short of funds. The vassal states, now locked in internecine wars, had stopped paying tributes. The state treasury had huge obligatory expenditurs, drawn from a small and shrinking income. Even the

Son of Heaven and his ministers were inadequately paid. Where are funds to repair the Archives to come from?

Explicitly, his words to the chief archivist were admonitory: "Be frugal. Frugality can help guard officials against corruption. It is better for scholars to lead a simple life under sparse conditions. True, the building has been deteriorating all these years, but learned scholars keep coming to it. It is a centre of culture without compare anywhere. I hear you have employed two archivists from Chu. They are well-educated persons, I presume?"

The chief archivist answered him with an equivocal "yes" which could mean "two archivists from Chu" or "well-educated persons".

As he followed the prince along a path, he was astonished to see two men straddling a stone table under a tree playing *go*!

Damn them, he thought. Why are they playing *go* during work hours? They get paid by the court but go fooling around like this. What sort of archivists are they anyway? Worst luck! Wouldn't this just happen when the prince is on a tour of inspection! Should he lose his temper, I'll be in for it.

As he approached them, he coughed deliberately and trod heavily on the path to signal them. Engrossed in their game, they did not hear a sound.

The prince went up to the players and stopped to watch. Behind him the chief archivist stood holding his breath, expecting to be rebuked at any moment.

Suddenly one of the players stood up, scattered the chess pieces all over the board, and ended the game.

"You messed them up because you were losing, eh?" accused his partner.

"Who was losing?"

"You were!"

"Not me! You! Don't you know you spoiled your game with the wrong move?"

"You can claim whatever you please, now that the pieces are

are all messed up!"

"So you don't admit you've lost?"

"Not unless you can put the pieces back in place and show me where I made the wrong move."

"You think I can't do that?"

"If you can, go ahead and do it!"

Just as he was going to sort out the pieces and replace them, the chief archivist interfered:

"Would you please stop all this nonsense and go back to work?"

Only then did they see the chief archivist. The player, who was to set up the pieces again, smiled at him:

"How come you're suddenly so serious today and say this is nonsense? Did you know *go* was invented by Emperor Yao? If you think playing this game is not serious, I take it Emperor Yao would be the first to blame. Is that what you mean?" His words were slightly sarcastic, half-serious and half-joking.

The archivist's face turned white with anger.

The other player looked up and remarked: "No wonder he's so serious today. He has a guest with him."

"Do you know who the honoured guest is?"

"Let's see how he restores the pieces," the prince cut in.

The players picked up the pieces and easily restored the unfinished game without putting a single piece in the wrong position.

"Is this correct?" he asked. His partner surveyed the board carefully and checked the pieces against their original positions as he remembered them, then nodded.

"Do you still believe your black side can win? Just one more move and I can take ten of your pieces. If you had not made that wrong move, the situation might have been different."

Prince Jin, watching, judged the strategy to be that of a genuine master player.

"Do you see the move I'm going to make?" the white side asked.

"What sort of trick are you trying?" the black side said, confident he had the upper hand. "It's your turn. Go ahead and move."

The white side put one piece at a position obviously overlooked both by his partner and the viewers.

They went on with the game. the black side pressed hard, launching repeated attacks, while the white kept retreating. It was an intense contest; neither player could disentangle himself.

After twenty moves or so, the critical move the white side had made earlier was now coming into play. The game began to undergo a dramatic change. The black side turned from the offensive to the defensive and remained in a passive position until the end. The white side won the game by ten pieces.

The prince clapped his hands in appreciation and asked the winner to comment on his strategy.

"There is nothing mysterious about it," he said. "Playing *go* is like conducting a battle. Military strategists say 'I dare not take the offensive, but prefer to take the defensive; I dare not advance an inch, but prefer to withdraw a foot.' They also say, 'Be brave in taking action and you will die; be brave in not taking action and you will live'. 'To bend in order to straighten out; to retreat in order to attack; to relinquish in order to take; to lose the west in order to gain the east.' This is the sort of strategy I applied in this game."

In admiration, the prince said, "The secret of *go* is not in *go* itself. I can describe your strategy with two words: plain and simple. You seem to take it easy. You do not try to be aggressive. There is strength in being simple. You take your time and in the end you win the game. Probably this is possible when one has attained the lofty realm many people seek, known as 'conquest without war'."

The player with the black pieces accepted his defeat gracefully. After listening to their analyses with great interest, he said, "I'm amazed to see that you know so much about *go*, young gentleman! Wouldn't you like to play a game with this brother of mine?"

"I can only talk about chess," said the prince. "It's like directing a battle on a military map."

"Are these two gentlemen from Chu?" Prince Jin asked the chief archivist. Indicating the white side player, he said, "This must be Li Er," and then nodding at the black side player, "You must be Yin Xi."

"You must have guessed who I am by my long ears," said Li Er.

"No, no," said the prince. "You are not the only one with long ears. In Luoyang alone I can find a dozen people with ears as long as yours, but I can never find another Li Er among them."

"Really?"

"I hear," the prince went on, "you are indifferent to fame and many other things also; you do not force anything and you do not contend. I can see this is also your approach to chess; you would rather stay on the defensive than go on the offensive, you would rather retreat one foot than advance one inch. As we tell a person by his writing, we can also tell a person by the way he plays *go*. So I don't have to look at your ears to tell who you are."

Yin Xi was surprised to find that the young man, still a teenager, was so learned and insightful.

"May I have the pleasure of knowing your name?"

"Prince Jin would not let me tell you his name," said the chief archivist. "This is Prince Jin. Come and kowtow to His Highness."

Li Er and Yin Xi hurried to show their respect but the prince said, "There's no need to stand on ceremony at a chess game and I've enjoyed this informal conversation with the two players."

"You live in the court, and we came to Luoyang just a short while ago. How did you get to know two humble subjects of yours like us?" Both Li Er and Yin Xi were puzzled.

"Do you call yourselves humble because your official rank is low?" said the prince. "I personally do not view it that way."

"There's a touching story based on this idea," the prince went on. "Once someone told me how Shusun Bao, prime minister of Lu, interpreted 'immortality'."

A few years ago, Shusun Bao visited the State of Jin and was received by the Jin prime minister Fan Xuanzi. One day Minister Fan asked him how to explain the old saying: 'to die yet live forever'. While Shusun Bao was thinking about it, the minister explained it himself:

"The surname of the Fans' ancestors was Gai and the Gais' ancestors dated back as far as the Tangtaos who lived before Emperor Shun of ancient times. The Tangtaos were known as the Yulongs in the Xia Dynasty, the Shiweis in the Shang, and the Tangdus in the Zhou Dynasty. They were all nobles with inheritable ranks and salaries. Since now the State of Jin is leader of the midland alliance and the Fans hold the state power, perhaps this is what 'immortality' means."

"So far as I know," said Shusun Bao, "this is not 'immortality', it's nothing but inheritance of ranks and salaries. In the State of Lu long ago there was a minister named Zang Wenzhong. He is still remembered by the people for what he said and did when he was alive. To me, this is 'immortality'."

"I think a person ought to be remembered for his virtue, his achievements and his sayings," he went on. "With these three things, he can endure. This is real 'immortality'. As for noble families, you can find them in any state, but are they all immortal people? Not necessarily."

"I agree with Shusun Bao," said the prince. "I believe people like you are immortal. I am not, though I am the Crown Prince with a high income. As archivists your position is not high and your salary is small but you are responsible for recording the great events of the day, and your recordings are kept in the Imperial Archives for posterity. This is what we mean when we say 'one is remembered by his sayings'. Isn't this immortality? You are widely-read, you are knowledgeable. You have your own ideas about life and the world. Write them down, pass them on and you will be remembered by what you say. This way, you will become immortal.''

At this, Li Er broke into a smile.

"Why are you smiling, Li Er?" asked the prince. "You don't agree with me?''

"Well, there is of course something like 'immortality' in the world,'' said Li Er. "He who dies unforgotten has longevity; this may be what you mean by 'immortality'. But do you really think one can seek to be immortal and succeed? Let me add one more thing — he who keeps to his roots endures.

"Keep to your roots and you will endure, or have immortality. If one does not keep to his roots and goes against the natural course, no matter how hard he seeks to be immortal, he can never achieve it.''

"Why, this rings a bell,'' said the prince. "I seem to have heard someone say this to me before.''

"Did you go to see Shi Kuang off when he left to return home?'' asked Li Er.

"I had a talk with him,'' said the prince, "but it left me feeling out of sorts. So I did not go to see him off that day. But this was quite in keeping with the proprieties. The Crown Prince is not supposed to go out of town to see off the diplomatic envoy of a vassal state. However, I did arrange for two officials of the east palace to send him off on my behalf. On returning, they reported that they had unexpectedly met up with two people who talked for quite a long time with Shi Kuang about 'immortality' or some such topic.''

Early that morning, said Li Er, we went to the North Gate. My friend Yin Xi felt it wasn't necessary to go all that way just to see him off since our talk with him in the market place had not gone off well. I told him the talk had not ended well because we had different views, but for all that, he is a man of rare talent and sincerity. For this alone we should see him off properly. We waited by the roadside, the new leaves of the willows rustling above our carriage. Soon we heard the clickety-click of horses' hooves and then saw carriages coming out of the gate. From the stately bearing of the entourage and equipage we knew the honourable guest Shi Kuang was setting out. We got out of our carriage and stood waiting to greet him. Suddenly our horse started neighing and the leading horse of the approaching carriage whinnied in response.

"Stop!" shouted someone inside the carriage.

The driver, not knowing what was happening, drew the reins but the momentum swept the carriage on for quite a distance.

The curtain was lifted and the same voice from inside inquired:

"Are you gentlemen Li Er and Yin Xi?"

"Yes, we are waiting here to see you off, sir."

"I knew you would come," Shi Kuang said as he was being helped from his carriage.

What happened was, the two officials from the east palace came up and said, "Since you are Shi Kuang's friends, wouldn't you like to join him in a farewell banquet? We have laid the table at the pavilion over there."

"We are only two humble scholars," said Li Er, "we should not join in a meal for a state guest. We'd like to say goodbye to Shi Kuang and then go back."

"There is no hurry to go back," said Shi Kuang. Turning to the two officials, he said, "I will have the wine in a minute."

"How did you know we were here to see you off?" Yin Xi asked Shi Kuang.

"Since we parted at the market that day," said Shi Kuang, "I've felt that we have not really said everything we have to say to each other and that some day we will meet again. I don't know why, but that's the feeling I have had all along."

"It's fate that brings us together," said Li Er. "For example our meeting at the market the other day and our meeting here today."

"I appreciate the word 'fate' you mentioned," said Shi Kuang. "Since we seem to have a common fate in some ways, how would you like to cross the river with me and go to the north?"

"To the State of Jin?"

Yin Xi glanced at Li Er to see what he would say, but he kept quiet.

"You are both such promising young men," said Shi Kuang. "You could give full play to your talents there, since Jin is the leader of the Midland Alliance."

"Can't make up your minds?" Shi Kuang urged them again, and continued to explain: "The State of Jin used to be the ancient Tangyu, the homeland of the Taotangs. They inherited the spirit of Emperor Yao's times, this includes concern for the welfare of the people and the future of the state. It is a vast stretch of fertile land between the Taihang Mountains in the north and the Yellow River in the south. The country has abundant crops, vast forests, and highly developed herds of livestock and fisheries. It keeps its doors open to capable people and capable people can give full play to their talents there. The *Book of Zhou Poetry* says, 'Life is too short to wait for the Yellow River to become clear.' While you are in your prime, establish yourself in some pursuit, win glory for the country, and you will be immortal."

Li Er and Yin Xi had not expected such a lengthy conversation with him. They had just wanted to bid farewell by presenting him with a willow branch according to the custom of the day. Yet since Shi Kuang had touched upon the subject of "immortality", Li Er felt like commenting.

"I believe there is such a thing as 'immortality'. One who dies and is remembered has longevity. One who dies whose fame and spirit live on for thousands of years, — such a person is 'immortal'.

"However, let me add one thing. He who keeps to his roots endures. Selfish desires are his biggest enemies. Man is often led by desires to go against Nature. Sometimes he cannot keep to his roots. In that case he cannot endure. He is short-lived."

"I thank you very much for your concern," he went on. "But I prefer following my own disposition and taking things as they come. As for 'establishing oneself in a pursuit and winning glory for the country' — this is fortuitous, you can't depend on it. Sometimes you bump into it with your eyes shut, but other times you can't search it out even with your eyes wide open!"

This gave Shi Kuang a jolt: People say Li Er is fond of speaking in paradoxes. Is he making fun of me — "eyes shut", "eyes open"? But he brushed it aside with a short laugh and said, "One tends to follow his own will. There is no sense in forcing him to go against it."

A gentle breeze arose, blowing a slim willow branch around Shi Kuang's arm as if appealing to him to stay.

Li Er broke the branch away from around Shi Kuang's arm and said, "Keep this willow as a souvenir. It will remind you of our friendship."

Shi Kuang accepted the willow with pleasure. What a delightful way of saying good-bye and what a unique souvenir! His ruffled feelings over Li Er's remarks on winning glory vanished.

......

"I must say, you've convinced me with the same argument you used with Shi Kuang," said the prince with a smile.

"That's because you tried to edify us the same way as Shi Kuang did," returned Li Er.

The chief archivist invited the prince to go inside to have a look at the books and the historical records the archivists had sorted out. The prince said he was already adequately rewarded by the trip and would find time to see them later. With that he motioned to his attendants and climbed into his carriage.

Watching the prince's carriage gradually disappear, the chief archivist was bewildered. Just as his visit was unannounced, his departure was unceremonial. Why had he come? Was he leaving with what he came for?

Yin Xi, on the other hand, was pleased with the visit. "He comes like the wind and is gone like the wind! He's a man of character, no doubt about it."

Li Er was silent, lost in thought.

16

Prince Jin lay in bed, short of breath, as if there were a heavy weight on his chest. He was wet with sweat, his cheeks burning.

In his semi-comatose state he seemed to see a man approaching. He looked like the craftsman who carved jade ornaments for him.

"I have pain in my chest and it feels like there's a heavy rock in there."

The jade sculptor looked closely and said with a gentle laugh:

"Congratulations Your Highness! It is not a rock, but a piece of rare jade that has never been seen before."

"A piece of jade? Are you sure?"

"I have carved jade all my life. I can't be wrong."

......

Jade, jade.

The prince awoke. The court servants and maids felt relieved.

A court doctor brought in a bowl of herb medicine, explaining that it was a decoction of walnut meats and dry persimmons and was not bitter.

The court doctors in their group consultations had concluded that the disease was caused by weakness of the lungs. They prescribed a concoction of walnut meats to moisten the lungs and dried persimmons to relieve internal heat.

There were other prescriptions for the lung ailment. One containing pig's lung, for example, was deemed highly effective. Two pig lungs were soaked in water until the air sacs were filled.

Then by patting them with the hand, all the dirt in them was to be removed. After washing them with clean water, they were sliced into small square pieces. After boiling them in water, they were washed again and again until there was not a speck of dirt left. Then they were stewed with almonds into a potion.

But the prince, brought up with the finest foods and delicacies, could not stand the idea of swallowing pig's lungs. After trying once, he refused flatly to take any more.

After a few sips of a walnut-meat and dried persimmon decoction he began calling "jade, jade..."

The attendants wondered why a bed-ridden patient would ask for jade!

They brought in a piece of jade and put it on his bedtable. "Your Highness, we've brought you a piece of jade."

"I don't want it. I want you to take the jade off my chest!" Raising his scrawny hands, he fumbled about on his chest.

"Take the jade off my chest," he kept calling.

The servants and maids were confused, but the court doctor seemed to catch on.

"Your Highness, do you feel pressure on your chest as if made by a rock?"

"Pressure yes, but it's not a rock, it's a piece of jade," said the prince. "The jade sculptor tells me it's a piece of rare jade that has never appeared in the world before."

The people around him looked at each other dubiously. They thought he was probably talking nonsense in his sleep.

The prince shook his head with a sigh: "You've been with me all these years, but you still don't seem to understand me. Go to the Imperial Archives and fetch Li Er here. He may be the only person in Luoyang who understands me."

A carriage was sent to the Archives and Li Er was brought to the east palace.

While Li Er was being ushered in by a chamber maid, he wondered why the prince wanted to see him. He knew nothing about medicine.

He walked up to the bed-side of the prince and wished him a speedy recovery.

"So you've come at last! I was afraid you wouldn't come," the prince said with a gloomy smile.

"How could I decline your summons?"

"You could if you didn't want to come. You're a man of great talent and you can find a place to establish yourself anywhere in the world."

"What can I do for Your Highness?" Li Er listened carefully, not to an imperial decree, but to a dying man's last words.

The Prince was only eighteen years old, and had not yet come of age. In those days when a young man reached twenty, a ceremony was held to mark his adulthood. Since ancient times imperial families attached great importance to the observance. Usually it was held at the ancestral temple. By divination the father set the date and chose the honourable guest who was to officiate. It was a complicated ritual carried out on a grand scale. After the ceremony he would be recognised and respected as a grown-up and expected to behave as such. At the rites he was given a literary name. The childhood name or forename was given at birth. The literary name was not given until the age of twenty. This name was used by historians in recording outstanding figures and events. But in very few cases did they use only the literary name without the formal name. Jin was the Prince's formal name. It was a pity that he had not yet been given a literary name.

The prince was a brilliant young man. Though not considered a grown-up, he was doing the work of an adult; though he was not old enough to rule the country, he had in fact begun ruling.

Chang (ordinary) is often misunderstood to mean mediocre, but *chang* (constant) is the root and home of everything in the world. The eternal Tao is the constant Tao; the eternal name is the constant name. To know it is constant, is wise; not to know it, is presumptuous and being presumptuous brings disaster.

......

"Li Er, are you listening to me?"

"Yes, Your Highness, I am all ears."

"What about the jade on my chest...?"

"I think the jade is still there."

"What does it mean, then, the jade?" He looked at Li Er with inquiring eyes, eager to find out.

The court had laid down very strict rules for designating the deaths of people of different status. For the Son of Heaven death was called *"beng"*; for the princess of states, it was called *"hong"*; for ministers, it was called *"zu"*; for scholars and officials, it was called *"bulu"*; and for the common people, it was called *"si"* — death. As for funeral rites, between the Son of Heaven and ordinary persons there was a world of difference even greater than mere words.

Nevertheless it was *"death"* that closed the immense gap between the prince and the scholar.

Keep the heart empty; keep the mind tranquil. While the ten thousand things thrive, I find them going back where they came from. All things go back to their roots. Going back to one's roots is called tranquillity, tranquillity is called returning to one's origin. The return to origin is called the constant. Knowing the constant is called wisdom.

Everyone must go back whence he came, whether he is the emperor, the prince, a scholar or an ordinary person. This is constant. This is the eternal Tao.

......

"To know what the jade on your chest means," said Li Er, "let me tell you a story about another piece of jade."

A man went to collect firewood on a hill. When he had collected two bundles of dry twigs, he thought he might as well have a rest before he started for home. While he was sitting under a tall tree, he saw a gleaming rock in front of him.

He thought it might be a piece of jade. He put it in an inside pocket of his coat and went down the hill. He hoped it would bring him a fortune.

Jade carving was done in a cottage at the foot of the hill. A sculptor famous far and near for his craftsmanship worked there. The firewood collector put down his bundles of twigs and went in.

The cottage assistant, seeing him dressed in rags and tatters, stopped him: "Get out of here! This is not a amusement place."

"I'm not here for amusement," said the wood-cutter. "I want to see the old jade sculptor behind the counter."

"You want to see the old jade sculptor, eh?" the assistant said with a sneer. "Do you know what his trade is?"

"I do," said the man. "He can tell the value of jade. I've got a piece of stone and I'd like to ask him to have a look at it."

"You've just picked up a rock on the hill and want to show it to the sculptor?" said the assistant. "Don't you see he's up to his neck in work at the moment? If you want him to have a look, you'll have to pay him. Have you got enough cash on you?"

"I don't have any cash with me, but I have one hundred *jin* of firewood lying here. It's worth some money, I suppose."

The old master carver called out from behind his workbench: "Let him in. Firewood collectors do bump into good jade sometimes."

The wood-cutter handed over the jade. The carver looked it over carefully, and said with a smile, "Young man, congratulations on your good luck!"

"Is it really jade?" the young man could hardly believed his ears.

"No mistake about it, and a very rare piece at that."

In great delight, the young man took the jade, tucked it inside his coat and left. He went tripping down the street, leaving his firewood behind.

"What's the matter with that young man? He seems to have gone out of his head!"

"He's found a rare piece of jade up on the hill, so I heard..."

The news spread like wild-fire. People on the street pointed at him saying, "There's the man who found the piece of rare jade!" He began to feel uneasy; it seemed that greedy eyes were looking right through his coat at his piece of jade. His excitement died down and fear took its place.

Coming toward him down the street was an old man with a long beard blowing in the wind, looking like a prophet, or like a saint.

The young man went up to him, saying, "Grandpa, let me give you this piece of jade." He produced the jade, and held it up with both hands for the old man to take.

The old man walked past him, without a glance.

The young man caught up with him: "I mean it, sir. I've had it appraised by a master jade carver and he says this is genuine jade."

The old man stopped and said, "You treasure jade, while I treasure being free of greed. If you give your jade to me, we'll both lose out. Better you go your way and I go mine; you keep your treasure and I'll keep mine!"

"Since leaving the carver's cottage, I have been followed by greedy eyes. I'm afraid I might get killed before I reach home. Let me give you the jade to save myself from danger."

"Now you understand that this rare jade may bring you trouble. Between fame and life, which is dearer? Between life and wealth, which is more important? Between gain and loss, which is more harmful? Some people never understand these questions. Since you understand them, you have learned Tao. Having learned Tao, you can take life and death in you stride." So saying, the old man went down the street and soon disappeared from view.

......

Prince Jin nodded, beginning to see the point.

"Do you still feel the jade on your chest?" Li Er asked.

"No, I feel much better there," answered the prince.

The servants and maids standing in attendance were surprised, but they dared not ask what had brought about the improvement. Whatever it was, they felt relieved so long as the prince was feeling better.

"Let me add a few words," said Li Er. "Tao is great, Heaven is great, earth is great and so is man. They are the 'four greats' in the universe and man is one of them. Man is subject to earth, earth is subject to Heaven, Heaven is subject to Tao and Tao is subject to its own way. Tao's way is the supreme law and let us follow it."

The prince nodded and said, "Your words do me more good than medicines."

After Li Er left, the prince seemed much better. The servants and maids all said Li Er's words had worked wonders. But the oldest court doctor did not believe it and decided to pay a call. When he went in the prince was surprised to see him.

"Why have I never seen you before?"

"I'm getting old," said the doctor. "I am asked to give advice in group consultations only, so I do not often have a chance to see Your Highness."

The old doctor's hair, beard and eyebrows had all turned white as if they were covered with frost.

"How old are you, doctor?" asked the prince.

"This humble subject of yours is a rather careless person," answered the old man. "I only remember I was born on the first *jiazi* (according to the Chinese ancient sexagenary cycle of sixty days, there are six *jiazi* in a Chinese lunar year) of that year, and I have passed four hundred and forty-five *jiazi* in my life. I celebrated my last birthday twenty days ago."

The attendants all looked at each other, baffled — none of them could figure out how old the doctor was.

The prince thought for a moment and them said, "You were

born in the year when the Quan Tower of Lu was demolished.
That year seventeen snakes crawled out from the Quan Palace
into Lu's capital. The number of snakes coincided with the
number of the previous princes of Lu, so Prince Wen of Lu believed it was a sign of bad luck and he decided to pull down the
tower. You must be seventy-three years old this year. The No.12
character of the Duodecimal Cycle of *dizhi* is *hai*. Its top component is the Chinese numeral two and its lower component is the
Chinese numeral six. Remove the top component and put it on
the left of the lower component and the numeral it makes is your
age which means you are twenty-six thousand six hundred and
sixty days old."

The prince turned to the doctor and the servants to question
whether his reckoning was correct. In a chorus, they all agreed
without any hesitation that it was a divine calculation.

The prince had a superb memory. At the age of four he astonished the grown-ups by giving the exact days on which the previous dynasties had risen and fallen.

Prince Jin laughed with pride and said, "So this disease has
not damaged my memory — it still works!"

At that the doctor and the attendants all knelt, congratulating
the prince on his recovery. There was no response to their congratulations. A deep silence reigned. When they looked up, they
found the prince lying in bed motionless.

"Your Highness..."

At first they called softly and then at the top of their voices,
but the prince lay still.

When they moved up on their knees to his bed-side, they saw
he had a serene smile on his face as if he had gone to sleep.
Everything about him was quiet and natural. They were reminded
of what Li Er said: Tao is subject to its own way.

17

The eighth month was the best season for observing the stars
and studying "aspect astrology". One evening Li Er and Yin

Xi sat cross-legged on a large straw mat spread out in the courtyard, watching the stars.

There is an imaginary belt in the universe along which the sun and the moon are apparent travellers. It is known as the Zodiac. Venus, associated with metal, Mars, associated with fire, Saturn, associated with earth, Mercury, associated with water, and Jupiter, associated with wood, all are seen to move along that orbit.

Many stars are stationary in the universe, arrayed in a certain order along the Zodiac, like a town's streets. Through the "streets" the sun, the moon and the five stars travel year in and year out. The stars in the universe can be divided into twenty-eight groups or constellations. The moon travels through one group a day and in twenty-eight days returns to where it started.

Jupiter moves at a slow but steady pace. It takes twelve years to travel one cycle, coinciding with the ancient Duodecimal Cycle of the Twelve Animals system. The cycle of the twelve years passes through the following order: *zi* (rat), *chou* (ox), *yin* (tiger), *mao* (hare), *chen* (dragon), *si* (serpent), *wu* (horse), *wei* (sheep), *shen* (monkey), *you* (rooster), *xu* (dog) and *hai* (pig). So Jupiter in ancient China was called the "Year Star". If the Zodiac is divided by the pace of the Year Star, it can be divided into twelve areas which are marked by the Twelve Signs of the Zodiac.

Li Er started to chant a passage from an ancient document about the changes of the four seasons:

When day and night are equally long and
The Rosefinch comes to the middle of the sky,
Spring is here.

When the sun comes overhead,
Throwing heat like a ball of fire,
Summer has arrived.

When the Star of Xu reaches the south,
Night as long as day,
The fruitful autumn has come.

When the Pleiades shines in the southern sky,
When days are short and nights are long,
Cold winter sets in.

Yin Xi searched for the Star of Xu in the southern sky. Suddenly he called to Li Er: "Look, the Year Star is going faster than usual, threatening the tail of the Rosefinch!"

Li Er looked in the direction Yin Xi was pointing. Sure enough, the Year Star was nearing the tail of the Rosefinch. It should not be approaching the Rosefinch until the coming year. Why is it going out of its orbit and travelling so fast? The Year Star occupied the most important position in the universe, like the Son of Heaven holding the most important position in the country.

"The Rosefinch is now somewhere over the State of Chu in the south," said Yin Xi. "The abnormal astrological phenomenon forecasts that some misfortune will befall the Son of Heaven and the Prince of Chu."

After Prince Jin died, Emperor Ling was overcome with grief. He had entrusted the talented and virtuous prince with the future of the country and the fate of the royal family, hoping he would accede to the throne after his death. But the son went earlier.

Soon Emperor Ling fell ill and was laid up in bed.

The news that the emperor was ailing had only lately been made known.

Since the reign of Prince Wen, the State of Jin had been the most powerful of the midland states. For the last few years, however, it had been declining. By contrast, the State of Chu in the south was coming up, extending its sphere of influence across the Yangtse River to the north. In their fight for control of other smaller states, Jin and Chu had been locked in one battle after another. Neither of them was powerful enough to dominate the midland, but the smaller states had been severely victimised by their conflicts.

Xiang Xu, prime minister of Song in the midland, was friends with Zhao Wenzi, prime minister of Jin, and Zi Mu, prime minister of Chu. He hoped to mediate between them and in alliance with them, to eliminate these internecine wars.

Xiang Xu first visited Jin to elicit the support of its prime minister Zhao Wenzi. The latter went into consultation with his ministers, during which Han Xuanzi pointed out how disastrous the wars had been, not only to people in general, but specially, to those of the smaller states. Since Xiang Xu had come with a proposal to put an end to wars, Jin felt obliged to accept, though he might not necessarily be successful. If Jin did not accept, Chu would in all probability, and would form an alliance with the other states. In that case, Jin would be kept out, and would lose its potential leadership of the alliance.

Therefore Jin accepted the proposal to join with other states to seek an agreement for the elimination of wars.

Xiang Xu then went to visit the State of Chu, where his proposal was readily accepted. Next he went to Qi and Qin, both of which were big states, but no match for Jin and Chu. Since the latter had agreed, Qi and Qin had no reason to refuse. So each of the four states notified their vassal states to attend a formal meeting of alliance to be held in Song.

At the meeting Jin and Chu vied to be the first to swear a blood oath of loyalty to the alliance. The envoys of Jin insisted that as leader of the former alliance, Jin had always been the first to swear the blood oath. But the envoys of Chu said: For one thing, Jin had already recognised Chu as an equal, for another, in the past the two states had been taking turns to preside over alliance meetings.

Senior minister Shu Xiang of Jin said to Zhao Wenzi that there was no point in striving to be the first; the other states had submitted to Jin because of its virtue, not because of its privilege of presiding over the ceremony. Both should continue with the practice of virtue and should not contend over who was first to take the blood oath. Chu became virtual leader of the alliance at this meeting and soon after, wars among the states came to an end.

The small states in the midland which had paid their respects only to Jin previously now began to pay their respects to Chu also.

Once when Zheng's senior minister You Jin went to pay respects to Chu, border officials stopped him at the Han River and turned him back. Since the Prince of Zheng had attended the alliance meeting in person, they said, why had he sent only a minister to pay his respects to the Prince of Chu?

You Ji retorted: "At the alliance meeting the Prince of Chu promised to guarantee security to the small states and to help them subdue social disorders. He also promised that the blessings of Heaven would be received according to the proprieties. This is exactly what the small states hope for."

"I have been entrusted with the mission of paying respects to Chu," You Ji went on, "but you want me to return and demand that our prince should take the trouble to journey here in person. Being a small state, Zheng expects to enjoy the favour of Chu. How dare it disobey Chu's will? But this was not written in the Agreement of the Alliance. Besides, it would sully the name of Chu's prince."

Chu's Chief of Protocol turned a deaf ear to his exposition and he went back to Zheng, seething with anger.

He reported to his prince: "I hear the Prince of Chu is seriously ill and may not live long. How can he expect to go on much longer if he doesn't mend his ways — if, instead of cultivating virtue, he only demands that other princes pay their respects to him to satisfy his vanity?

"I have divined for him, and the hexagram that emerged is *fu*. It says: He who does not return after losing his way has trouble in store. This is contrary to the doctrine of the ruler. The upper part of the hexagram consists of five *yin* lines — a sign of losing the way, and the lower part a *yang* line — a sign that warns him to return to the right course, otherwise he will meet with trouble.

"He does not accept my advice and insists that Your Majesty in person go to pay respects to him. This alone shows he is losing his way and does not want to return. How can he expect to have good luck?"

You Ji encouraged the Prince of Zheng to go there and pay his respects just to keep the Prince of Chu content for a few days, since he did not have much longer to live. He also advised the prince not to return until the funeral was over. Chu needed at least ten years to strengthen its forces before it could hope to contend successfully for hegemony over the midland. Meantime the people of Zheng would be able to live in peace.

As Yin Xi informed Li Er, the various states in the midland soon got to know that the Prince of Chu had fallen ill. With Duke Xiang of Lu in the lead, the princes of all the states went south to express their concern and solicitude. At this time the Son of Heaven also happened to fall ill. He was still nominally supreme ruler of the country, but none of the princes went to see him. The comparison was not to be overlooked; it was only too obvious.

"Unfair, you think?" Li Er said with a smile.

"We are on Zhou's payroll after all," countered Yin Xi.

"But we are from Chu," rejoined Li Er.

"I have always admired your indifferent attitude towards the world," said Yin Xi, "and I never would have expected you to feel so attached to your own home state."

"Don't take me too seriously," said Li Er. "What I meant is that Chu has been unfairly scorned as a backward place. None of the midland princes has ever set foot on Chu territory. Therefore I think their visits to the south will widen their vision.

As for Luoyang, they have visited it any number of times!"

Yin Xi listened in amazement; he had never heard such remarks before. The more he thought about it, the more he found there was to think about.

While Li Er gazed up at the starry sky, he began to speak, as if thinking out loud:

> Saying little fits in with Nature.
> Strong winds do not last for a whole morning,
> Nor does a rainstorm last a whole day.
> What is behind these phenomena?
> Heaven and earth.
> If Heaven and earth cannot act enduringly,
> How much less can Man?

He enjoyed using metaphors and allegories. Yin Xi, being his close friend, was accustomed to his manner of expression and usually understood what he meant. "Do you appreciate the way things change?" Yin Xi asked tentatively.

"Not necessarily appreciate," Li Er said. "I just like to follow the natural course of things, to use my own cliche. Or let me put it this way: He who pursues Tao identifies with Tao."

"Does Tao determine the movements of the sun, the moon, the stars and the changes in human affairs?" asked Yin Xi.

Li Er nodded and explained: "Tao gives birth to the One, the One gives birth to the Two, the Two give birth to three, three give birth to the ten thousand creatures. The thousand creatures have *yin* and *yang* as their components and the joining together of *yin* and *yang* creates harmony."

Yin Xi was still gazing at the stars that grouped themselves in various shapes — a winnowing fan (a grain container), a *dou* (a grain measure), a bird or a cow; some formed streets, others resembled a town. Since ancient times the stars had been observed, studied, given a variety of names by numerous people. Some divided the stars into twenty-eight mansions. But the number of stars in each mansion was different, some containing a large number of stars and others a small number. Why the difference? Were they like the hostels and inns along the streets, some standing close to each other, others standing far apart?

There were any number of legends about the birth of Heaven and earth, the formation of the sun and the moon, most of them fantastic and contradictory. However, this Li Er managed to describe the universe in such simple terms: Tao gives birth to the One, the One gives birth to the Two, the Two give birth to three and three give birth to the ten thousand creatures.

As compared with those mysterious and self-contradictory legends, Li Er's interpretation is easier to understand. But since Tao is invisible, inaudible and intangible, how does it produce the Two and then the three and then the ten thousand creatures?

Yin Xi felt like asking more questions when Li Er said, "It's getting late. The autumn chill may be unhealthy. Let's go in and go to bed."

18

Emperor Ling of Zhou was lying in his sick-bed. When he closed his eyes, the image of Prince Jin seemed to appear before him. Father King, he heard a voice say, I hear Your Majesty is going to build a dam across the Gu River.

The Gu River flowed through the Guyang Valley to join the Jian River, and then ran by the capital on the east side. Recent heavy rains in the upper reaches had caused the water to rise threatening to break the banks at any time. As the capital was in danger, there was a plan to build a dam to protect it.

"Have you heard people discuss the possibility of a clash between the Gu and the Luo rivers? It is all very upsetting."

The Emperor was silent.

We must not build the dam on the Gu River, the voice continued. If the ruler does not force the people to move mountains and fill rivers, the people will have no worries about hunger and cold. Leave the mountains and rivers alone, leave the people undisturbed, and the ruler and his people will live in harmony; the country will be consolidated and, therefore, we will be able to tide over any crisis.

Ancient sages and emperors were careful about things of this kind. If we change the course of the rivers, the river gods might be provoked into fighting each other. In that case, the capital will be flooded, including the court palace.

Jin, say no more about it. I have already issued the decree to build the dam and I cannot revoke it now. Thousands of labourers are working day and night and I'm sure the river will soon be blocked — it's only a small one.

Couriers on horseback or in carriages kept coming with reports that the dam had been raised several times higher than the city wall of Luoyang, but the water in the river continued to rise. To make matters worse, heavy rains kept pouring down continually...

More decrees were issued: Block the river to protect the capital. Hold out in spite of all. Live or die with the dam.

Deafening noises resounded in the northern part of the capital. Tumultuous roaring filled the air as if thousands of oxen and cows, set on fire with oil, were charging into the city, braying like thunder.

Shouts of panic arose above the hubbub: The Gu and Luo are locked in battle!

......

Has the dam given way? Is the city threatened? Jin, my dearest son, come quickly! Help me! Help me!

"Please wake up, Your Majesty. What is it? Is something the matter?"

Opening his eyes, he saw the court doctors, maids and servants all standing round his bed, full of concern, but Prince Jin was not among them. The emperor sighed.

Ah, my son's already gone, he realised, he's gone ahead of me.

A painful thought crossed his mind: Jin, I blame myself for not taking your advice. I should never have issued the decree to build the dam. Just as you predicted, the river gods are incensed and the capital is being destroyed.

Fortunately the flood waters of the Gu River, having swept across the northern part of Luoyang, turned west and raged southward to join the Luo River. When the two rivers joined, the water went up dozens of feet and the roar of the mounting waves could be heard a hundred *li* away. The court palace, in the southern part of the capital, was not seriously damaged. Prince Jin had taken safety precautions and the court staff were out of danger. Only a few buildings on low ground were slightly damaged.

Not long after, the State of Qi offered to help reconstruct Luoyang, but the offer was misconstrued as an insinuating gesture derogatory to the Son of Heaven, because Qi at that time was uneasy about threats from the Jin Kingdom.

In less than a year after the capital was restored, the young prince died.

My dear Jin, I have been thinking that your untimely death had to do with the wild tossing of the rivers, lamented the emperor to himself. You were too weak to stand the panic when the floods rushed in, and later your illness got worse when you had to stand in the cold water directing relief work.

I should have been punished for disturbing the mountains and rivers and provoking the river gods. Why did they take it out on you?

"Have any of the states sent envoys to Luoyang?" Emperor Ling, gasping for breath, asked his servants.

"None so far," the official in charge had to tell the truth.

"If only my son were alive," the emperor sighed again. "None of them would dare to neglect me like this!"

In the Imperial Archives Yin Xi, his burin poised, gazed blankly at the bamboo strip. After a long pause he turned to Li Er:

"What shall we put down as the date of Emperor Ling's death?"

Li Er was at a loss for an answer.

The emperor had died on the 25th of the 11th month. The royal family, engaged in conflict over the succession, neglected to issue obituaries to the vassal states. Some court official actually failed to recall the exact date when questioned. When a messenger was finally sent to Lu with the announcement, the date he gave was the 26th of the 12th month.

In fact, Lu had learned of the actual death date. As it had not received the official obituary from Luoyang, its historians refused to file the date. Now when a different date was announced, *Spring and Autumn*, the official chronicle of Lu, deliberately entered it as a form of punishment for such an absurd mistake.

"This is a disgrace to the reputation of Zhou," said Yin Xi.

"But this is not its only disgrace," said Li Er with an enigmatic smile.

"Shall we put down the date as recorded in *Spring and Autumn*, since that's considered the authoritative chronicle by the other states?"

"*Spring and Autumn* is authoritative because it records historical events faithfully," said Li Er. "We, however, should note it down just as it happened."

"I simply don't understand how the messenger of Zhou could have forgotten such an important date!

"The messenger may have been ashamed to announce the true date lest he should be questioned why he had taken so long to deliver the obituary, and therefore advanced the date by one month. Or he may have been confused about the date. One easily gets things muddled up when he is already confused."

Yin Xi engraved the date as follows: Emperor Ling died on the 25th day of the 11th month, having reigned for 27 years.

Putting down his burin, Yin Xi heaved a sigh of despair:

"It is said the emperor died of frustration."

"Frustration?"

"When the emperor was dying," went on Yin Xi, "he asked

his ministers and officials why none of the states had sent envoys to call on him. They had to tell him the truth. At that time Qi was involved in civil strife. After Cui Shu killed the prince, he seized control of the state. Then he and his family were annihilated by Minister Qing Feng. No one could restore order. The contenders were too deeply immersed in their internal affairs to think of the emperor.

"Duke Xiang of Lu and five or six princes of the eastern states had gone south to pay their respects to the Prince of Chu. This was in accordance with the Agreement of the Alliance. Hearing this, the emperor turned pale with anger, raging that Duke Xiang of Lu, as a descendant of Duke Zhou, should have come to see him but instead went to visit the Prince of Chu. Where was his respect for the proprieties formulated by his exalted ancestor? In this pitch of anger and frustration the emperor breathed his last."

"This Emperor Ling should not have taken the matter so seriously," observed Li Er. "Tao goes in a cycle. What is strong today will become weak tomorrow. Zhou has been a strong country for several hundred years and now it is turning weak. This is the way of Tao.

"What is meant by 'strong'? Keeping to the weak is strong. Even when you are strong, you should keep to the weak. But the fact is that the country is now going from the strong to the weak. If you don't understand Heaven's Way and the way of the world, if you don't pursue the doctrine of keeping to the weak and of not contending, how can you endure?"

"Emperor Ling and Prince Kang of Chu died and were buried just a few days apart," Yin Xi said. "The funeral of Emperor Ling should have been a grand one in keeping with his status but it was attended by none of the princes, while that of Prince Kang should not have been so impressive yet it was unprecedentedly grandiose, really too ostentatious."

When Prince Kang was laid in his coffin, one of the ministers asked Duke Xiang of Lu to put sacraments on the dead. In Lu this procedure was usually carried out by servants. Besides, northerners believed that it was inauspicious, or even disastrous, to touch the corpse in the coffin. Duke Xiang was caught in a dilemma.

Southerners on the other hand viewed the matter in a different light. They did not regard putting cerements on the dead as servile in any way. In the south this was done by members of the family to express their grief. Though death was counted a grievous thing, it was not considered totally inauspicious, or disastrous, in Chu. As there is life, there is death. Death is where life returns. Having lived for so long, one is tired; death provides a permanent rest and relieves him of his heavy burden. At funerals in Chu, people of course wept, but they also sang and danced to the accompaniment of gongs and drums. Birth was celebrated as a happy event to mark the advent of life, and so was death, to mark life's return to its origin.

To relieve Xiang of his embarrassment, his minister Mu Shu advised him to exorcise evil spirits from around the coffin before putting the shroud on the corpse. Accordingly, a witch was called in to perform the exorcism. She danced about at random, occasionally swinging a peachwood stick and a broom over the coffin. The Chu officials did not interfere, taking the action to represent a customary burial rite of the Lu Kingdom. By the time they realised what the witch was doing, the exorcism was already over.

When the service was finished and the princes from the north had fulfilled their duties, it was nearing the first month of the Zhou calendar. It was time for Duke Xiang, who had been away for several months, to return home for the New Year. But neither he nor the other princes returned home. They stayed on, waiting for the burial of Prince Kang scheduled for the fourth month of the year. On the day of the burial, Duke Xiang of Lu, the Marquis of Chen, the Earl of Zheng and the Baron of Xu and their entourages all joined the procession to the cemetery on the hill.

Emperor Ling of Zhou was buried in the fifth month of the year in the hill southwest of Luoyang. In the funeral procession there was only a young junior official from Zheng by the name of Yin Duan. Senior Minister Zi Zhan begged to be excused because of another engagement. Some ministers demurred on grounds of Yin Duan's youth and low status. Zi Zhan insisted that at least somebody was better than nobody at all. Times had changed: Emperor Ling's funeral turned out lonely and forlorn as compared with that of Prince Kang.

Duke Xiang lingered on in Chu for almost a whole year.

"He has not stayed in Chu all this time just for Prince Kang's funeral," remarked Li Er. "He has other reasons."

"What are they, do you suppose?" wondered Yin Xi.

"He is probably intrigued by Chu's rich and beautiful landscapes, or enamoured of the luxurious palaces and attractive maids, the songs and dances, the exotic but fascinating culture and customs. Probably at this very moment visiting the Dragon and Phoenix Palace in Chu's capital Ying."

Li Er guessed right. Duke Xiang did linger on Chu to see the Dragon and Phoenix Palace. His earlier requests to see it had been declined, because the Chu officials were busy. He was asked to wait until the burial was over. His entourage kept reminding him that he had been away from home for nearly a year. Such a prolonged absence could give rise to trouble at home. But Duke Xiang insisted on staying longer, since he had come all the way from Lu, he ought to remain until all the funeral ceremonies were finished.

On visiting the palace, he was enthralled: How huge it is! Its walls stretch all of half a *li*. No palace in Qufu can match it! I have visited all the major northern capitals: of Zhou, Jin, Qin and Qi, but have never seen one of this size.

The red paint, among other things, is quite different from that in the north. The Chu people, as descendants of Emperor Yan and Shu Rong, the fire god, worship fire and the colour red that breathe warmth and animation. Is that the fire god over there? The figure with a man's face but an animal's body riding twin dragons? The fire god is believed to be the ancestor of the Chu people. No wonder they worship dragons! The beams, columns, eaves, screens, doors and windows are all carved with dragons, phoenixes and serpents — an architectural style not to be found in any other state.

One of the city gates, maybe the east gate or the south, was named Dragon Gate for reasons of safety, since dragons were protective gods of the Chu people. What an exquisite screen beautifully engraved with many-coloured dragons, serpents and phoenixes! See that mural with a man astride a long dragon riding against the wind? What an impressive face! What an elegant bearing, in his high hat, long gown and sword hanging from his waist. Flying above the world he represents the ideal image of a southerner.

There was a popular legend about a man who was fond of dragons. As magistrate of Yexian County in Chu, he was known as Magistrate Ye. He had dragons painted and carved all over his house — on the roofs, beams, columns, eaves and even on ordinary household utensils. His love of dragons touched a real dragon in Heaven. One day the real dragon descended from Heaven, flew over to his house, poked its head through the living-room window and dangled its body and tail across the hall. At sight of the dragon Magistrate Ye was frightened out of his wits. He turned and fled in a panic.

The legend had its origin in banter: It was made up by northerners to satirize the dragon-worshippers in the south. Still, northerners also worshipped dragons but there was a difference of degree: they were not as idolatrous as southerners.

Another image also stood out prominently in the palace — that of the phoenix. The people of Chu regarded the phoenix as a divine bird the way the people of Lu respected the unicorn as a divine animal. The male phoenix was named "feng" and the female was "huang". Both dragons and phoenixes were beautiful creatures and flew about gracefully in Heaven.

The Dragon and Phoenix Palace opened up a new world to Duke Xiang. Where else in the world could one find such architecture, such decorative engravings and paintings! They were great! Fantastic! he exclaimed.

......

In the State of Chen the songs and dances of Chu had become popular and so had *The Book of Changes* (*I Ching*).

"Duke Xiang is now ready to build a spacious palace modelled on the Chu architectural style on his return to Lu," said Li Er. "You'll see it painted, engraved, or carved all over with dragons and phoenixes."

"In the past," Yin Xi said, "it was the culture of the north which influenced the south, but now it's the other way round!"

"The south and the north should exchange cultures; why should one dominate the other?" said Li Er. "The Yellow and the Yangtse rivers flow from one and the same mountain region. Like water the Great Tao flows right and left. Why differentiate between the south and the north?" They both laughed.

"'Like water the Great Tao flows right and left.' What a great statement!" Yin Xi exclaimed.

After a moment's thought, Yin Xi had another question to ask Li Ee:

"Now the date of the emperor's death is settled, right? Shouldn't we add a few words about accession to the throne?"

"And would you propose to write?" countered Li Er.

"Prince Jin died early. His younger brother Prince Gui succeeded to the throne. Like that," said Yin Xi.

"According to the inheritance system, it should of course be recorded that way," said Li Er. "But as far as I know, there is strife brewing within the royal family over the succession."

"You mean someone is contending with Prince Gui for the throne?"

"So it seems," Li Er said.

172

"Then there's plenty of excitement in store," said Yin Xi.
"Shall we hold on till the situation settles?"
"We had better wait and see what happens."

19

In mid-winter the days were short and nightfall came in late afternoon. Quiet reigned throughout the southern end of the capital,
especially around the court palace. The stillness of the night was
broken only by the fitful howling of the wind sweeping in from
the north.

Ordinarily, day and night, winter and summer, music was
played at the large mansions around the court area. But these
days, as Emperor Ling lay dying, singing and dancing were prohibited. When the light faded, people shut their doors, blew out
the candles and lamps and retired.

The emperor's brother Ning Fu tossed in bed, unable to
sleep for worry. He was upset by Minister Dan Kuo's secret
visit to the emperor's chamber. Dan Kuo was one of the few
ministers whom the emperor really trusted. The first time he
came to see Ning Fu, he reported only on the emperor's condition.

Ning Fu was filled with anxiety over his brother's critical
illness. Lying in bed, he reflected on all the good things he had
accomplished as emperor. He was not only honest, and kind-
hearted, but during his twenty-seven years on the throne, the people of Luoyang had enjoyed peace and prosperity. For these, in
such unsettled times, they were especially grateful to him.

Dan Kuo told Ning Fu that his brother was a good, honest,
outstanding ruler. But for the emperor's help, he himself would
have been murdered long ago.

"What happened?" Ning Fu asked in surprise.

"When my father Dan Ji died, it was I who was sent to inform the emperor of the sad news. As you know, my father had
served the emperor with great devotion for years and years and

the emperor always took him into his confidence without reservation. It was my first visit with His Majesty. He was very sorry on hearing of my father's death. He assigned me as my father's replacement to serve him in the court. I fell on my knees before him in gratitude.

"I returned home and waited for the announcement. A long time passed, but there was no report of the appointment. While I was wondering why it should take so long, someone came to inform me that I had narrowly escaped an attempt on my life.

"When I asked what had happened, he explained that the emperor had a bodyguard named Qian Qi. He is the son of the prince of a small state, Shan (in today's Shandong Province). After I left the court, this Qian Qi told the emperor that Dan Kuo was wicked and disloyal.

"The emperor asked him to prove it. He said that when I went to see the emperor in the court I was dazzled by the magnificent palaces and the rich, luxurious living. I openly gasped with astonishment and greed. I obviously wanted it all.

"The emperor expressed his doubts, saying I was only intrigued by the brilliance of the court on my first visit. Qian Qi urged the emperor to get rid of me. He said I did not show any signs of grief over my father's death. He also said I was snooping about everywhere in the court with stealthy steps and furtive eyes. He insisted I must have gone to the court with evil motives. He goaded the emperor on to have me killed. Otherwise, he said, I would surely be a source of trouble.

"The emperor brushed him off, telling him it was all foolishness. This is how he saved my life."

"Generally he does not see people in a bad light," said Ning Fu, "and seldom punishes people without adequate evidence. This is part of his honesty."

"I understand that your father, former Emperor Jian, of all your brothers, loved you best."

"How did you know about that?"

"Not only do I know that, but all the other senior ministers do as well. I can tell it from the names he gave you. Emperor Ling's name is Yi Xin. Yi means genial and Xin means the heart. Since childhood he has been an agreeable character. His name matches his personality. But your name is Ning, meaning 'talent', 'intelligent'. From the name he gave you I can see how he doted on you."

His flattery set Ning Fu's head spinning. "Yes, of all my brothers, some of them of different mothers, my father loved me best."

"I hear the former emperor originally intended to pass the throne on to you but, according to the royal inheritance system, the throne has to be taken over by the queen's first son or the eldest son of a concubine. So Yi Xin was made heir to the throne. As to whom he intended to pass on the throne to, I am not supposed to guess or comment."

"Anyway, there is no sense in talking about the past," Dan Kuo went on. "Let's have a look at the present. Emperor Ling's time is limited. This is Heaven's will and we can do nothing about it. In fact he had set his eyes on the precocious and talented Prince Jin. In his early teens, Jin was entrusted with important state affairs, both internal and external. He dealt with them so neatly that the other ministers admired him from the bottom of their hearts. Especially after he refuted Shu Xiang, the minister of Jin, with only one sentence, and convinced Shi Kuang, the envoy of Jin, the two border towns were regained from Jin without a battle. His reputation was acknowledged all over the country.

"The emperor believed that with Prince Jin in charge of state affairs, he need have no worries about the country after he was gone. Flowers that blossom early may wither early, apples that ripen early may fall early. Precocity may end up in early death. The emperor ought to have known it and been prepared for it. Prince Jin's death cost the emperor's health and morale. He broke down in the end. Who will take the throne and what will become of the dynasty after him? The ministers are worried, the whole city of Luoyang is worried."

"Maybe Prince Gui can bring stability to the country?" said Ning Fu.

"That depends," said Dan Kuo. "The mediocre Prince Gui is a dwarf compared with Prince Jin. If all of a sudden he ascends the throne, it remains to be seen if the ministers will accept him. When the kind-hearted emperor was assisted by the intelligent and perceptive Prince Jin, wicked people in the court dared not plot and intrigue. When the young mediocre Prince Gui takes over, I am afraid mean people like Qian Qi will emerge and, with these people around him, anything could happen."

"You have a point," said Ning Fu. "But what do you think I should do?"

"I think, in the interest of the court and the country," Dan Kuo said, "you should stand up and take it over."

"How?" Ning Fu was hesitant.

"The Son of Heaven could be succeeded either by his son or his brother. This has been the tradition since ancient times. In most cases the crown prince succeeds, but still there are instances of the emperor's brother taking over. I think you are now being called upon to rise to the occasion."

"Is it...a legal thing to do?" Ning Fu was full of reservations.

"What's illegal about it?" Dan Kuo went on with irresistible persuasiveness. "Your reputation in the court is impeccable; the ministers are all looking forward to seeing you settled on the throne."

"This carries a tremendous risk," said Ning Fu. "Could we just let the matter rest for now? I need time to think it over."

......

Suddenly a low, urgent voice was heard at the door.

"Who is it?"

"Minister Dan Kuo is here. He says he has an important message for you and must come in."

"Let him in."

Ning Fu slipped into his clothes and, on entering the outer room, found Dan Kuo already waiting there in the dim light, agitated and trembling.

"The emperor has just passed away; he breathed his last only a moment ago."

Ning Fu was grief-stricken. The tears welled up in his eyes and spilled down his cheeks. As he strained to bring his emotions under control, he broke down. Wailing between sobs, he cried that his brother should not have gone so soon and that he himself should have been by his side when he was dying.

"This was a trick played by Qian Qi," said Dan Kuo in a fit of suppressed indignation. He told everyone the emperor wished to be left alone and, accordingly, his relatives and ministers were kept away form him."

Ning Fu was anxious to learn in detail exactly under what circumstances the emperor breathed his last.

As one of the few ministers in close touch with the emperor, Dan Kuo knew the whole situation. The emperor was quiet when he was dying. During the day, he slept most of the time. Toward evening he woke up and said Prince Jin had come riding a white crane to take him away.

"It's a dream, Your Majesty," his attendants told him.

"Yes, it is a dream," said the emperor, "but it's as clear as day. He is perched on a white crane, playing a *sheng* (a wind instrument). 'Father,' he said, 'I live on Mount Song and I am very happy there...'"

"What is in your mind during the day returns in a dream at night," the attendants explained to soothe him. "You dream of the prince because you miss him. A dream is a dream after all. Please do not take it too seriously."

"But listen! He is playing his *sheng* outside the window..."

They listened but heard nothing.

Suddenly his eyes flashed bright. "My son's come and I am going!" These were his last words. He dropped his head to one side and died.

"Did he leave a will?" asked Ning Fu.

"No, he left no will," said Dan Kuo, "and that is so much the better."

Before Ning Fu could take in what he said, Dan Kuo went on: "It's just what we wish for. You can go ahead and take over with complete justification."

"What about the ministers? Won't they be opposed to me?" Ning Fu could not make up his mind.

"Except for that scoundrel Qian Qi, no one will object. He is the number one stumbling-block on your way to the throne. I have arranged to get rid of him tonight!"

With that he left, confident that he could take action since Ning Fu had acquiesced.

However, Ning Fu was left in a quandary, unable to sit still. He began to regret not having stopped Dan Kuo from taking such a risk.

His mind in a turmoil, he reconsidered:

Am I interested in the throne? To be frank, I am not. The Son of Heaven had spacious palaces to live in, but he can't live in all of them at the same time; he has a great deal of delicious food to eat, but with too much tasty food he will be overfed; he can take as many concubines as he pleases, but too many women can exhaust his vitality. That's not the right lifestyle for achieving longevity.

What's more, the Son of Heaven has too much to worry about. He's weighed down by countless state affairs. It's like placing a heavy yoke on your shoulders. Come to think of it, I really enjoy my carefree life. As emperor I wouldn't have a tranquil moment — it's better to remain where I am...

Dan Kuo and Qian Qi have unsettled scores between them. Whichever one takes advantage of state power to gain personal revenge, the law will bring to justice. Why should I get involved in their altercations?

As it is, regrets are now useless, he concluded. If by luck things turn out well, so much the better. If, on the other hand, Dan Kuo fails, I will not be responsible, because he is the one who cooked up the plot and took action. I have kept shut up indoors all these days. Anyone can testify to this.

He waited anxiously for dawn. In the morning he planned to offer condolences at the deceased emperor's shrine and to pay a call on Prince Gui.

He was about to doze off when he heard the pounding of running feet and hoof-beats of horses galloping toward his gate.

He sprang out of bed. Can it be Dan Kuo returning in triumph?

Shouts rang out over the noises: Don't let Ning Fu escape!

As he listened more carefully, the shouts grew more shrill and insistent. He trembled in fear. Obviously Dan Kuo has failed and brought disaster on me!

The banging on the gate continued. People began climbing over the walls and entering the house shouting and rampaging.

How dare they break into my house like this! he said to himself. After all, I am the late emperor's brother and the new emperor's uncle. Rushing out of his chamber to call for help, he saw that the courtyard was packed with hundreds of — strangers! Where are my stewards, where are my servants? Have they all fled now that I'm in trouble?

He shouted to the crowds: "Stop! Stop this lawlessness! Traitors! You will all be punished for this!"

Someone in the crowd recognised him. "Ning Fu! This is the usurper Ning Fu! Whoever gets his head will be awarded one thousand taels of gold!"

The marauders swarmed up, swinging their swords and slashing at him wildly. In an instant Ning Fu, the brother of Emperor Ling, was cut to pieces.

20

Yin Xi walked along the street, looking right and left at the blacksmiths' and carpenters'. To his disappointment, he did not find the cottage till the end of the street. Suddenly he heard someone calling him from behind. "Master Yin Xi!

Turning, he saw Chang Xiang, the court official in charge of the handicraft industry. They had become acquainted during sword exercises and gradually became good friends.

"I went to see you at the guesthouse, where they told me you had just left for the market," said Chang Xiang.

"I hear some blacksmiths have come from Wu and Yue," said Yin Xi. "Some of them are expert sword-makers. I need to have a new sword made and I have looked for them along the street here, but so far I haven't found them."

"I can tell you why," said Chang Xiang. "I've rounded them all up and put them to work in the court cottages."

"You've got long arms," observed Yin Xi. "But you must ask them to make a sword for me. It must be first-rate, whatever the cost."

"Don't worry, I'll see to it personally. But there is something else I have come to see you about."

"What is it?"

"We need to find a quiet place where we can talk," said Chang Xiang. He led Yin Xi to a tavern down the street. They chose a table at a quiet corner and presently wine and dishes were brought along by the assistant.

"Quick service!" said Yin Xi approvingly. "A court official makes a real difference here, right?" he whispered.

"Not only that — I'm a frequent customer here, and we're on the best of terms. Sometimes they ask me for wine-making tips since I'm a well-known connoisseur."

As Yin Xi took a sip, the tavern owner bent over him and asked: "How do you like it, sir?"

"Sweet and mellow." He examined the wine in the cup. It was crystal-clear except for some distiller's grains floating in it.

"Have you started making *koji* wine?"

Previously wine made by small wineries was fermented but not filtered and therefore still contained distiller's grains.

"We learned to make *koji* wine from the court wineries," said the keeper. "Our filtering technique is not good enough. That's why you still find a few grains in it. It's not real *koji* wine."

"For the past few years," said Chang Xiang, "Chu has not presented filtered wine to the court, so we have had to invent a new filtering technique to make our own *koji* wine. Actually it is just as clear. I'll send one or two technicians here to show you how to do it."

The keeper thanked him again and again. It was a generous offer.

Chang Xiang urged Yin Xi to take one more sip and asked how he enjoyed it.

"Sweet and fragrant," said Yin Xi. "This wine is subtle and slightly intoxicating. No wonder in ancient times when Yi Di presented his mellow wine to Emperor Yu, Yu drank it up and remarked: There will be people who indulge in wine and lose their country. After that Yu kept away from Yi Di and abstained from drinking."

"Let's find some other time to talk about wine," Chang Xiang suggested. "Right now I have something important to discuss with you."

"Please go ahead. What is it?"

"Down this cup first and then I have a favour to ask of you," Chang Xiang said, filling another cup for Yin Xi.

Chang Xiang was serious. Yin Xi thought something might have come up and his help was needed. He took the cup and drained it at one go. He wiped his mouth with the back of his hand, turning to his friend with an attentive look.

"You've always been straightforward with me," said Chang Xiang, "and I'll be frank with you. I have a younger sister; she's very pretty. I think you've met her once or twice. Minister Liu Ziwu has sent a go-between with betrothal presents. He wants to marry her. My sister simply does not want to be married to him and I can't afford to cross him. So I've told the go-between with apologies that my sister is already engaged to Yin Xi."

"This is a joke, but not funny!" Yin Xi was desperately flustered. "I'm already married and I have a wife at home."

"Don't worry," said Chang Xiang. "No one in Luoyang knows you are married. Even if some people know about it, it doesn't matter. So long as Liu Ziwu doesn't know, we'll slide by somehow and the matter will be dropped."

"Is Liu Ziwu so easy to fool that way?"

"No, absolutely not," said Chang Xiang. "He has visited Minister Wangsun Yi, asking him to persuade you to cancel your engagement; he knows you are close friends with the minister.

"Minister Wangsun is a sensible man. He has declined to become involved and said the decision is entirely up to the girl and her choice has to be respected. So I asked Liu Ziwu to follow Minister Wangsun's advice. He agreed, though with great reluctance. I've set the date with him and I want you also to come to my house on that day. My sister will watch from behind a curtain and choose which one of you she prefers. So please, I beg you to come and help us fend off this Liu Ziwu. That will be a great relief to our family, greater than anything else I can possibly think of!"

"Don't worry, brother," agreed Yin Xi. "I'll go along with you through fire and water. Besides, isn't this like a play? It ought to be fun. I'll act in it for your sake — why not?"

At this moment several small children were passing by the tavern, chanting a rhyme:

Aiyiwuhu, wuhuwuhu,
Have you heard what's new?
Who spilled blood? Who? Who?

The Son of Heaven
Killed his brother Ning Fu.

A historian like Yin Xi was sensitive to children's rhymes; he hurried to the door. The children had gone past the tavern, their chanting still faintly discernable.

"What's happened to Ning Fu?" Yin Xi asked Chang Xiang in surprise.

"Murdered in his chambers last night," answered Chang Xiang briefly.

"By whom? Who did it?"

"Didn't you hear the rhyme?"

"The emperor is dead, so how could he have killed his brother Ning Fu?" Yin Xi was puzzled.

Chang Xiang gave him a detailed account of the disputes between Dan Kuo and Qian Qi, adding in conclusion:

"Ning Fu was killed by a gang of unknown armed soldiers. I hear Dan Kuo fled to Jin this morning, accompanied by some trusted subordinates. Dan Kuo must have had a hand in it. If the late emperor had taken Qian Qi's advice and done away with Dan Kuo, there wouldn't have been such trouble today and Ning Fu would not have been murdered either."

Yin Xi nodded thoughtfully and said, "That's why folk songs and children's rhymes are called *feng* (wind). They spread as quickly as the wind. Even before the ministers learn of the event, the rhyme is revealing it outside the court. Since this happening is being bruited about via a children's rhyme, we historians should note it down and file it among the records."

"Why bother about it? You'll only get in trouble!" Chang Xiang looked around to make sure their conversation had not been overheard. He assumed a jovial air, picked up his cup and urged Yin Xi to have another drink.

Yin Xi had had enough, and so saying, pushed his cup aside.

"Are you afraid you'll get drunk?"

"Me? Afraid to get drunk? Give me ten more cups and see

how quickly I down them!"

"Why not drink as much as you can?"

"Do you happen to know my friend Li Er?"

"Why, certainly! I've known him for ages! A great name like that?"

"He often admonishes me: Don't rely on your boldness, don't show your strength, don't take credit for your success, don't indulge in sensualities..."

"When friends get together, a little wine just for fun is nothing to worry about — one or two cups is good for the health. If you drink too much, go on a binge and get drunk, it means you have lost control. Such indulgence in wine will surely lead to trouble."

"I see. I didn't mean to force you."

As they left the tavern, Chang Xiang reminded him to be sure to appear for the visit at his house on the set date, and not to forget, under any circumstances.

Back at the Imperial Archives, Yin Xi's ears were still ringing with the rhyme he had heard. He picked up a bamboo strip and engraved on it:

The late emperor has killed his brother Ning Fu.

He went to show Li Er the engraved bamboo strip, and found him busy in his room packing.

"Are you leaving?" asked Yin Xi.

"Not now. I am getting prepared in case I have to."

"So you know what's happened in the court?"

"Even the deaf must know of it by now."

"What do you think of it, Li Er?"

"Ning Fu had no ambitions to rule," said Li Er. "His life was untrammelled and he was happy, but some ruthless person, out of evil motives, tried to incite him and kindle his desire for power. The scheme failed, the schemer fled, but Ning Fu lost his life."

"I think, it's the late emperor's fault," said Yin Xi, "If he had dismissed Dan Kuo and nipped his plot in the bud, nothing of the kind would have happened.''

"Is this how you see it?"

"Yes, and I've already noted it down just as I see it.'' He produced the bamboo strip inscribed with a line of clearly cut characters.

Li Er, about to say something, changed his mind. Yin Xi, bursting with indignation, had not expected Li Er to view the matter in a different light. He strung the engraved bamboo strip with the others in chronological order.

"Whatever the risk, I intend to tell the truth.'' Yin Xi was moved by an irresistible sense of justice, typical of a qualified historian.

On the appointed day, he set out in his carriage to see Chang Xiang's sister. He had not taken the trouble to dress up in elegant attire, but went in his everyday outfit.

Liu Ziwu had arrived earlier. Extravagantly dressed and escorted by liveried servants, he entered the reception hall and laid out an abundance of betrothal presents and then backed out with carefully worked-out formalities.

Yin Xi, in his ordinary clothes, went in carrying a bow and two arrows, completely forgetting to bring presents. Aware that Chang Xiang's sister was watching from behind the curtain, he raised his bow and, with one arrow, he shot the tassel of a lantern and, with the other, he shot the tassel of the other lantern. Walking back to the gate, he jumped onto his carriage and drove off.

When Chang Xiang asked his sister which of the two she was in favour of, she said though Liu Ziwu was handsome and wealthy, Yin Xi was manly. She was impressed by his archery and charioteering. No one in Luoyang could possibly match him in these two arts.

"The wife should be tender, the husband manly,'' the girl went on. "A tender wife and a manly husband get along well with each other, with Heaven and earth, and with Nature.''

"So you choose Liu Ziwu, I take it?" asked Chang Xiang.

"Who ever said that!"

"You yourself. You say a husband should be like a husband. Liu Ziwu is handsome and wealthy. Hasn't he got all you expect in a husband?"

"But I said something different!"

"What else did you say?"

"The husband should be a real man. A real man is what I expect a husband to be."

"I'm confused. Which one do you choose?"

"I choose Yin Xi..." the girl answered firmly.

Not waiting for his sister to finish, Chang Xiang broke into a laugh.

"You've tricked me into saying his name!" the girl flushed crimson with embarrassment.

Her choice, as it turned out, was the same as her brother's.

21

One summer evening as Yin Xi sat in the refreshing coolness of the courtyard he happened to look up at the sky. The planet Mars was moving westward.

A folk rhyme went like this: Mars sinks west in the seventh month; people make winter clothes in the ninth. In the fifth month Mars is high in the sky; in the sixth it slants toward the west; in the seventh it sinks lower down and in the ninth when autumn winds arise it is time to prepare winter clothes.

Be that as it may, it was not winter clothes that Yin Xi was concerned about, but his ice cellar.

In the twelfth month it was bitterly cold with fierce winds howling and heavy snows sweeping down. Lakes and rivers were frozen. Ice in the mountains was crystal clear. Mountain people were ordered by the court to cut the ice into regular-size blocks to be taken to the capital and stored in the state ice cellar.

When Mars appeared in early summer, royal families began to

slaughter sheep for sacrifices and the ice needed for that purpose was rationed out.

It went first to the emperor and then the court ministers and officials, including those who were retired or on sick leave. By the time Mars appeared lower down in the sky, all the ice had been given out. Individual families had small cellars for keeping their ice rations from the state cellar. It was used not only at banquets and sacrifices, but particularly at funeral ceremonies, because in those days when court officials and their wives died, the corpses were scraped with ice blocks before burial according to the proprieties.

With the ice safely stored in the cellar, black sheep and black millet were offered to the god of coldness for the ice he provided. Prayers were said to keep the cellar in good condition. A peachwood bow and bramble arrows were hung at the cellar door to exorcise evil spirits and avert possible disasters.

Yin Xi had a cellar in his house, but several places had caved in and the cellar door did not fit properly. Repairs had to be done before the coming storage season.

Suddenly there was a knock on the door. His servant opened it and Li Er came in, expressing his congratulations.

"What for?" Yin Xi was confused.

"Don't pretend to be innocent. You paid a visit to your future bride, didn't you?"

"Oh, you mean that. It was a visit I paid against my will. I went there just to warn Liu Ziwu that he had to give up his silly idea. I have now clean forgotten all about it, but you seem to be taking it seriously."

"It's not me who is all that serious, but Miss Chang."

"How do you know?"

"Chang Xiang told me all about it this afternoon. He asked me to propose to you on his behalf. That's why I am here tonight."

"Chang Xiang is carrying this joke too far!" Yin Xi's face took on a grave look. "This simply won't do."

"Why not? This Miss Chang makes even me feel jealous. You wouldn't find such a woman in ten thousand. Do you think she is no match for you?"

"Not that she's no match for me; it's the other way round. You know me better than anyone else, why quibble? I'm already married as you know, and I have a wife at home."

Li Er digressed a bit.

"Have you heard of the battle between the Jin armies and the Di tribesmen? The Di came out badly beaten."

"I've heard about it," said Yin Xi. "Really an extraordinary event! But what does this have to do with the case?"

"The Di tribesmen in the western border have been harassing the State of Jin," Li Er went on. "The Jin armies went out with one hundred chariots to confront the Dis. General Wei Shu said to the commander-in-chief that they planned to encounter the Di infantry with charioteers. In hilly area the chariots were as slow as snails. If the Di tribesmen fought with ten foot soldiers against one chariot, it would be like ten fighting cocks pecking at one snail. If the charioteers were to win the battle they had to become foot soldiers. As they outnumbered the Dis by a large margin and their weapons were better, they could round them up and annihilated them on the ground in a strategic spot. General Wei Shu jumped off his chariot first and, waving his halberd, shouted: 'Get off the chariots and fight on the ground!'

"All the men under his command immediately followed his example. The other contingents followed suit and turned into foot soldiers, each group of five chariots transforming themselves into three combat units. One charioteer from a noble family who refused to leave his chariot was beheaded on the spot as a warning. The three combat units were deployed in five different formations to meet any possible emergency.

"When the Di soldiers saw the Jin armies march up, they laughed. In their eyes, the Jin soldiers were all spoilt charioteers with tender feet who could not fight on the ground. The tough-

footed Di tribesmen seriously underestimated the newly-trans-
formed foot soldiers, and were crushed before they could spring
into action against the onslaught of the Jin armies.''

"All well and good," said Yin Xi, "but what are you telling me all this for?''

"The story is different, but the lesson is the same — that of
'changed circumstances'. That is, you should change your notion of marriage according to changed circumstances. It's true
you are married and you have a wife at home. But you haven't
been together with her for more than ten years, you cannot go
home to reunite with her until you retire from your post, and
there is no likelihood that she can come all the way here to join
you. You are husband and wife in name only. In reality you
have no wife and she has no husband. The law of the Tao is its
being what it is. It's better to disentangle yourself from the yoke
of your nominal marriage. You regain the freedom of a single
man, and she the freedom of a single woman.''

Enlightened, Yin Xi began to reconsider.

Liu Ziwu, of course, was jealous of Yin Xi's marriage to
Miss Chang. One day, with a dagger tucked inside his jacket,
he went to call on Yin Xi.

"What can I do for you?" Yin Xi asked warily.

Casting a glance round the room, the visitor said with a note
of sarcasm in his voice: "Is this where you and Miss Chang
got married? Don't you feel rather sorry for her?''

"That's none of your business! Tell me straight: what are
you here for?''

"All right. I'll tell you straight: I want to borrow that newly-
engraved bamboo strip of yours for a look.''

"Which one?''

"The one containing the record that the Son of Heaven killed
his brother.''

"What right does an idling official like you have to ask to
see a bamboo strip?''

"You sound scared. Afraid to show it to me, eh?"

"Afraid? What is there to be afraid of? I take responsibility for what I do. I refuse to show it to you because you're being rude. Your rank as an official and mine as an archivist are the same under the prime minister. We are both working for the Son of Heaven. Do you realise that by ordering me around you are violating the proprieties?"

"Me? Violating what proprieties? You've committed an unpardonable crime by slandering the Son of Heaven! Do you know that?"

"You are talking nonsense! Get out of here!"

"I stay until the issue is settled. Would you like to solve it in public or in private?"

"What do you mean, public or in private?"

"Either I take the issue up to the court and get you relegated to a remote backward place where, I am sure, Miss Chang would refuse to go — in that case she will be mine after you are gone — or I can hush up your crime on condition that you give up Miss Chang to me. Then you can go your way and I go mine. As for the bamboo strip, you can destroy it and we'll all forget about it."

"You are an outrageous rascal," Yin Xi shouted in a fit of anger.

"How dare you insult me?" Liu Ziwu drew a dagger and stabbed at Yin Xi, taking him unawares. Yin Xi, highly trained in martial arts, neatly dodged the thrust. Liu Ziwu, realising that he was no match for Yin Xi in close combat, turned and fled.

Yin Xi snatched a dagger-axe off the wall and ran out in swift pursuit. Catching up with him at the cross-roads, he slashed him in the shoulder, immediately drawing blood.

Yin Xi stopped in his tracks. Spitting on the ground, he warned:

"I'll spare you your life this time." On his way back, he caught sight of Miss Chang at the gate, holding a sword in her hand.

The people of a country were usually divided into six categories according to their respective functions. Some sat back and talked about how to rule — they were kings and lords; some carried out policy, enforced traditions and regulations, administered and supervised public affairs — they were ministers and officials; some worked with raw material and made things — they were craftsmen; some bought things in one place and sold them in another — they were merchants; some worked in the fields and grew grain — they were farmers; some raised silkworms, grew hemp and wove cloth — they were women.

In Luoyang the court had gathered together experts of the different trades and put Chang Xiang in charge. Thus he often had blacksmiths and swordsmen visiting him at his home. Miss Chang, who had a lively, outgoing personality, watched them practice swordsmanship or skill in the use of halberds. Gradually she became interested in trying out these weapons herself.

She had been in the backyard practising martial arts with her sword when she heard a fracas in the front hall. Sword in hand, she rushed in to see what was wrong.

"What's going on?" she asked Yin Xi at the gate.

"Nothing. Liu Ziwu was here a moment ago."

"What was he here for?"

"Not to say congratulations, you can be sure," said Yin Xi with a smile. He told her in detail what had transpired.

"What a shameless interloper!" said Miss Chang. "Why didn't you call me! I would have been glad to give him a couple of thrusts with this sword!"

"What is more despicable is that he came with a dagger hidden inside a protective leather vest. He planned to leave me dead and take you away with him."

"But why in the world did you let him off so easily?"

"In the past I would have finished him off," said Yin Xi. "But after some cultivation in Li Er's teachings, I now believe in following his way of life. He often says when one is alive, his body is soft and flexible; when he is dead, his body becomes hard and rigid. This is true with plants and all other living things. When grass and trees are alive, their leaves and stems are soft and bendable; when they are dead, they become withered and hard. So the strong and hard are nearing death, while the weak and soft have much longer to live. The strong is down and the weak is up. This is the way things are in the world. Forbearance and tolerance, though seemingly weak, enable one to endure."

"Very well," said Miss Chang. "I'll try to remember this. Next time..." So saying, she went in with Yin Xi.

22

Yin Xi felt as if he was living in a dream.

Away from home all these years and living alone, he now found himself at middle age suddenly together with a beautiful, intelligent young woman who had come into his life and become his wife. Was this real or was it a dream?

At least it was like a fairy tale, and there were plenty of similar fairy tales to hear about if one would only stop to listen:

In Quanqiu of Lu there lived a woman — young, well-bred, beautiful, rich. One night she dreamed of dancing out in the forest with her maid. A sudden shower came down and they were drenched.

The clouds dispersed, the sun came out, the air was fresh and clear. Suddenly not far off they saw a palatial edifice of exquisite design. They entered. It was small and quiet with no one inside. The young woman suggested that they take off their skirts and hang them on the carved stone balustrade to dry.

The maid, being shy, was reluctant to take off hers, but the young woman did, seeing there was no one else around. Standing in the refreshing breeze, her legs felt as if caressed by a rough hand.

"Sister, your legs are so white! Like lotus roots," observed the maid.

"Oh, yes, they are, aren't they? They have never been exposed to the sun before. The inner sides are even whiter."

"What a shameful thing to say!" exclaimed the maid, embarrassed, covering her face with her hands.

"What's shameful about that? It's so, isn't it? That's all I'm saying." With that, she took off her shirt also and draped it over the balustrade.

What high breasts she has, her maid mused. My legs may be just as white as hers, but my breasts are not as high. They say men are more attracted to women with high breasts. She felt a bit envious. Since there was no one else around, she thought she might as well take off her skirt too. It was irritating to have wet clothes sticking to one's skin. Besides, she was curious about what being naked felt like.

"Who is drying skirts in front of my ancestral temple?" Suddenly out popped a man, like a ghost.

Panic-stricken, the two women grabbed their garments from the balustrade and pulled them on hastily. The young woman, fearfully standing behind her frightened maid, queried: "Who are... you? Are you man... or ghost?"

The man burst into laughter: "Who ever saw a ghost in broad daylight! I am Meng Xizi. Have you ever heard of me? This is my ancestral temple."

The young woman heard the name in surprise, for she knew he was one of the three powerful noblemen in the State of Lu.

"Ha, ha! I have your skirt right here in my hand!" he said.

It was not until then that the young woman realised in consternation that her lower half was still naked. She recalled having put on her skirt; how come it was there in his hand? Did I grab only the shirt and miss the skirt?

"Give me my skirt!" she demanded, on the verge of tears.

"You put your skirt on my ancestral temple and now you want to have it back, eh? No way," he said teasingly.

"Give it back to me, I want it back!" the young woman

cried again and again.

When she awoke she realised it was all a dream.

Not long after that the young woman left home, taking her maid with her, to find Meng Xizi. Meng Xizi in real life looked exactly the same as the man she had seen in her dream. Ecstatic when the two arrived, he put them up at Wei as his concubines.

Meng Xizi and the young woman got married, pledging lifelong faithfulness to each other at the temple. She gave birth to two sons, one was named Meng Yizi, the other Nangong Jingshu. Meng Xizi was delighted, since he had had no sons with his first wife.

Yin Xi had heard the story about Meng Xizi and now the same course of events happened to him. Such a splendid fortune smiled on him, and he was only afraid that he might lose it some day.

As Li Er often said: Bad fortune is something in which good fortune lies; good fortune is something in which bad fortune hides. Who knows why this is so? It's hard to tell. The upright can become crooked; the good can become evil. People have long been puzzled about it.

This presentiment now became a reality. One day the Minister of History and Calendar, a high-ranking court official, summoned Yin Xi for a private talk. In the beginning of the dynasty the Minister of History and Calendar, Duke Zhou, Duke Zhao and Duke Tai were esteemed as the "Four Sages". Toward the end of the dynasty the status of this ministry declined, but nevertheless, he was still head of the court historians. Yin Xi went to the minister's office, wondering what he was being called in for. After the preliminary exchange of greetings the minister, a kindhearted official, asked Yin Xi with concern: "Have you offended anyone in power recently?"

"What's happened?"

"The Son of Heaven has decided to transfer you to Hangu Pass to serve as military commander there. I must obey his order and I've asked the secretary to engrave his decree on a bamboo strip. It will be issued presently. The reason given for the transfer is that you are highly trained in charioteering and archery; your talents can be brought into full play in the military service. That's a high-sounding excuse, I know. Because if he really thinks so, why not promote you to be an army general of the court garrison? A transfer to this remote pass is a form of banishment, exile in disguise. That's why I wonder if you've offended anyone in power..."

After a moment's thought, Yin Xi told him about his romance with Miss Chang.

"A romantic story, indeed," mused the minister.

"If there's someone I've offended, it's Liu Ziwu. He threatened to accuse me of slandering the Son of Heaven."

The minister nodded perceptively, but did not comment. Yin Xi said no more for fear of compromising the minister's credibility at court. But he could not help asking: "What about that inscribed bamboo strip? Does the Son of Heaven want to have it destroyed?"

It's easy to find an excuse to transfer an official, but it's not so easy to destroy an inscribed bamboo strip. Even the Son of Heaven cannot risk being condemned by the people. In the various states there have been many who insisted on telling the truth at the risk of their heads, leaving emperors and princes highly embarrassed.

The responsibility of a historian is to record honestly what the emperor and the three dukes say and do as well as report important state affairs. If he can destroy something just because he is unhappy about it, there will be no truth in historical records. Later generations will not be able to tell what is true and what is untrue, what is correct and what is incorrect.

"So long as he does not destroy that engraved bamboo strip," said Yin Xi, "I don't care where he transfers me."

Yin Xi went back home, heavy of heart. Usually he was of an

optimistic and expansive turn of mind and could view a complicated scenario in perspective.

Why am I feeling dejected? He could not explain.

A transfer from the capital to Hangu Pass is nothing to worry
about, he felt. Luoyang, as the capital, is a prosperous city, but
on the other hand, it is also troublesome. Hangu Pass may be
far out at the frontier, but going there means going out of reach
of the emperor. In this sense my transfer is a release, and one
does not come by such a release easily.

It was not Luoyang that he found hard to leave, it was his
young wife.

That year when he came to Luoyang, he had left his newly
married wife behind resolutely. Though she wept for several
days, he was not softened by her tears. When she said she
should not have come to his family and that it was she who was
driving him away, he knew she was speaking the truth,
something which he himself did not have the courage to say at
the time. In fact, he did not know what to say, so he kept
quiet. However, the impasse was not her fault, because the
marriage was not one of her own choice.

That last night she curled up in the corner of the bed like an
innocent lamb. He thought if he moved over closer as a consola-
tion to her before he departed, she would not refuse him. But,
unable to pluck up his courage, he kept his distance. The night
was unbearably long and, when the first rays of dawn slipped
through the window, he got up quietly and left. The moment he
was out of the house, he felt like an uncaged bird.

This time was different. He was irresolute in his actions. He
lacked the courage to tell her about his transfer. Miss Chang did
not fail to detect his change of mood. One day she asked:

"What's the matter with you today?"

"I am being sent to a far-off place and must leave you behind."

Miss Chang was surprised: "You have to go? But where and
why?"

"To Hangu Pass. There is not much 'why' to ask. The court thinks I am more fit to be a military commander than a civil official."

"Not much 'why' to ask?" Miss Chang smiled knowingly. "Don't try to hide it from me. I suspected something inauspicious was brewing when that minister summoned you!" Taking the sword down from the wall, she said, "That rascal Liu Ziwu! I won't let him off easily!"

Before she could go any farther, Yin Xi stopped her and said, "Forget it, forget it. Li Er often says no matter how much you are wronged, repay it with virtue."

"But if this scoundrel is not punished, he will become all the more vicious."

"Vicious people will be punished. Heaven's Way is to benefit but not harm. Our principle of repaying wrong with virtue is in line with Heaven's Way. We only benefit but not harm others. Vicious people go against Heaven's Way to do evil. Therefore, they will be punished. Let us wait for them to be punished. It will be punishment meted out by Heaven."

With a sigh of disappointment, Miss Chang slowly hung her sword back on the wall.

"If you have to go," she said, "we'll go together! Why should you leave me behind? I won't clip your wings, do whatever you wish to do."

"What are you talking about? I come from the grass roots, I can certainly go back to the grass roots. But with you it's a different story. You were born in Luoyang, a prosperous city, and brought up in a wealthy family. How can I drag you to the frontier to spend the rest of your life in a barren wilderness?"

"Is there really no way you can go and take me along?"

"I can't think of any."

"I have a method in mind."

"All right, tell me, let me hear what it is."

"The old saying that 'Every inch of the land under Heaven is the king's land; everyone on the land is the king's subject' has become an empty motto. Today the Son of Heaven has little power beyond the confines of the capital. Beyond the capital he has little control. You don't have to go to Hangu. You can go anywhere and you will be welcome. You are learned and well trained in martial arts. You can find a job anywhere. At the moment the states are contending for hegemony and in any of them you can call your talents into full play. Let's go to some other place and our problems will be solved."

The idea was good, but Yin Xi was hard put to agree to it.

"In my younger days, I could have sought positions among the states and gone anywhere. I would not have come to Luoyang. Now that I am more advanced in years, if I go looking for positions here and there, the world will laugh at me!

"Yours is undoubtedly good advice, but I cannot take it. I'm fed up with life in Luoyang. I don't mind going to Hangu at all. Remote as it is, it's a quiet place in which to spend the rest of my life. I prefer to obey the court order and leave you behind in Luoyang."

"Oh, don't take everything so seriously," cried Miss Chang. "It was only a casual suggestion. If I had been interested in wealth and position, I would not have chosen you as my husband..."

"You mean you really want to go to Hangu with me?"

"That's right! Once with you, always with you!"

"But you're still young. You haven't even begun to enjoy the hustle and bustle of a city like Luoyang."

"Not all young people enjoy 'hustle and bustle' — some of them prefer tranquillity. Just as not all old people enjoy tranquillity — some of them go in for 'hustle and bustle' all their lives."

"Well said," Yin Xi exclaimed in admiration. "Your wonderful remark has a note of Tao in it."

"If I'm getting anywhere near Tao," said Miss Chang, "the credit is all yours."

23

> You lovely, naughty child,
> Stop crying and calm down.
> If you don't fall asleep,
> I cannot bear to eat!
>
> You lovely, naughty child,
> Stop crying and calm down.
> If you don't fall asleep,
> I must your vigil keep.

Gently rocking the cradle, Zhen Gu hummed the lullaby in soft, soothing tones. Li Er turned toward her. She had recovered after giving birth and her pinkish cheeks made her more attractive than ever. The lullaby had a calming effect on the baby and on Li Er too.

"You sing wonderfully well," said Li Er.

Zhen Gu looked up, her eyes sparkling.

"You think so? I'm just humming the baby to sleep. I'm glad you enjoy it."

"Yes, I do, very much!" said Li Er. "When I passed your home state on my way to Luoyang, I heard someone singing in the fields. It was a beautiful song. I still remember it. In some way it resembles the one you just sang, but it was not a lullaby."

"Really? Can you sing it?"

"I can't sing the song, but I can repeat the words to you:

> You handsome, crafty guy
> Won't speak to me at all;
> Because of you is why
> I cannot eat at all.
>
> You handsome, crafty guy,

At meals you pass me by,
Because of you is why
I can not sleep at night.

"You're not particularly fond of songs," said Zhen Gu. "How is it you remember this one so well? Is it because you found the singer quite attractive?"

"No, no," Li Er hastened to explain. "I only heard the song drifting over from the fields. The singer was out of sight. Of course it did occur to me that since she sang so well, she had to be a very charming girl. However, what appealed to me was the typical flavour of the Zheng folk music. Almost every line of it ended with a long drawn out cadence. But you sang it without that slow ending. Maybe yours is a more traditional version?"

"It doesn't matter which is traditional; it's nothing but a song. You can sing it any way you like."

Zhen Gu had been preoccupied with something other than songs. With a sigh she changed the topic: "You look a bit lonesome these days."

"What makes you think so?"

"There are more signs than one. Before, when I sang the song, you paid no attention. But now you do, because you feel lonely."

"You are very observant."

"We have been married for so many years, your moods cannot come and go in front of my eyes without my noticing them."

......

"Yin Xi is gone. He was such good company! Without him you feel lonely, right?"

"I guess you're right. Since we came to Luoyang, we have been working and studying together. Now suddenly he is gone. I feel lost."

On the day Li Er saw him off, they both kept their feelings

under control.

Li Er's carriage approached the roadside pavilion and the driver halted the horses. Li Er got off and walked to the pavilion; there was no one there. Suddenly he realised that he had come to the wrong place. Yin Xi was to go to Hangu Pass from the West Gate, but he had come to the North Gate.

Li Er asked the driver, who told him the messenger from Yin Xi's house said that he was to set out on his journey from the North Gate.

Li Er stood by the roadside, waiting. Presently a horse-drawn carriage came rumbling up the road. Li Er wondered: Who can this be? Is it Yin Xi or Chang Xiang?

When the carriage came to a screeching halt at the pavilion, two men, both in army uniform, jumped off and walked straight toward the pavilion. Li Er, who had no connections with army people, turned and was about to go when he heard his name called:

"Brother Li Er, I'm sorry to keep you waiting!"

"Why, it's Yin Xi! You are simply unrecognisable in that uniform. You look like an army officer. Is this young soldier your assistant? Was he appointed by the court or did you find him yourself?"

"I found him myself," said Yin Xi, looking serious.

"Did you? At such short notice you're fully equipped with everything, assistant and all…"

The young warrior exploded with a laugh.

Li Er wondered what was so funny.

Yin Xi told him the "assistant" was Miss Chang disguised in uniform.

"Oh, it's Miss Chang!" Li Er was surprised. "I was wondering where you managed to find such a handsome assistant!"

At this moment Chang Xiang came with a few servants carrying wine and dishes. They all entered the pavilion. Wiping the sweat off his forehead, Chang Xiang apologised for being late saying that he had been delayed by the Yellow River carp.

When the chef found out that Yin Xi and Miss Chang were leaving for Hangu Pass, he insisted on cooking Yellow River carp for their farewell feast. The fish had to be caught with a net before sunrise and cooked alive; that was why he was late.

Chang Xiang and the servants began to lay the table. Half way through, he turned to Yin Xi: "Where is my sister? Isn't she going with you?"

They all looked at each other and laughed.

"She fooled me a moment ago," Li Er said, "and now she has fooled her brother!"

Chang Xiang stared at his sister in disbelief and annoyance: "What! This is sheer tomfoolery."

Yin Xi explained with a smile that the uniform was a disguise for reasons of safety, because on their way to Hangu Pass they had to cross mountains frequented by bandits. Travellers, especially young women, were often attacked and robbed.

"Let me ask you something," Li Er said to Yin Xi. "Why do you go to Hangu Pass through the North Gate, and not the West Gate?"

"It's a court regulation," said Yin Xi. "All diplomatic envoys, and court officials as well, must arrive and depart through the North Gate when they travel to the west. They leave by the North Gate and travel westward by boat along the Yellow River. This may be because travelling by boat is thought to be more stylish, or because the road from the West Gate is rugged in the hilly areas and, apt to be frequented by robbers."

"I see," said Li Er. "I didn't know that. When I go to visit you in Hangu Pass some day, I would like to leave from the West Gate. Not ride in a carriage, of course. I'll ride an ox, which can only amble along slowly while I enjoy the mountain scenery." His face glowed with anticipation.

"That would be an ideal pleasure trip!" said Chang Xiang.

"I'm looking forward to that day," said Yin Xi. "I can hardly wait!"

......

Li Er sat motionless, lost in thought.

"You must be feeling depressed, shut up indoors all day," remarked Zhen Gu. "Why not go away somewhere for a change and pull yourself together?"

Zhen Gu's "why not go somewhere" struck a chord.

"That's a great idea!" said Li Er. "As a matter of fact, I've been planning to tour some places and look around to see how things are. We have the same thing in mind. It's decided!"

"You are planning to travel?" Zhen Gu was taken aback. "But I am only suggesting you go out for a stroll in Luoyang!"

"In Luoyang? No, I'm going outside Luoyang," said Li Er.

"But why should you? You are not involved in the complications that drove Yin Xi away. In Luoyang you have work to do, you have books to read, life is comfortable. What's the point? The Yins went because they had to."

"Don't you see I also have to go?"

"What do you mean! There is nothing that compels you to go!"

"Do you remember the bamboo-strip engraving recording the death of the late emperor? It was carved by Yin Xi, but with my approval, do you see? The court has not mentioned it, nor has any of the court officials, but the court knows and all the officials know the part I played. This we must keep in mind. Since Yin Xi has gone, what's the point of my hanging around here? People will say I'm staying only because I want to keep my job and they will call me a spineless coward."

Li Er, usually calm, was growing more and more excited.

"Is it that serious?" Zhen Gu was astonished. "If you feel you must go, let's go then. Tell me when, so that I can prepare winter clothes for the child. Grown-ups can take the rough with the smooth on the road, but a child cannot stand the cold."

"Why, you mean you want to go with me?"

"Of course," Zhen Gu looked at her husband with large

innocent eyes.

"That's all very well, but you are not going with me. I am going by myself."

"Why not? Miss Chang went with Yin Xi."

"Remember, you are different from Miss Chang. She is not a mother yet and has no burden whatsoever to carry around. Also, I'm different from Yin Xi. He has been relegated to the Hangu Pass. Remote and desolate as it is, he has at least a permanent place to live, a life-long position, and a regular income, if not the prospect of great riches. But look at me — I have to run from place to place, from state to state. It's hard enough to earn my own keep; how can I manage to feed you and our child? It's better for both of you to stay in Luoyang. The little money we have saved over the years should last for some time and you don't have to worry about food and clothing here."

"How can you get along travelling on your own with no one to cook for you or mend your clothes! That way, I cannot set my mind at rest!"

"I can take care of myself. If you stay here to bring up our child, I won't have to worry about you. For that alone I'll be ever so grateful to you..."

Zhen Gu knew that once he had made up his mind, no one could make him change it. Li Er decided to leave without saying goodbye, not even to Minister Wangsun Yi.

The newly-enthroned Son of Heaven had "solved" Yin Xi's case by transferring him. Naturally he still felt resentful of Li Er. This was a thorn in his flesh, but he could find no real excuse to expel him from Luoyang.

Leaving Luoyang meant Li Er had virtually resigned from his post. Therefore he had to go unannounced and unnoticed. If he made it known, people would come and urge him to stay, either in good faith or as a gesture. They would ask him "Why? Why?" What was worse, speculation could arise that though he said he was going, he really wished to stay on.

On the day of his departure, there were no friends to see him off, no farewell feast to grace the occasion. The leave-taking was even more solitary than when Yin Xi had left for Hangu Pass. When the carriage arrived at the East Gate, Li Er told his driver to halt. His servant Xu Jia got down first and then helped Li Er and his family.

"Yin Xi went west," said Li Er, "but I am heading east."

Zhen Gu handed over the child to him. The child flung his arms out and kicked his feet in the air, but he did not cry. Li Er did not know how to placate the child or comfort him.

"When I return, you'll be able to babble and toddle, I expect," Li Er said.

Zhen Gu, forcing a smile, teased the baby playfully until it laughed.

"Say good luck to your daddy!"

The child smiled brightly, two dimples dancing in his chubby cheeks.

Li Er laughed heartily; he had not laughed like that for a long time. "That means I am going to have a great journey." Giving the child back to Zhen Gu he said, "I must be on my way."

Zhen Gu dropped her eyelids and asked:

"Have you anything else to say to me?"

Li Er thought for a moment and then spoke as if from memory:

> "Cautious as if crossing a frozen river in winter;
> Watchful as if confronted with danger from all sides;
> Reserved and courteous like a guest;
> Yielding and compliant like melting ice;
> True and simple like uncarved wood;
> Open and broad-minded like a valley;
> Indiscriminating like muddy water;
> Tranquil like the depth of the sea;
> Free and elegant like drifting winds.

Who can make the muddy water clear? As it quietens down it will become clear. Who can make stillness last? Let movement go on and stillness will gradually prevail. He who has mastered Tao does not seek abundance and because he does not seek abundance, he can succeed continually, though appearing shabby."

He seemed to be commenting on life in general, and at the same time encouraging himself. Zhen Gu nodded understandingly. He urged her to go back into the carriage and return home with the child.

"Me?" Zhen Gu was puzzled. "It's for you. You get into it."

"I have left my post. I should not use the court carriage any more," said Li Er.

Here the driver interposed. "Sir, you have a long trip to make," he said earnestly. "But without a carriage, how can you make it? Let me go with you. The court has lots of carriages. It won't be missed."

"No," said Li Er. "You don't use things you are not entitled to. This is the code of life. I'll hire one myself on the way."

He helped Zhen Gu, in tears with the child in her arms, into the carriage.

Li Er, wiping away her tears, said encouragingly, "Don't cry. Look, our child is smiling. I'm just going to have a look around. I'll come back before long. When I find a place to stay, I'll come back to fetch you."

He dropped the carriage curtain, gave the horse a slap on the rump and told the driver to start back.

When the carriage disappeared through the gate tower, Li Er and his servant Xu Jia set out on foot.

24

Soon Li Er and his servant entered the State of Zheng. There they gazed on level, meticulously cultivated fields which were divided into squares by narrow waterways. These ditches were for irrigation during droughts and drainage in times of flood. How different they looked from the fields around Luoyang. Li Er thought the difference must have been brought about by Zi Chan.

It had not rained for a long time; the ruts on the road were full of dry dust. Li Er dozed off as the ox-drawn cart jolted along, leaving the farm houses and fields behind in the hazy distance.

Suddenly someone in the street called out: "Stop a moment! Is that Li Er from Luoyang?"

Xu Jia, who was driving, turned to tell his passenger that someone was asking about him.

"En, Well..." Li Er mumbled half asleep. "Who can that be?"

Xu Jia drew the reins and the ox stopped abruptly.

Li Er wondered if anyone in Zheng could possibly know about his arrival, for he had not told a soul in Luoyang where he was going.

The man in the street now came up and, seeing that Li Er was puzzled, explained: "Minister Zi Chan has asked me to meet you here. I assume you have heard of Minister Zi Chan?"

Li Er nodded.

"He is now staying at a guesthouse nearby," the messenger said, "and will be coming here shortly to meet you."

"We have never met. I cannot trouble him to come way out here to meet me." Li Er told Xu Jia to drive on.

The messenger stopped the carriage. "It is just because you have never met that the minister would like to see you," he said. "He has been waiting here for you several days. Please do not go."

Further ahead, some people were standing in the middle of the road. Obviously the minister was intent on seeing him. Li Er disliked meeting with officials; he could not put up with their formal greetings and ceremonies. But out of courtesy, he stopped and waited in the carriage.

"Since the minister took office, what have the people of Zheng been saying about him?" Li Er asked the messenger.

"They've had plenty to say. Before the end of his first year, they complained: 'He taxes my property, he taxes my land. Whoever kills Zi Chan, I'll lend him a hand!'"

"The people really hate him? Is he that bad?" Li Er inquired.

Then he promulgated the *qiu* tax law. According to this system land was taxed according to acreage for military expenditures. Land was measured in *jing* (one *jing* was one square *li* — a *li* is roughly one-third of a mile) and *qiu* (sixteen *jing*). The tax on one *qiu* of land was one horse and three oxen. This, of course, was not Minister Zi Chan's invention. It had been the practice since ancient times. The people did not understand him. They said that his father had died a dishonourable death on the road while travelling and now he himself had turned out to be as precious as a scorpion's tail: If he kept issuing decrees like this at random, what would become of the State of Zheng?

"I assume his father was Duke Cheng, wasn't he?" asked Li Er. "And Zi Chan was Duke Cheng's youngest son, right? The people even spoke of his father's death on the road? Wasn't it disappointing to him?"

"No, he was not disappointed at all. He said so long as it was in the interest of the country, what did it matter if he had to die? If his system was a good one, it would work out, whether the people liked it or not. He'd stick to it, he maintained. The *Book of Poetry* says 'If it does not violate the proprieties, why worry about gossip?'"

"No matter what happens," Li Er commented, "he persists in going his way. People in power need to have the tenacity to enforce their policies."

"Sure enough, in three years' time conditions improved in Zheng and people began to understand. Now they say 'Zi

Chan educates my children and cultivates my land. When Zi Chan is gone, who can take over?'''

Li Er was about to ask more questions when a horse-drawn carriage appeared and the man told him Minister Zi Chan was coming.

The horses slowed to a halt quite a distance from where Li Er was waiting. When the carriage curtain was lifted, a man, formally dressed, jumped out and walked straight toward him. Li Er hastily jumped down from his carriage.

"Welcome to Zheng, Mast Li Er. I have been waiting for you here for quite a few days!"

Zi Chan was about Li Er's age. Though his clothes were not richly ornate, his refined and elegant bearing defined him as a confident ruler.

"Why should Li Er leave Luoyang and come to Zheng?" Li Er asked with a smile. "Have you checked on the report that Li Er was really coming here?"

Zi Chan looked into Li Er's eyes — eyes full of insight and dignity. Only people with wisdom and strength could have such eyes, he judged.

"I cannot be mistaken about it," Zi Chan said firmly. "After your colleague Yin Xi was exiled to Hangu Pass, I had the feeling that you would have to leave Luoyang before long. Since Yin Xi went to the west, logically you would come to the east, and the first place you would have to pass through would be this humble State of Zheng. How would I have been wrong about it?"

"So you are aware of what's happened to Yin Xi?"

"How could we have remained ignorant of a person like him, who had the courage to record the emperor's murder of his own brother Ning Fu in the Zhou chronicles?"

"Your ox cart is a unique vehicle," Zi Chan went on. "Court officials ride in four-horse carriages with guards of honour, wealthy merchants ride elegant horses accompanied by attendants. Only people like you ride in an ox-drawn buggy.

When I arranged for my people to come and meet you here, I told them to watch for it as it would be heading eastward."

Leave it to an official; he is really good at figuring things out, Li Er mused.

"Sir, where are you going this time, may I ask?" Zi Chan inquired.

"I have no particular destination in mind," said Li Er. "After coming to Luoyang I had no chance to go about to see other places. I'll go wherever the wind sweeps me and see whatever there is to be seen."

"In that case," said Zi Chan, "why not stay with me for a while and let me have a chance to learn from you?"

Li Er was put up at a guesthouse in the Zheng capital.

In fact the country was known as the New Zheng (with its capital at Xinzheng County, Henan Province today). Earlier, Emperor Xuan had enfeoffed his brother Ji You as Duke Huan of Zheng along the Wei River, near Fenghao, capital of Western Zhou. Zheng was originally a county under Fenghao. Since it was granted to Ji You, it had become a subordinate state — the State of Zheng, or the Old Zheng.

Ji You, being a competent duke, gained the support of the Zheng people. In the eighth year of Emperor You's reign, Ji You was transferred from Zheng to the capital and appointed minister of culture. In one year's time he performed his duties so well that he became a popular figure among the local people and enjoyed an excellent reputation all over the country.

Emperor You, preoccupied with his concubine Bao, neglected state affairs and the country was faced with impending disintegration. The subordinate states began to fall away from the central government. Ji You, sensing imminent danger, went to seek advice from the minister of history as how to steer clear of the internal political strife.

The minister of history advised him to go to the east and establish himself in the region east of Luoyang and south of the

Yellow River. He said this was a safe area occupied by the two small states of Guo and Gui. The princes of the two states were busy taking advantage of their position to seek their own private interests. People were very unhappy about their rule and there were widespread complaints.

As an accomplished court official, the minister of history said to Ji You, "You enjoy great popularity and a fine reputation among the people. If you ask for a fief from the Son of Heaven and obtain a piece of territory from Guo and Gui, you won't be refused, and the people there will be only too happy to become your subjects."

"What about going south to the Yangtse River?" Ji You asked.

"The Yangtse River Valley is Chu territory. The Kingdom of Chu has a long historical background and is now coming up fast. If you go there, you will find yourself in a passive position, subject to its beck and call."

"What about the west?"

"West of Fenghao there is a rather desolate area inhabited by unfriendly people. In the long run it would not be a good place to go."

Ji You petitioned Emperor You to grant him a fief in New Zheng. The states of Guo and Gui, either deferring to the authority of the emperor or confused by the enfeoffment, readily offered ten counties as additional territory. Thus Ji You went to settle there with his people.

The next year the Rong tribesmen invaded Zhou and killed Emperor You at the foot of Mount Li. Pushing further east, they reached Zheng and killed Ji You. His son Jue Tu succeeded him as Duke Wu. Ten generations later, when Duke Jian took office, he appointed Zi Chan prime minister, with whose help the prolonged internal strife was brought to an end and peace and stability restored in Zheng.

Li Er was put up at the guesthouse outside the south gate of the Zheng capital. The guesthouse was named after a towering plant — the peony, which had two species — one, the herbaceous peony and the other, the common peony. The former was a herb and the latter an ordinary plant with beautiful flowers. Li Er wondered which the guesthouse was named after and how it acquired such a name.

The guesthouse was set amidst a grove of trees at the junction of two rapid rivers flowing southeast. Suddenly it occurred to Li Er: These were none other than the Zhen and Wei, long familiar to him through Zheng folk songs. His marriage to Zhen Gu had made him feel particularly partial to them.

He stood at the confluence, the willows bending low along the banks. Gazing at the smooth currents flowing past, Li Er was touched. They seemed to murmur a message from him to Zhen Gu:

These are the rivers you grew up with and have always remembered so fondly. It's so many years since you've seen them! Let me take a fond look at them on your behalf.

It was now winter in the south. The clear, cold waters flowed calmly along. The willows, still swinging gracefully in the wind, had lost their exuberance. It was the custom in Zheng that, when the rivers ran high again and the peach trees were in blossom, people went on excursions along the rivers. They bathed in the water to exorcise bad luck and evil spirits. Li Er could see in his mind's eye the festive mood of the occasion:

> When Zhen and Wei waters are high,
> Young men and women come strolling by.
> ......
> Teasing and bantering all the way,
> "Accept a peony from me", they'll say.

Does the name of his guesthouse have anything to do with this folk song? Li Er wondered. As the attractive common peony does not blossom in summer, it is not the "peony" referred to in the folk song. It has to be the "herbaceous peony" which has a lovely fragrance and a harmonising effect on the internal organs when eaten. And besides, it can exorcise evil spirits. In this sense, the plant serves the purpose of the custom very well.

Li Er decided to accept the offer to stay at the quiet, attractive "Peony Guesthouse".

25

In spring when poplars and willows turned green and exuberant, Li Er liked to stroll along the Zhen and Wei rivers.

One day as he was ambling along the shore through the willows, his mind turned to Tao again. What was Tao really, the unnamable, formless mystery that was in existence before the universe? He had pondered over this for decades, still unable to find an answer. He might remain ignorant of the answer for the rest of his life, he conjectured. Nevertheless one could feel its existence, the great power with which it controlled and nurtured all creatures.

Isn't Tao like the flowing water in the river, both figuratively and literally?

Gazing at the running water, he broke into a chant:

The Great Tao flows everywhere. It may go left or right. All creatures lean on it for existence and it does not refuse them. When it achieves success, it does not claim credit for it. It nourishes all creatures but does not act like a master — which may be called Small. All creatures turn to it but it does not claim mastery over them — which may be called Great. Because it does not regard itself as great, it achieves greatness.

As he walked along, he thought he heard voices of children reciting something. Led on by curiosity, he turned into an alleyway where the sound came from. In the alley looking through a gate he saw a hall. In it an old scholar was teaching three or four children to read aloud.

Of the three kinds of schools — private, run by a family,

village-sponsored ones, and those run by the state — this was clearly a family school. Village schools were usually staffed with retired court officials. Schools run by the state were found only in the capital. They were better equipped and staffed than private schools, and attended only by children of noble families.

In Luoyang Li Er had seen how state schools operated, but he did not know how private schools were conducted. He stood outside the gate and watched the scholar teach his pupils reading.

It was getting late and the sun was setting. Farmers were returning from the fields with their cows and sheep. Some of them stopped to watch and listen to the pupils. Meanwhile they kept up a lively chatter among themselves.

"I hear Feng Juan has returned from exile in the State of Jin."

"Which Feng Juan?"

"The one involved in the plot to murder Zi Chan three years ago."

"Why did he want to do that?"

"Feng needed game for a sacrificial offering and asked Zi Chan for permission to hunt on the state hunting ground. Zi Chan who had just taken over the office of prime minister from Zi Pi wouldn't hear of it, saying, 'No one but the prince is allowed to enter the state hunting grounds, not even the nobles!' Infuriated by this peremptory refusal, Feng Juan, who was from a big family of powerful nobles, began to organise his servants and enlist recruits in preparation for a showdown by force of arms. Zi Chan was intimidated because, newly in office, he had not managed to establish himself on a firm footing. He was planning to flee from the capital. Zi Pi, who had offered the premiership to Zi Chan, went to call on him. 'Why run away?' he said to Zi Chan. 'You can exile him from the capital. If you are afraid you are not strong enough, remember I'm with you; I'll help you.'

"He had served the court as prime minister for many years and his reputation among the people was impeccable. With reliable backing, Zi Chan put down Feng Juan's rebellion and drove him out of the capital.''

"Why, then, should Zi Chan allow him to return?''

"This is where tolerance and benevolence prevailed. When Feng Juan fled to Jin three years earlier, Zi Pi had insisted that his estate and houses be confiscated, but Zi Chan disagreed, 'in case he returned to atone for his mistake.'

"Having lived in Jin for three years, he could no longer bear the loneliness and hardships of life in exile. He sent a message to Zi Chan, expressing regret over what he had done and asking to be allowed to return to Zheng to mend his ways. Zi Chan approved the request, restored his official post and had his estate, houses and salaries returned to him.''

"That's not the way to bring him to justice; it will only encourage more rebellions.''

"But isn't turning enmity into amity in the interest of the state?''

......

Li Er suddenly felt a powerful hand on his shoulder. Turning around he was surprised to see none other than Zi Chan behind him. He was about to greet him when Zi Chan hushed him with a decisive shake of his hand, signalling him not to speak there. Leaving the crowd they retired to a quiet corner.

"I went to see you at Peony Guesthouse but you were not in. So I came out looking for you.''

"Have you been here for some time?'' Li Er asked.

"Quite a while.''

"Did you hear what they were saying?''

"Yes, I did,'' Zi Chan said with a smile. "This was but a casual exchange of information on the way back home from the fields. If you come in the evening, you will hear heated discussions. After supper, they usually gather in front of the school to relax. That's when you will hear plenty of exciting gossip.''

"You seem to be quite familiar with their evening activities.''

"Oh, yes. Do you have anything like this in Luoyang?''

"Not that I know of. People in power do not like to be the subject of discussions among the common people. Are officials in Zheng the same?"

"More or less," said Zi Chan. "Some ministers are driven to exasperation. They even ask me for permission to have the school pulled down."

"Why pull down the school, after all?"

"They say these doughty farmers gather here in the evening just to fool around and talk nonsense. It's not enough that they stir up trouble among themselves; they also comment on court affairs and criticise officials. They sometimes have their say about you, too, Minister Zi Chan, behind your back.

"So what? In my opinion, it's only natural that they should have comments to make on the government and its officials. Is there any harm in finding out what they think about us and what we do? If what they think is good, we stick to it; if what they think is not good, we do away with it. Their comments can help us judge what is right and what is wrong. Why pull down the school? I believe people's complaints can be eased only through kindness, not harshness. If you want to stop them making comments, it's very easy. But stopping them from speaking their minds is like trying to stop a flood. Floods have to be dealt with through dredging and channelling. If you go on putting up dams here and there, the banks will break some day and in the end, the damage will be much more severe. it's better to open a small gap and let the water flow out gradually. Their comments can cure our diseases."

"Did you convince them eventually?" Li Er asked.

"Yes, I did. They believed I was reasonable. An awful blunder was prevented."

Li Er listened in silence.

"What do you think of the way I went about it, sir?" Zi Chan asked.

Li Er nodded in approval. "When the people refuse to be intimidated by threats great calamities will arise," he said. "Do not oppress them so hard as to reduce their dwellings and strip them of their livelihood. Only when the ruler does not oppress them will they not abhor him. Therefore, the Sage knows himself but does not show off. He loves himself but does not exalt himself."

"I'm very glad to hear it," said Zi Chan. "You and I think alike."

They say, this old man is a bit queer, Zi Chan thought to himself, as a scholar he tends to be somewhat ironical and hardly ever agrees with anyone. But he is not always that way, by any means.

"You've got something to talk about with me, I take it?" Li Er said.

"You guessed right," said Zi Chan. "Let's go and talk about it at the guesthouse."

They left the school for the guesthouse, chatting about minor topics on the way. The moment they were outside the village, a four-horse carriage came up to them from among the trees. It was Zi Chan's carriage, which he had left there for fear he would disturb the school. He suggested they go back in it, but Li Er preferred to walk.

"In Luoyang I believe you were provided with a carriage," said Zi Chan. "If you insist on walking, people will think you are not properly treated here and that we are lacking in hospitality. Please take the carriage, sir."

It is not important to me, Li Er thought, but it violates the rule of the court for the prime minister to walk back. Besides, as prime minister, he must have political opponents and his safety has to be ensured.

They both got into the carriage and soon they were back at the guesthouse.

"What did you wish to talk to me about?" Li Er asked.

"It's very simple. We have just finished casting our Law Tripod," said Zi Chan. "I'd like to invite you to the dedication tomorrow."

"Your Law Tripod?"

"It's a bronze tripod inscribed with the clauses of the Criminal Law," explained Zi Chan. "We are going to place it in front of the court to inform the officials and the people of the legal stipulations."

"I heard the casting of the tripod had been postponed because many were opposed to it," said Li Er. "So you've gone ahead with it regardless."

"I thought about it for a long time," said Zi Chan, "and finally decided to let nothing get in the way because it's in the interest of the state.

"Since ancient times legal judgements have been made by emperors," said Zi Chan. "As state affairs become more complicated, the minister of law makes judgements on his behalf, except in important cases. But so far there has been no written law, so that whatever the emperor or the minister of law says is law."

"The tripod is a good idea! A daring undertaking I must say," Li Er exclaimed approvingly. "Still, I am not sure whether it can be implemented or not," said Zi Chan.

"I wouldn't want to miss such a world-shaking event," said Li Er. "I'll be sure to attend the dedication tomorrow."

Zi Chan had doubted whether he would accept the invitation because he knew Li Er did not like to show up on formal occasions. Delighted at his favourable response the prime minister went on to ask how he was getting along at the guesthouse.

"I know you enjoy tranquillity. But things always go in pairs. For instance, tranquillity and activity, movement and quiescence, being and nonbeing, *yin* and *yang*. If there is only one without the other, it may not comply with your Tao. When you have too much tranquillity, you need some activity. That's why, I suppose, you left the guesthouse and went to the village school."

"Well..." Li Er was at a loss, not knowing exactly what the prime minister meant by such a prelude.

"What I mean is that you need some 'spice' in your life, say, some lively young girls to take care of you. That will make your life more harmonious."

Zi Chan laughed and Li Er was amused by his down-to-earth interpretation of Tao. The minister was quick to realise he had brought his guest round by the path of humour. He rose and said, "I'll send a carriage to fetch you tomorrow morning."

"There's a carriage at the guesthouse, don't trouble..."

"But you are an honoured guest from afar," said Zi Chan, "and the dedication is a grand ceremony. You must have an official carriage to take you there."

26

When Zi Chan left Peony Guesthouse the sky was spangled with stars. The brightest one at the zenith was Mars — the star associated with fire.

Back in Emperor Yao's time people knew how to tell the season by the position of the brightest star in the sky. According to The Book of Yao: "When day and night are equally long and the Rosefinch appears in the middle of the sky, spring comes; when the sun shines overhead, emitting heat like a ball of fire, summer has arrived."

It is spring. The Rosefinch should appear at the zenith of the sky, because birds herald the opening season of the year. Mars is expected to hold that position in summer. Why has it come there so early?

As the houses galloped along, Zi Chan sat in the carriage, thinking of the rumours he had heard at court: The untimely appearance of Mars foretells that fires will break out in the State of Zheng. Zi Chan should not have cast the Law Tripod before Mars came. Mars must have taken offence. And the legal stipulations inscribed on the tripod will surely cause confusion among the people.

This is all nonsense, he thought. Take no notice of it. They are all rumour-mongers. How do they know so much about the relations between the stars in the universe and men on earth? Although Zheng is a small state, it has a territory of several hundred *li*. It is possible that some parts of it might suffer from drought or flood and that fires might break out in others. They might guess what will happen here or there. When Mars comes at the wrong time, there might be fires. But when it comes at the right time, who can guarantee that not a single fire will break out in the state?

When Zi Chan got back home, the doorman told him that there was a letter on his desk from Shu Xiang, prime minister of Jin.

Zi Chan asked about the messenger, and the doorman said he was at the guesthouse waiting for an answer.

The letter written on silk and sealed with wax was highly confidential. He opened it and read:

At the beginning I had confidence in you, but now my confidence is shattered.

Zi Chan was startled at the blunt, unrestrained wording. He read on:

In the past there were no written laws — princes passed judgement according to the gravity of the offences — lest people should argue over the wording and meaning of clauses. They did not believe written laws could eliminate crimes, so they issued orders and decrees to keep the people from committing crimes. They instilled into their heads the notion of justice, mutual trust, love, benevolence and proprieties. They encouraged orderliness. Lack of discipline and disorderliness were severely punished. They taught the people to be loyal, setting examples for them to follow.

In addition, they appointed virtuous people as prime ministers, perceptive people as court officials, loyal and trustworthy people as village heads, and kind-hearted, intelligent people as teachers, so that the people were brought under control and kept from making trouble.

It has always been difficult to govern the people even without stipulated provisions of law, you see.

What will happen when they themselves know the provisions of the Criminal Law? They will cease to fear the authorities. They will try to justify their evil deeds by interpreting the stipulations in their own interests. In that case, it will be even more difficult to govern them.

When the Xia Dynasty was in trouble, there was the Criminal Law of Yu; when the Shang Dynasty was in trouble, there was the Criminal Law of Tang; when the Zhou Dynasty was in trouble, there was the Criminal Law of the Nine Provisions. However, none of them were carved out in written form.

Now as prime minister of Zheng, you have promulgated the cursed new tax policy and cast the Criminal Law on the tripod, believing that in this way you can make the people humble and submissive. Do you think you can do that?

The *Book of Poetry* says, "Follow the example of Emperor Wen of Zhou and the country can be pacified in one day." It also says, "Follow the example of Emperor Wen and you win the trust of the neighbouring states." You see, the book says nothing about the enforcement of laws. When the people know the legal provisions, they will quote them to justify their own ends. Officials will be bribed and jails will fall into chaos. Your career will be ruined and the State of Zheng headed for collapse.

I hear when the state is declining laws are promulgated. That settles it.

When Zi Chan finished reading the letter his forehead was covered with perspiration.

Zheng, a small state wedged between two powerful states — Jin to the west and Chu to the south — had to maintain a certain air of subservience toward them. Since the prime minister of Jin was so strongly opposed to the promulgation of the Criminal Law, Zi Chan had definite qualms about the opening ceremony of the Law Tripod. At the same time, if Zheng intended to survive under the shadow of the two powers, it had to push ahead with its own independent policies.

He answered the letter as follows:

Your kind persuasion understood. This humble Zi Chan is but a mediocre mortal. I am hardly qualified to be of benefit to future generations, but to those of the present, I can perhaps be of some small service. I forgo your kindness, with apologies.

It was brief and concise, its sharp edge buffered in mild tones. He sealed it and had it delivered to the Jin messenger the next morning.

The moment he finished the letter, his wife Song Shu came in, announcing that she had just returned from her uncle's. Song Shu's uncle was the former prime minister, Zi Pi. Her mother was Mrs Zi Pi's younger sister, who died when Song Shu was small. She was brought up by her aunt.

When the royal families of Zheng were contending among themselves for control of the state, Zi Chan, also of royal lineage, kept out of the melee. Later, he was instrumental in restoring order. Zi Pi had a very high opinion of him.

One day Zi Pi invited Zi Chan to his house for a private talk. Considering his advanced years, he explained he would like to retire and have Zi Chan take over as prime minister to assist the Earl of Zheng.

Zi Chan declined the offer on certain grounds: for one thing, Zheng was a small state squeezed in between two larger ones; for another, the royal families were exerting a baneful influence over the court while their sons were still locked in rivalry over power; and finally he himself was neither qualified nor able to handle the situation.

Nevertheless, Zi Pi had strongly recommended him to the earl, who readily agreed, therefore he had little choice but to accept.

Zi Pi encouraged him: "I'll stand by you and so will the young people of the royal families. We'll just see who dares give you trouble! Small as it is, Zheng, with a trustworthy administrator in charge, I'm sure can achieve lasting stability and establish good relations with its neighbours."

So Zi Chan had little chance to remonstrate.

Song Shu had heard every word of their conversation from behind a curtain. She told her aunt how impressed she was by Zi Chan's virtue and talent and confessed she would like to spend the rest of her life with him. When her uncle was informed about it, he told her Zi Chan was a married man.

"I don't mind his being married," she said. "If you are against this match, I'll never marry. I've made up my mind." That was how Song Shu happened to be married to Zi Chan. Being a woman of virtue, she got along well with Zi Chan's other wives.

Zi Chan asked Song Shu if Zi Pi would be willing to attend the opening ceremony the next day. "He was reluctant at first," Song Shu said, "but I managed to talk him into it."

Zi Chan was grateful to her for that.

"I don't need your gratitude," said Song Shu, "I just want you to listen to me about one thing, just this once."

"What is it?"

"You are not to go to any of your wives tonight," she said in an authoritative tone of voice. "Sleep right here by yourself in your study, to store up energy for tomorrow's ceremony. It's an occasion of great significance!"

"As a matter of fact," Zi Chan said with a smile, "I was planning to visit you tonight."

"No, I won't let you in!" So saying, she left the study and shut the door behind her.

Li Er got up long before dawn. He washed and dressed more carefully than usual. When he thought he was ready to go, he sat down to meditate, closing his eyes. This had been a practice of his since entering middle age.

Tao does nothing, yet there is nothing left undone. If kings and princes keep to it, all things will transform themselves. If, in the course of transformation, they are aroused by the desire to act, I will restrain them with the simplicity of Tao. The simplicity of Tao can keep them free from desires. Being free from desires can bring about tranquillity. Therefore, the world will follow the right track of its own accord.

This is true of governing a country and just as true of keeping fit.

The human body is like the world and the heart is its king. If one can keep his heart utterly empty and his mind completely tranquil, the parts and organs of the body will grow in harmony. In the course of harmonious growth some of them tend to go wrong as a result of desire, such as the desire for food, sensual pleasure or fame and profit.

When the harmony of the body is upset by desires, the only thing that can restrain them is the "nameless simplicity", or the simplicity of Tao.

Li Er was now awakening from his state of emptiness and tranquillity. He stood up slowly, rubbed his hands and face and began to pace up and down in his room.

There came a knock at the door.

"Your carriage had come, sir."

"Oh, it's still early," Li Er mumbled. "The opening ceremony of the Law Tripod is after the morning session of the court, isn't it?"

The carriage started off, with two lanterns in front lighting the way. When it arrived at the court, day was breaking. Some people had gathered under the gate tower. Along the street across the square people who had come to see the ceremony were waiting for it to start. They began making comments.

"That big thing draped with silk must be the Law Tripod, I suppose."

"Zheng has never cast such a big tripod before. I wonder if it was cast by Zheng itself..."

"Of course it was. I hear the neighbouring states are all opposed to it. Naturally they made no offer of help in any way."

"It's quite a feat to cast such a huge thing. Zheng craftsmen have certainly improved their techniques."

"Aren't tripods supposed to be used for cooking? How come they cast the law on it?"

"You don't understand anything! Ordinary small families use tripods as cooking utensils, but in the court or in big families, tripods can be used for any purpose. Rich people use them to show off. They say they have 'hundreds of carriages to travel in, ten thousand pots of grain in store, piles of comfortable straw mats to sit on and rows of tripods to eat out of.' They eat beef, mutton, pork, fish and venison, the 'five tripods' as they call them. Some people even use tripods to talk big. They say 'If you don't have five tripods to eat out of, you'll be boiled alive in a tripod.' Boiling alive in a tripod is a cruel punishment used by the court."

"Tripods are also used in burying the dead. This is very much in vogue these days. But now rich people are beginning to use bronze tripods instead of pottery ones for burial."

"Since King Yu of ancient times cast the nine tripods to represent the nine states, the tripod has become a symbol of state power. When the Xia Dynasty fell, the nine tripods were taken away by the Shang Dynasty. When the Shang fell, they were taken away by the Zhou Dynasty."

"Tripods have never been inscribed with laws before. This is Minister Zi Chan's invention — a new use for tripods."

"Well, if they can be used for boiling people alive, they can certainly be imprinted with law. Perhaps this is how Zi Chan first conceived the idea..."

Zi Chan did not hear what the people were saying. He was

busy receiving those who were participating in the ceremony. When former prime minister Zi Pi came, Zi Chan went up to greet him. He noticed that some people who had promised to come did not show up.

"Some ministers did not even attend the morning session of the court," said Zi Chan, "let alone the opening ceremony of the Law Tripod. As a retired senior minister of the court, you were not required to come, but you have come, and come early at that. I am really grateful for your concern."

"I should come," said Zi Pi. "It is nothing to speak of. Look! There comes another guest."

It was Li Er. Zi Chan greeted him: "Welcome! I knew you would come."

"Since I promised to come, I should come."

"Many people promised to come, but they have not shown up. It reminds me of what you often say: True words are not high-sounding, high-sounding words are not true.

"That is the way things are," Zi Chan went on. "Though you are a man of few words, you keep your word. Some people talk big and make tripodfuls of promises, but their actions do not fit their words."

"But not all who have come are necessarily your supporters," Li Er said with a sly smile.

"That I know," said Zi Chan. "So long as they have come, I have hopes they will eventually come to understand me at least, if not support me."

A formal announcement proclaimed that the ceremony was to begin. Cows, sheep and pigs were sacrificed as offerings to the gods — the richest and grandest offerings ever.

When the Tripod was unveiled, the opening passage of the Law appeared in prominent display:

In governing a state, only men of virtue can win over the people with lenience and tolerance. Men lacking in virtue resort to harshness. Fire burns; few people enter it to be consumed by flames. Water is soft and yielding; people play in it and many drown. Therefore, it is difficult to govern with lenience and tolerance.

Zi Chan had asked Zi Pi to give the opening address but Zi Pi declined:

"You are the proper one to make the speech because the Law Tripod was your idea. You must have seriously considered every aspect of this innovation."

Others also urged him to come forward to describe how he had conceived the idea, how it had developed, and so on. Accordingly, Zi Chan began:

A state must be governed by people of great virtue. Only people of virtue can win over the population with lenience and tolerance. When you know you are not a man of virtue and cannot govern the state with lenience and tolerance, you resort to harshness. People fear the flames of fire and keep away, therefore few die by fire. Water being soft and yielding, people don't worry and play in it, so that many drown. Thus, governing with lenience and tolerance is not at all easy.

If I relied on lenience and tolerance alone the people and the state would suffer. I must resort to the blaze of fire, so to speak, though it is taking a step backward. This is how I decided to cast the Criminal Law Tripod.

Unwarranted harshness would hurt the people. Harshness has to be tempered with a certain measure of mildness. If too much mildness renders them negligent, you use harshness to command respect.

This is how you achieve harmony and balance in government. All this is stamped on the Tripod, but as you ask me to speak, I can only repeat what is there. When I retire and hand over the government, the people who take over from me will ask what advice I have to give them; I will say the same thing.

Some day I'll die and I'll say the same things in my will: A state has to be governed by people of great virtue and only people of virtue can win over the people with lenience and tolerance. When you know you are not a man of virtue and cannot govern the state with lenience and tolerance, you resort to harshness. Fire burns, few people enter it to be consumed by flames. Water being soft and yielding, people play in it freely and many drown. Therefore, it is difficult to govern with lenience and tolerance...

Zi Chan spoke with eloquence and passion, leaving the audience deeply moved.

Li Er listened in silence throughout the speech.

The ceremony is a success, he reflected. A clever and experienced senior minister like Zi Chan is bound to be good at making speeches. With his sincerity he has won over the audience and skirted some sensitive issues.

27

On arriving at the guesthouse after the ceremony, Li Er happened to glance in at the window and was surprised to see a young woman in his room. He wondered who she was and why she was there. Hesitating to go in, he met his servant Xu Jia who came forward and said, "Why don't you come in, sir?"

"I thought I had come to the wrong place," said Li Er. "Who is the woman in my room?"

"Minister Zi Chan has sent her to you. He says she is here to take care of you. I've been waiting for you and wondering what to do with her."

"Zi Chan often says that I am bored and lonely here and I need some spice to balance the yin and yang of my life. I thought he was only joking, but I see he was really serious."

When Li Er entered his room, the young woman came up to greet him. She was seventeen or eighteen, pretty and well-mannered. There was nothing about her to suggest the role of a maid servant.

"You are not native to Zheng, are you?" Li Er asked.

"Your accent is not typical."

She raised limpid eyes and countered: "Where do you guess I come from then?"

He detected a tinge of his hometown dialect in her question, but was not certain about it, for he had not heard it for quite a long time. "Are you from the south?" Li Er asked tentatively, stressing the southern way of speaking.

"As a matter of fact I am from your hometown," the woman said with a sparkle in her eyes.

"From my hometown? But do you know where I am from?"

"Yes, Minister Zi Chan says you are from Chen, and I can tell right away by your accent."

"I've been wandering around for several decades. I now speak with a mixed accent."

"But you still have your hometown accent. I could tell it the first word you spoke."

Is she flattering me or is she sensitive to accents? Either way, Li Er was not particularly concerned. He was more interested in what had happened to the girl and in news of his hometown.

"But tell me why have you come here? What brought you here in the first place?"

"I am a refugee here, but thank heaven, I have ended up in the hands of good people. Minister Zi Chan has been very good to me and you are good-natured too. Chen has been eliminated by Chu. Have you heard that, sir?"

"Yes, I have, recently. But I am not very well informed about the details. What happened?"

"The trouble began with a power struggle among the royal families," the girl said.

Duke Ai of Chen married the princess of Zheng and had a son who was named Dao. But he doted more on Liu, the son he had with his concubine. Duke Ai once said to his brother Zhao, minister of culture, that if anything unexpected happened to him, he would like him to help Liu succeed to the throne.

Soon Duke Ai fell ill. Zhao had Dao put to death and set Liu up as heir to the throne. That infuriated Duke Ai, for Zhao had carried his behest too far. Duke Ai was planning to do away with Zhao.

When Zhao got wind of it, he besieged Duke Ai's palace. Laid up in bed, Duke Ai could not break through the siege. He hanged himself. Zhao set Liu up as the Prince of Chen, then sent an envoy to Chu to report on the succession. Prince Ling of Chu was shocked to hear that Duke Ai had hanged himself, that the crown prince had been killed and Liu had usurped power.

Prince Ling, assuming the envoy must have been party to the plot, had him put to death. He then ordered his son Qi Ji to launch a punitive attack on Chen. Chen being no match for Chu, its capital was soon taken and the State of Chen was conquered.

When Qi Ji broke into Chen's palace it was already dark. Icy moonlight flooded the compound and mournful winter winds howled, tossing fallen leaves about, together with valuables scattered about at random.

Some people were killed, others fled. The palace was deserted. Suddenly they heard a sad lament sung in a faint voice:

> The moon rose bright in the east,
> The handsome man was tied,
> Like an oak entangled in branches.
> I am worried, I am upset.

> The moon rose high in the sky,
> The handsome man was killed in its light,
> The wind howling on high,
> Blows sorrow and grief into my heart.

> The moon glowed bright from afar,
> In flames of fire the man was burnt.

Trees swayed in the palace yard,
As if mourning for the dead.

Qi Ji, escorted by his bodyguards, turned in the direction from which the song came. He passed one palace hall after another until he entered a compound where a man was singing by a fire and offering a sacrifice.

There was a slaughtered horse and some broken jade ornaments taken from a carriage standing behind him. When Qi Ji went up to him and asked his name, the man answered:

"I am Yu Bi."

"Yu" was a carriage and "Bi" someone's favour. Qi Ji said, "I guess you must be an excellent driver and in favour with your master. But to whom are you offering the sacrifice and singing this mournful song?"

"I hear the Marquis of Chen has been killed," said the man. "Since I have been driving for him over several decades, I am offering a sacrifice and singing this song to him."

At that Qi Ji flew into a rage: "This song is dedicated to martyrs and is sung only for them. What do you think your marquis is? How dare you sing this song to him? Are you purposely setting yourself up against the righteous armies of Chu?" Qi Ji ordered his men to bind and take the culprit away and cut off his head in the public square.

Yu Bi fell on his knees, begging forgiveness: "How dare I set myself up against the Chu armies, sir? I am offering sacrifice only to repay the kindnesses of the Marquis toward me. I do not know which songs are for martyrs and which for the condemned. I'm only a foolish old man and have no idea about such things. I beg of you to forgive me." Working up a stupid look on his face, he fooled Qi Ji into believing he was completely muddle-headed.

"All right for now," Qi Ji said. "Arrest him and I'll take care of him tomorrow."

In the middle of the right Yu Bi asked for permission to

relieve himself outside. The guard, to keep the stench of excreta out of the cell, let him out, making sure his hands were tied behind his back with a hemp rope. Once he was outside, he broke the rope by scraping it against the edge of a rock and fled. Running swiftly, he was soon outside Chen's capital Huaiyang. He wound the hemp rope round his head as a sign of mourning.

"You certainly are acquainted with all the details." Li Er observed.

"On the way out to Zheng, we met a strange-looking man with a rope tied around his head," the girl continued. "He was very good to us. When we asked him why he had that odd-looking rope on his head, he told us the whole story."

"Then was he the Marquis' driver?" Li Er asked.

"Yes, he was Yu Bi. He came to Zheng together with us. Somehow he found out the marquis had also fled from Chen and was still alive; therefore he parted with us and went to look for him."

With a sigh of admiration, Li Er said, "With such a sense of loyalty, the driver is a man of sterling character. He is many times better than those princes who fight and kill each other for power. His fine deeds mark him as a man of integrity. Tao is pursued by both good men and bad. Some say Tao is mysterious. In fact there is nothing mysterious about it. This humble driver's conduct is in conformity with Tao."

The girl did not fully comprehend the words of Li Er, but she understood he was praising the old man and fully agreed with him.

"Do you think this is the end of Chen?" The girl asked Li Er, deeply concerned as she was about the fate of her country.

"The end of Chen? Not necessarily. Chu conquered Chen once before and, like this time, made it one of its counties. Later on they restored its position as a state and searched everywhere for descendants of the marquis who would inherit the throne."

"That was then," the girl said. "This time many of the

royal princes were killed in the internal turmoil, more perished in the war with Chu. The rest who survived fled. Do you think Chen can possibly have any descendants left?''

"When Emperor Wu established the Zhou Dynasty," related Li Er, "he set about looking for the descendants of the three Sage Kings. Finally he found Shun's descendant Gui Man, then living along the Wei River, and enfeoffed Huaiyang to him and granted him the title of Duke Chen. If you go back in time from Emperor Shun, you can trace up to the ancient Emperor Zhuanxu and along his line you can find many descendants of Chen. If I had not been named Li after the plum tree but had taken my mother's surname, that is, my maternal grandpa's surname, I could have identified myself as a descendant of the house of Chen — a branch of Gui Man's family tree."

Li Er said this in all seriousness but the girl did not seem interested. "The princes of the house of Chen and the ministers of the court all wish to preserve Chen as a state, but as far as the ordinary people are concerned, it's all the same whether it's a state or a county. What is the difference between a state in name and a county in reality? To my mind, it would be better if Chen became a county of Chu. Neither the princes nor the neighbouring states would fight over it and the people would be spared the suffering from endless wars.

Li Er listened in silence. He had not expected the girl to view the situation from that angle, but what she said was not without merit...

28

Li Er had a bowl of crucian carp soup for breakfast and his appetite was greatly whetted. His maid, the girl from Chen, was an expert at southern cuisine. Zi Chan had arranged for Li Er to have Yellow River carp regularly, but the chef could not cook it properly and he had yet to develop a taste for it. One day the maid asked the fishmonger if he could bring some crucian carp on his next round.

"But crucian carp is not as good as Yellow River carp," put in the tradesman.

"Can you get crucian carp in the market?" insisted the maid, ignoring his suggestion.

"Oh, yes," said the man. "But the local people do not care for it particularly. It's not a great delicacy here."

"Well, we southerners consider it a great delicacy," said the maid. "Could you bring some tomorrow?"

The crucian carp soup the maid cooked was delicious. It was stewed with oil, salt and shreds of ginger until it turned white. It was simple to cook, and to homesick southerners, tasted divine. The fish peddler allowed himself a sip and was elated at the rich flavour. He asked the maid in detail about the spices she added and said he intended to try making some as soon as he got home.

Since the maid came, Li Er had become more talkative — a change he himself grew gradually aware of. In the company of his servant Xu Jia, he did not have much to say. He spent his time reading or meditating while the servant found all sorts of chores to busy himself with. They had been together too long to have much to talk about. They knew each other too well. They could make themselves understood with a simple look or gesture. There was little need for words.

But these days he found himself in a loquacious mood.

Has the young woman invigorated my life or has her refined speech stimulated my interest in conversation? Or is it because I am concerned about what has happened in my home state? He did not know what accounted for the change, but he was engaged in a discussion with her. A folk song he used to hear at home was now beginning to ring in his ears:

The pond at the east gate,
Is good for steeping hemp.

Fair lady so sedate,
I'd like to sing with you.

The pond at the east gate,
Where people steep ramie,
Fair lady so sedate,
I'd like to speak with you.

The pond at the east gate,
Steeps villous themeda.
Fair lady so sedate,
My heart calls out to you.

But Li Er was determined to leave Zheng. He was planning to say good-bye to Zi Chan after breakfast.

"Why do you want to leave? You're enjoying your stay here..."

"Yes, that's exactly why I want to leave." He had a faint notion that some subtle desire was burrowing in him and he felt he ought to be on the alert.

No evil is greater than selfish desires, he thought. Selfish desires must be restrained before they rise. Indulgence in them will bring trouble.

The maid laid Li Er's favourite fish soup on the table and watched while he took the first sip.

"Isn't it delicious?" she said, in more of a statement than a question.

"Very," Li Er agreed, wiping his mouth with the back of his hand. "Since I left home, I have not tasted such wonderful soup."

His compliment made the young woman happy. "Shall we have more tomorrow?" she suggested.

"Tomorrow?" Li Er repeated mechanically. "I think we can do without it tomorrow."

"You don't want crucian carp soup tomorrow?" the maid did not understand. "Perhaps you'd prefer Yellow River carp soup for a change? Yellow River carp is very good too."

"Well, we'll see when tomorrow comes."

The maid, perplexed, returned to her own room.

When Li Er got up the next morning he asked Xu Jia to have the driver get the carriage ready.

"Where are you going, sir?" Xu Jia asked. "Since coming to Zheng, you've never used the carriage in the morning except for the trip to the Law Tripod opening ceremony."

"I am going to see Minister Zi Chan," said Li Er.

"Are you planning to leave here?" Xu Jia asked tentatively.

"Don't try to be smart with me." Li Er spoke in a grave tone of voice partly to himself. The maid did not seem to hear him; he went out quietly.

While he was riding along the street, a strong whirlwind arose, darkening the sky with fine dust.

Shouting broke out: "Bo You is coming!"

People in the street dashed here and there looking for hiding places. The doors along the street were all slammed shut one after the other.

Li Er's carriage horse was startled and broke into a gallop. It was quite a while before the driver was able to halt it.

"Is this Bo You a Zheng minister?" Li Er asked the driver. "What's happened to him? Why are the people so frightened at the mere mention of his name?"

"He's dead," said the driver. "He died quite a number of years ago and his ghost has been haunting the streets. People get panic-stricken when they hear his name."

Bo You was a powerful minister and a terrible drunkard as well. He had a cellar in his house for storing aged wines. He often drank in his cellar while singers and musicians entertained him. He drank every night and sometimes during the day, too. If you went to visit him while he was drinking, he would not receive you. If you asked where he was, his servants would say he was in the mountain. You did not know what they meant. You had to turn around and go back.

When Prince Kang of Chu died that year, the princes of Lu, Song, Chen, Xu and Zheng all went to attend his funeral. Being the senior minister of Zheng, Bo You should have been at the funeral with the Earl of Zheng, but, instead, he sent Zi Xi in his place while he went back home to drink.

Zi Xi was angry. He gathered together several princes of the royal families to launch an attack on Bo You. They burned down his house, leaving him out on the street with no roof over his head. The drunkard fled the capital in panic, not knowing what was happening. He had to find refuge living in exile in the State of Xu. Not long afterward Bo You came back with a band of warriors. They slipped into Zheng through the sewers.

His brother Si Dai drove him out of the Zheng capital. The brothers had been crossing swords for a long time in bitter rivalry. While they were locked in battle, they both appealed to Zi Chan for help. Zi Chan said things had gone too far between them; he would rather steer clear of the issue rather than take sides in their conflict. Let them ask Heaven for help. Bo You was outnumbered by far, so that in the end, he was defeated and killed by his brother in a fierce clash that took place at the sheep market.

The battle over, Zi Chan offered to put cerements on the dead. He laid his head on the leg of the corpse and cried bitterly, in ritual style. Then he clothed the corpse for burial at Doucheng.

Zi Chan's gesture of help at Bo You's funeral enraged Si Dai. He planned an attack on Zi Chan with his own private armed forces. Zi Pi threatened and cajoled him into cancelling his plan. He explained that Zi Chan had helped with Bo You's funeral in compliance with the proprieties; complying with the proprieties was a matter of life and death for the state, and so on. Whoever attacked Zi Chan was the worst enemy of Zheng. Zi Pi, who was an influential, powerful figure in Zheng, managed to deter Si Dai from rushing pell-mell into yet another rash mêlée.

When the driver paused, Li Er asked if anyone had seen Bo

You's ghost.

The driver explained: "Not long after the opening ceremony of the Law Tripod, someone did actually see his ghost walking down the street in his armour and helmet. The ghost threatened to kill Si Dai on the second of the third lunar month and Gongsun Duan on the twenty-seventh of the first lunar month the next year. It so happened that on the second of the third month Si Dai died. People believed that he was killed by Bo You's ghost. On the twenty-seventh of the first month the next year, Gongsun Duan died, and people were even more strongly convinced that he was also killed by Bo You's ghost."

Soon they arrived at Zi Chan's house and Li Er found it was an ordinary dwelling, just like most of the others in the capital.

Zi Chan often granted land or towns to officials for excellent performance of their duties. When some officials complained about it, he said, "It is difficult to be free from desires. However, if their reasonable desires are satisfied, they will do their best to carry out their tasks. When their tasks are successfully completed, it is I who will take the credit. Whoever the land or towns are granted to will remain on the territory of Zheng; they cannot be taken out of it."

Since Zi Chan had the right to grant land and towns to other officials, he certainly had the right to build a better house for himself. But his house was just a commonplace dwelling like most of the others.

Li Er looked at the matter from a different angle: What are "reasonable desires"? Is there a standard to measure which desire is reasonable and which is not? Once there is a desire, there is no end to it.

Li Er believed in being simple, free from selfish desires and careful not to display things that could excite desires so as not to disturb the people. Therefore it was best to keep the people without knowledge and without selfish desires.

Being free from desires and being contented consummate each

other, he believed. Man tends to pursue wealth, but what is wealth and who is wealthy really? He who is contented is wealthy. No disaster is greater than discontent and no evil is greater than desire. He who knows what contentment is, is always contented.

To be contented means not to be humiliated; to know where to stop is to be free of danger. Thus he can endure.

Unless one is contented, he cannot be free from desires. The Sage's desire is not to desire. If Zi Chan, as prime minister, is free from desires, the people will become plain and simple.

Being free from desires can bring about tranquillity, and the world will be on the right track. Zi Chan restrains his own desires but makes allowances for those of others so that they will be willing to work for him. When the work is well done he takes the credit. Is he really keeping free from desires? It's hard to say.

Different people crave different things. Some crave expensive clothes, some magnificent houses, some power and position and others fame. In this world there are few people without desires. People without desires are hard to find.

When Li Er arrived, Zi Chan came out to the gate to meet him.

Li Er asked him about the strange sights he had seen and heard in the street on his way:

"Do you believe Bo You has turned into a ghost?"

"Yes, I do," Zi Chan replied.

They began to discuss why a man turned into a ghost when he died.

"When an infant is born," Zi Chan said, "he can see with his eyes and hear with his ears, he can swing his arms and kick his feet. He can cry to make himself heard; this is called 'po' — the physique. As the infant grows, his mind develops and his vitality matures; this is called 'hun' — the soul. 'Po' is associated with the physique and 'hun' or vitality with spirit. When the soul matures it can detach itself from the physique. Therefore, when a person dies, this soul leaves his body and travels around. If a person has expensive clothes and delicious food all his life he develops a strong physique and vigorous soul. If an evil person, man or woman, dies in his or her boots, not to mention Bo You and his like, his or her soul will lodge in the body of another person who is alive. Bo You, his father and his grandfather, being the descendants of our previous Duke Mu, have all been senior ministers of Zheng. They must have used abundant gold and jade vessels and appliances and, therefore, absorbed profuse vitality from them. Bo You was killed by his own brother and, naturally, his soul was pent up with bitterness. So it's not hard to imagine why his soul turned into a ghost that haunts the streets from time to time," concluded Zi Chan.

"Do you agree with me, sir?" he asked.

"I am not certain if souls exist or not," Li Er said. "When the ten thousand creatures thrive, I watch them go back where they come from. Everything goes back to its root — the place it came from. Existence comes from non-existence and goes back to non-existence in the end. Going back to one's root is called tranquillity. Tranquillity means returning to the origin. When a person is back at his root, when his every fiber is finished, does his soul still linger on? I'm not sure."

"But I hear," Li Er went one, "you have appointed his son Liangzhi as minister. By that do you mean to pacify the soul of the deceased?"

"When he knows someone from his family is appointed minister and that he will be remembered and offered sacrifices," Zi Chan explained, "he will not be a bad ghost."

"But why have you also appointed Gongsun Xie minister?" Li Er asked. "So far as I know, he is Prince Jia's son. Prince Jia took the office of the senior minister several decades ago and, after his death, he did not turn into a ghost to haunt the streets.

"I know," said Zi Chan, "there are complaints about it.

The people are scared by his ghost. I am scared too. But by appointing Gongsun Xie minister I can show the world that I am impartial to both former senior ministers."

With an embarrassed smile Zi Chan went on: "Sometimes you need to play up to the public against your will. When they believe in ghosts and you don't, they won't listen to you."

"Do you mean," asked Li Er, "by feigning belief in souls and ghosts you can win over the public? And by appointing certain persons' sons as ministers you can pacify their ghosts? So you've done all this just for the eyes of the public, right?"

Zi Chan did not deny it.

"All right, I think we've talked enough about 'souls' and 'ghosts'," said Li Er. "As a matter of fact I have another reason for coming."

"What is it?"

"I have come to say good-bye."

"To say good-bye? But why?" Zi Chan was not prepared for this. "As I had the feeling that you might feel lonely here, I found the young girl from your home state to serve you as a maid. I hear you two are getting along very well. I thought you would be happy to settle here. Why do you want to leave?"

"Our 'getting along very well' is beside the point. I have been away from home for so long and I did not even know Chen had been conquered by Chu. Being a refugee herself, she cannot go back to Chen, though she has a home there. In fact, we are in the same boat. How can I bear to have her serve me as a maid? This is one of the reasons why I want to leave."

"Why do you take it all so seriously?" said Zi Chan. "I understand you assume a very detached attitude toward things in general. When people say you are of Chu origin, you do not even argue about it. Besides, this is not the first time that Chen has been conquered by Chu; it was conquered once before. It can be made either a state or a county as the Prince of Chu pleases. When in a bad mood, he can have Chen annexed to Chu as a county. In a good mood, he can restore Chen as a a state again. But either way, it is all the same. Sooner or later, Chen will become part of Chu's territory."

"It is understandable that the young woman resents having been forced to flee from her home. But you, sir, being a learned philosopher, you can penetrate the mysteries of the universe. You often say: While others are so brilliant, I alone seem to be dull-witted; while others are all so demanding, I alone seem bored and listless. "As I see it, your 'dull-wittedness' and 'listlessness' are actually great wisdom. "We might just as well view this matter through your 'dull-wittedness' and 'listlessness'."

"Yet how much difference is there between good and bad?" Li Er said with an embarrassed smile. "'What others fear cannot but be feared.' This is the way people have been since ancient times."

"If that is the case," said Zi Chan, "I am not alone in 'playing up to the public'. The reason you want to leave is also 'to show the public', right?"

"No wonder people admire your silver tongue," Li Er said.

"Thank you for your compliment," said Zi Chan. "If you insist on leaving just because 'what others fear cannot but be feared', I won't keep you. But don't hesitate to let me know if there is anything you need on the road."

"I have already given you too much trouble during my stay here," said Li Er, "but I do have a favour to ask. Please take good care of the woman from Chen after I'm gone."

"Why not take her with you?" Zi Chan suggested. "That would be the best way to take care of her."

"No, that won't do."

"There you go again. 'What others fear cannot but be feared', eh? All right, you go ahead and leave her with me. I'll take good care of her."

Reassured, Li Er said good-bye to him and left.

29

Li Er is coming to Lu.

The news was bruited about in Lu's capital Qufu before he arrived. Although he had held only an ordinary position in the Imperial Archives of Zhou, and had resigned at that, Lu ministers followed his whereabouts with interest.

It was clear he was not an ordinary archivist, for he had been in charge of the great collections of books in the Archives. In this regard, Jin, Chu, Qi and Qin were no match for Zhou, though they were stronger in military prowess. Li Er had carried out intensive studies in Luoyang and had emerged as the best-read and most learned scholar of the day in that country. For this reason his coming to Lu became the topic of the day.

Why would Li Er come to Lu, of all places? Speculations were rife in Qufu. One reason was known to all. After Emperor Ling of Zhou died, his brother Ning Fu was murdered in the ensuing rivalry over the succession. The event was noted down as a murder implicating the Son of Heaven. In fact, *The Spring and Autumn Annuals*, the chronicles of Lu, recorded it in this manner:

> The Son of Heaven killed his brother Ning Fu.

Quite conceivably it had been written under the influence of the Zhou archivists' version.

Li Er had left Luoyang because he was not on convivial terms with the house of Zhou. But why did he choose to come to Lu? Only one reason could explain this — his compulsive interest in reading. He was not interested in official positions, perquisites, or salaries, but in the study of classical works and historical relics. As Lu was first enfeoffed to Duke Zhou, who had formulated Zhou proprieties and composed Zhou music, Qufu became a centre of classical learning second only to Luoyang. None of the other states could compare with it in this respect. To fulfill his purpose, he naturally chose to come to Qufu.

On arriving at the western city gate, he was met by a gathering of people who were waiting to take him to the guesthouse.

"Who arranged for you to meet me here?" Li Er was suspicious.

"Minister Ji Wuzi," they told him.

"Ji Wuzi is the senior minister of Lu," said Li Er. "I cannot afford to accept his kindness. Please go back and tell him I am planning to stay with a friend of mine. When I am settled, I'll find time to call on him."

Seeing that Li Er meant what he said, they went back.

"Where are we going then?" Li Er's companion Xu Jia asked.

"We'll go to Master Gongye."

"To Master Gongye? I hear he has annoyed Ji Wuzi recently. Is it proper to refuse Ji Wuzi and go to Master Gongye?"

"It is not Master Gongye who has annoyed Ji Wuzi but the other way round. There is nothing improper involved. Let's go."

As they proceeded, Xu Jia asked about the altercation between Gongye and Ji Wuzi. Li Er said, "Once when Gongye visited Zhou, he dropped in at the Imperial Archives. He told me what had happened."

Prince Xiang of Lu attended the funeral of Prince Kang of Chu that year, remember? On his way back from Chu he was met by Gongye at Fangchengshan, a small town on the border. Ji Wuzi had sent him to meet the prince there as a gesture of courtesy.

Not long after Gongye had set out, Ji Wuzi sent an official to catch up with him and hand him a letter. It was highly confidential, and he was asked to deliver it personally to the prince. Assuming it was but a formal message of greetings and salutations, Gongye did not ask what it was about. When the prince received the letter at the border town, he read it out in a low voice:

I hear the general stationed at Bian is planning a mutiny. I am prepared to put him down and take back the town. I will keep you informed.

Gongye was shocked. "When I set out," he reflected, "he said nothing about this. I doubt if he's telling the truth."

That night at his lodging house, he heard that Ji Wuzi had already taken over the town of Bian.

Prince Xiang knew what Ji Wuzi was up to, but he was helpless. His only option was clear: "Ji Wuzi wants to take over the town and keep it in his control, but he says the general of Bian is rebelling. The Prince of Lu is nothing in his eyes. From now on I intend to keep my distance from him."

Nearing the border he had qualms about going back to his own country. He consulted Gongye: "Can I go back to Lu? Would it be safe?"

Gongye was highly indignant. "You are the Prince of Lu — who dares raise a finger to stop you?"

For Gongye, a minister under Ji Wuzi, to speak like that showed his loyalty and integrity were beyond question. Prince Xiang presented him with a set of minister's official robes as a reward. Gongye at first declined, but as the prince insisted, he took it with gratitude. At the border, the prince hesitated again. Rong Chengbo, an official in his entourage, struck up a song:

> Sunset, the daylight dims,
> Why do we not return?
> If not on your behalf,
> Why sleep under the stars?

> Sunset, the daylight dims,
> Why do we not return?
> If not on your behalf,
> Why do we trudge through mud?

The effect of Rong Chengbo's song was positive. The prince made up his mind to go back.

Gongye, returning from the trip, gave his fief back to Ji Wuzi and never entered his house again. The thought filled him with indignation: Why did he use me to deceive the prince?

Later whenever Gongye and Ji Wuzi met, they exchanged pleasantries as if nothing had happened. Otherwise, Gongye made it a point never to mention his name.

On hearing of Li Er's arrival, Gongye, accompanied by his servants, went out to the gate to welcome him.

Li Er was surprised to see how much he had changed.

"Why are you looking so pale?" Li Er asked. "Are you feeling all right?"

"Since returning from Chu with the prince," Gongye said, "I have been feeling out of sorts."

Gongye was wearing a raw silk cap, the ribbons tied under his chin with an extra length dangling down his chest, and a set of old-fashioned two-in-one, a jacket and a pair of pants of coarse cloth sewn together. It was a fashionable garment as early as Emperor Shun's time, popular among people from all walks of life including civil officials, armymen and the ordinary civilians.

"With ribbons hanging five inches down, it's an idle man's way of wearing cap." This old saying came to Li Er's mind at the sight of Gongye's woebegone expression. "An idle man" could refer to a lazy loafer or a gentleman sitting idly at home in comfort. Gongye fell into the latter category.

"Although you have returned the fief to Ji Wuzi," said Li Er, "and made up your mind never to enter his house, he seems to bear you no ill will. The way he talks with you suggests that he still recognises you as his minister. It's clear you don't relish the position. But the prince, by giving you a set of minister's robes, has in fact appointed you a minister of Lu. Why make yourself look like an idler?"

Pointing up at the wall, Gongye said, "This is the outfit the prince has granted me — something that makes me feel guilty to accept and impolite to refuse. So I hang it on the wall.''

"Speaking of 'idler','' he continued, his anger rising, "do you know how many upright people are turning into idlers these days? Look at you for example. You are the most learned scholar of the day, a man with the strongest sense of justice, but aren't you becoming an idler like so many others?''

"I admit I have become an idler,'' said Li Er. "I know the strength of the male but keep to the weakness of the female. I know the brilliance of the white, but keep to the obscurity of the black. I know what is glory but keep to what is humble. I take everything with indifference and preserve my vitality by not worrying. This is the principle I abide by.

"You choose to be an idler,'' he continued, "because you don't want to associate with evil-doers; you want to help the state get on track, but there's nothing you can do. You want to be of service to the state, but you can't. So you are pent up with worries. That's why you have been feeling unwell. Thus, there are two kinds of 'idlers' in the world and this is where they differ.''

"It's good you've come,'' said Gongye with a dry smile. "Stay with me — perhaps you can help change my outlook.''

30

When Gongye began to feel better, he went to pay a call on Li Er. The latter did his best to ease his friend of mental strain but was helpless in face of an illness which was already too far gone.

Aware that his end was drawing near, Gongye called his family members and servants to his sickbed and said, "After I am gone, dress me in the minister's robes presented to me by the prince. If Ji Wuzi offers anything for my funeral, do not accept it.''

The listeners nodded with tears in their eyes.

After a pause, he said to Li Er, "I am sorry, my old friend,

I have not been able to act according to your edifying precpts. I am a real stick-in-the-mud, hard to change…''

Li Er, who was about to offer some comforting words, was cut short when he saw that the minister had breathed his last. The family members and servants all burst into tears, overcome with grief.

Li Er's eyes filled with tears, too. His thoughts were meditative: Block the openings, shut the gates, blunt the sharpness, and stay out of tangles; tune down the glare, be one with the dusty world. This is called identifying with Tao. He who has achieved it cannot be favoured or distanced, benefited or harmed, honoured or disgraced. Therefore he is highly esteemed by the world. This is complete freedom. If it is esteemed by everyone in the world, there is no reason to grieve over death. And no more tears fell from the eyes of Li Er.

The day came for the funeral procession. It was made up mostly of his personal admirers, for Gongye had enjoined his family not to inform the court or Ji Wuzi about his death. Among the mourners was a young man named Kong Qiu (Confucius), who lived in Qufu. His father Kong He was held in high esteem among the states. He was a renowned warrior, and for the outstanding services he had rendered to Lu, he was granted the small town of Zou about two or three dozen *li* southeast of Qufu.

When Kong Qiu was three years old, his father died. As Zou had been enfeoffed to him as a reward for his excellent military services, the enfeoffment was not inheritable. Zou was taken back by the court. Kong Qiu's mother was compelled to move the family to Qufu where they settled in a place on Que Street. Since childhood Kong Qiu had been reading and studying Zhou proprieties with the help of his mother. He admired Gongye for his sense of propriety and moral integrity and had learned that the great scholar Li Er was staying at Gongye's house. So he offered to officiate at the funeral.

Kong Qiu was introduced to Li Er.

Although Kong Qiu had learned Zhou proprieties from his mother, his knowledge of that sphere was necessarily limited as his family collection was scanty and he had not been sufficiently exposed to many classical works. Li Er, who was much older and more widely-read, was learned enough to be the young man's teacher.

For the first few moments Kong Qiu seemed to be proceeding under a sense of restraint, but the older man's amiable personality soon set him at ease. He explained: "Gongye's death has caused great sorrow among the people. With his admirable integrity he could have filled a higher position with a better salary, but he wouldn't accept anything that violated righteousness. He had the moral integrity of the ancient sages. As I respect Gongye, I've come to help with his funeral. I've offered to draw the hearse or play the dirge but they ask me to conduct the ceremony. This is really a good opportunity for me to practise proprieties. But in your presence, I am hesitant to take on such an important function."

Li Er said, "I have read some classical works about the proprieties, but to tell you the truth, I am more concerned with history and culture. However, this is not the time for us to discuss it as a subject. Why not just go ahead and do your best? If there is anything you are not sure of, I would be pleased to help."

"You are really modest," said Kong Qiu. "No wonder you compare Tao to a 'valley' and prefer being the low valley, not the high mountain peak."

"It is not a matter of modesty," said Li Er, "you see Tao is profound and I know very little about it. The Imperial Archives of Zhou has a large collection of classical works, but there are many scattered about among the people outside the court and I have not had a chance to read them yet. When Duke Zhou came to Lu, he brought along a wide range of classical writings and relics. This is why I came to Lu. I came to learn. One seldom finds a young man of your age so dedicated to studies. You were born and grew up here and you must know much more about Lu classics and relics than I do. In this regard I need your help."

"It's my pleasure to be of any help to you," said Kong Qiu. "I have a friend by the name of Nangong Jingshu. His father, Meng Xizi, is one of the three nobles of Lu. Through their good offices, you can easily obtain access to the collections of the Lu court."

"I see; so he is Meng Xizi's son," said Li Er. "I've heard of him. If I remember correctly, his mother was the woman who ran away from home with her maid and went to find Meng Xizi. The nobleman married the two runaways as concubines and one of them gave birth to two sons, one of whom, I believe, is Nangong Jingshu. This romantic story is well known among all the states." Li Er noticed that Kong Qiu blushed. He wondered if the young man was unaccustomed to hearing romantic stories, or if he himself had said anything indelicate.

"Although Nangong Jingshu is from a noble family," Kong Qiu explained, "he is unusually keen on studying. He respects learned people. When he finds out you are in Qufu, he will surely come to you for advice. If there is anything he can do to help you, I'm sure he will be very pleased to oblige."

"With his help," said Li Er, "my stay in Qufu will certainly be made easier and more pleasant, but I'll try not to bother him."

The funeral procession set off under Kong Qiu's direction. Li Er followed with the others.

Aloft at the head of the file was a white streamer. What did it signify? It reminded Li Er of what Zi Chan had once told him: When alive, man absorbed the vitality of Heaven and earth; when he died, his soul would detach from the body. Once it was out of the body, it wandered away. The white streamer was supposed to lead the soul of the dead.

After the streamer came the hearse. This was followed by a

band of musicians playing sad funeral music and singers chanting a dirge adapted from a Lu folk song. Gongye's family, relatives and friends brought up the rear.

The sun, shining in the sky, shed its golden rays over the long procession. The white streamer gradually turned into a light orange, while the sad music through some influence took on a trill of joy.

The brilliant sun suddenly turned into an opaque orange plate stuck up on the arched curtain of the sky. Was this an ominous sign presaging an imminent catastrophe? Doomsday presentiments arose in the minds of many mourners. When clouds rose around the sun, covering it inch by inch until it was fully obscured, some of the more astute realised it was an eclipse of the sun. They recalled a poem:

> Eclipse of the sun
> Means disaster.
> The moon is darkened
> The sun obscured.
> Humble commoners
> Are filled with gloom.
> An ominous sign
> When sun and moon
> Swing off their orbits.
> Countries are run
> By evil persons.
> Moon's eclipse is bad,
> The sun's is worse.
> Now what shall we do?
> What shall we do?

Soon the funeral procession was engulfed in complete darkness and the mourners were breaking ranks in confusion. Li Er called to Kong Qiu: "Halt the hearse by the roadside and advise everyone to stop crying. Let us just wait and see what happens."

Kong Qiu hurried up and down, directing the bearers to halt and the mourners to remain quiet.

From the distance sounded the beating of drums, gongs, cymbals, and metal pans. This clatter was raised by the local people to drive away "The Heavenly Dog that was eating the sun". Frightened, the "Heavenly Dog" began to release the sun from its jaws. Soon, inch by inch, the sun began to squirm its way out and shine again.

Li Er looked up at the sky and advised Kong Qiu to let the hearse and the funeral procession move on. The hearse started up. The mourners began their ritual crying again, but with muted intensity. The coffin was buried in the family graveyard on the hill.

When it was all over, Kong Qiu accompanied Li Er on the way back to Gongye's house. It seemed a good chance to ask the elderly scholar a few questions.

"Sir, once the hearse starts out, it is not supposed to return. What if the eclipse had lasted long and we were stranded by the roadside for the whole day? I think we should have continued the journey in spite of the darkness."

"According to the proprieties," said Li Er, "when the princes of states go to pay tribute to the Son of Heaven, they set out at sunrise and stop at sunset. When court ministers are out on diplomatic missions, they set out at sunrise and stop at sunset. But with funeral processions it's different. Funeral processions can go on after sunset. If we had been delayed too long by the eclipse, we could have continued the journey at night under the stars. If we had gone on in the darkness we might have had an accident, say, the hearse might have overturned or someone been hurt. As master of the procession your responsibility is to see that nothing of this kind happens to the participants."

Kong Qiu nodded: "You are right. But what you are saying concerns the participants of the procession only. You haven't touched on what a solar eclipse might bring about. On our way back from the burial I heard some speculation:

One said he was afraid the eclipse was a sign of some disaster but he didn't know where the disaster would fall.

Another said, 'I'm sure it will fall on the State of Lu and the State of Wei, but Wei will suffer more than Lu!'

The first one asked why.

The other said, 'When the eclipse started, the sun was over Wei, and when it ended it was over Lu. If it really means disaster, harm will be inflicted on both. For Wei it's the prince who will take it and for Lu only a minister. Mark my words.'

These speculations are about celestial-human relations. What do you think of them?''

"The *Book of Songs* says," Kong Qiu quoted, "'The eclipse of the moon is bad, but the eclipse of the sun is worse. What shall we do about it?' Generally speaking, the foreboded disaster will be inflicted on the prince of the state or the senior minister. People in power have to be careful about their conduct and examine their policies, or Heaven will punish them.

"I wonder if you look at this matter the same way, sir?" Kong Qiu asked.

Li Er was listening with his eyes slightly closed. After a moment he opened his eyes slowly and spoke with great deliberation: "This is an abstruse question. I have pondered over it day and night for years. Maybe I can describe it in this way: There was something formless yet complete in itself that was in existence before Heaven and earth. It is soundless and shapeless, independent and unchanging. It goes cyclically and ceaselessly. It can be the mother of all beings in the world. I do not know its name, but I call it Tao or passably name it Great. The Great goes on and on; going in cycles it extends far and wide; extending far and wide it comes back to its origin. Therefore Tao is great, Heaven is great, Earth is great and so is Man. Man is one of the four greats in the universe. Man is subject to Earth, Earth is subject to Heaven, Heaven is subject to Tao and Tao is subject to its own way.''

Kong Qiu listened intently, turning the ideas over and over in his mind.

"You mean," he said, "that Heaven, earth and man are all under the influence of Tao? As it is all-powerful, you call it great. If Heaven and earth or, all natural phenomena for that matter, are related to man, the movements of the sun and moon must have an impact on human life."

"There is no doubt that Heaven and earth have an impact on man," said Li Er, "but whether the impact is as simple and direct as you've described is not clear. Are you sure about it, Qiu? I am not very sure."

Kong Qiu thought for a moment and said frankly, "Neither am I."

"That's right," Li Er said with a smile.

When Kong Qiu left, Li Er saw him off at the gate. Kong Qiu was touched: Master Li Er is much older, more learned and more experienced than I am, but he is so easy to get along with.

When I was learning the *I Ching* from my mother in my childhood, the hexagram *qian* included a line: "With the dragon flying in Heaven, it furthers one to meet with a great man." Mother said it was a propitious interpretation but I had my doubts. I thought a great man was unapproachable, if not beyond reach. But today I suddenly realised that sometimes a great man is not so difficult to meet with. That is, sounds in tune are harmonious, breaths of the same length keep pace, water flows where it is low and wet, fire burns where it is high and dry; clouds drift after the dragon, winds blow with the tiger. When the Sage acts, the ten thousand creatures respond. The free and the light elements ascend to Heaven, the stable and heavy ones descend to earth and take root. This is how things of the same nature go together.

31

After Gongye was buried, Li Er felt obliged to move out of his house, but Gongye's son would not hear of it.

"You've been my father's good friend and honoured guest all this time, and you have helped us so much with his funeral. If you leave right after the burial, what will outsiders think of us? And the memory of my deceased father will make me feel guilty."

Li Er was persuaded to stay on. He spent his time reading. The historian in charge of *Spring and Autumn Annals* often visited him with questions concerning the writing of history. Sometimes he brought along books from Lu's Archives which were of interest to Li Er.

Before long Ji Wuzi died and people said it was a punishment inflicted by the recent solar eclipse.

Someone asked Li Er: "This solar eclipse punished the senior minister as predicted. If there is another solar eclipse or some other celestial phenomenon, can we predict who will be punished the same way?"

"No," said Li Er.

"But why not?"

"Because the time will be different, so will the people and the circumstances. If there is another eclipse it may not cover the same place on the sun. Even if it comes again the same way as it did last time, it may not end up the same way. You certainly must know this poem:

......
Some pass their time at leisure,
Others live for their country.
Some enjoy their days in bed,
Others spend theirs on the run.

Some hide away in their shells,
Others never stop toiling.
Some sleep away their whole lives,
Others spend it on horseback.

Some drink and make merry, too,
Others always feel guilty.
Some get by with empty talk,
Others sweat to hoe their row.

"Different people have different lots," Li Er continued, "It's difficult to make correct predictions based on experience."

After Ji Wuzi died, his son Ji Daozi took over as the senior minister of culture. Being weak and sickly, he did not accomplish much in that capacity. Before long he also died.

Following the death of the father and son, the Ji family went into decline and their influence on the state began to dwindle. When the young Ji Pingzi — Ji Daozi's son — became the senior minister, he took radical measures to revive the family fortunes. His actions led to trouble in Lu.

In recent times the accustomed serenity of Qufu had become unsettled. War chariots were seen rumbling down the streets, rattling the doors and window-frames. The people of Qufu began to have the jitters. Rumours spread that Nan Kuai, the magistrate of Feiyi, a small town south of Qufu, was rising in rebellion and that Qufu had sent Minister Shu Gong to subdue him. Shu Gong's soldiers besieged Feiyi, but Nan Kuai managed to break through and defeat them. He was now leading his rebels in a counterattack on the capital.

Under the circumstances, Li Er could no longer keep "tranquil". He wondered if he should not get ready to leave Qufu as soon as possible. The court historian of Lu came to call on him with a load of bamboo-strip books. He piled them on Li Er's writing table. Li Er asked him what was happening in Lu these days.

Nan Kuai had been Ji Wuzi's subordinate. After Ji Wuzi died, his son, Ji Pingzi failed to treat the old man with respect. Therefore Nan Kuai, distressed over this treatment, said to Ji Pingzi: "When I was in full charge of all the Ji household affairs and what's more, providing military training to their private army at Feiyi, you were still a baby. Now that you have become the senior minister you look down on me. What do you think you are — the trunk of a tree that can shake me up and down like a branch? Don't be too sure — just remember you can't shake this branch just as you please!''

Nan Kuai approached a few ministers who were not on good terms with the Jis and said to them in the utmost privacy: ''I'll kick Ji Pingzi out and take his property! Then you can replace him as the senior minister.''

As schemes are apt to do, this one leaked out. Ji Pingzi ordered Shu Gong to besiege Feiyi. Nan Kuai, while in charge of Feiyi for many years, had constructed defensive walls and trained military forces in Feiyi. Earlier, Ji Pingzi had suggested that the middle wing of the court's armies be split into four divisions with two put under the Jis' command, one under the Shusuns' and another under the Mengsuns'. Obviously by this division, he intended to undermine the prince's military strength and increase his own armed forces. But in only two or three years, he began to feel the backlash, for his military forces were all under the command of subordinates who were not turning in hostility against him.

Listening to the court historian's account, Li Er became more concerned about the possibility of Nan Kuai's attack on Qufu. ''You don't need to worry, sir,'' said the history officer. ''Nan Kuai cannot take Qufu.''

''Has the situation changed?''

''Nan Kuai's accomplices have backed down and one of them has informed against him. Without coordination from within, he can not even launch the attack, to say nothing of winning. His scheme is shattered and he has fled to Qi. Some unofficial scholars say this is an important event in Lu history and must be entered in *The Spring and Autumn Annals*. But we are not sure how to enter it. Shall we simply note down the event, or add a word or two about its rebellious nature? I've come to seek your advice, sir.''

Li Er after a moment's thought expressed his opinion without reservation: "Nan Kuai is only an official of the Ji family, but the court ordered a minister to subdue him with state troops. Instead of overcoming him, the minister himself was defeated. The situation is quite clear: Nan Kuai came out stronger than the Jis, and Lu is moving toward disintegration. If you ask who has justice and righteousness on his side, I would say no one.

"The family official rebelled against the Ji family, not the State of Lu. *The Spring and Autumn Annals*, as the official record of important state events, has no space for the episode. If you want to know my opinion, it's sufficient to note down the occurrence as it took place and leave judgement to future generations."

"Thank you — a very penetrating and profound analysis," remarked the court historian: "I am impressed."

An official of the Gongye family came to tell Li Er that an envoy from Luoyang had come to see him.

An envoy from Luoyang? What for? Li Er wondered.

With Li Er about to receive a new guest, the court historian stood up to leave. Li Er saw him off. When he returned, the announced envoy was waiting for him in his room. "How have you been, Master Li Er?" he inquired. The man looked familiar.

Li Er suddenly remembered: "Ah, isn't this Minister Chu? What a pleasant surprise!"

"What a good memory you have," the envoy said with a smile, "you still remember me after so many years!"

Li Er, so pleased to see his old friend from Luoyang, took him by the shoulders, and holding him at arm's length, sighed happily: "How can I forget you, my friend? When you were a family official of Minister Wangsun's and I was his guest, we saw each other almost every day!"

Gazing into each other's eyes, they laughed heartily over their shared memories.

"It's very kind of you to come and see me while you are on an official mission," Li Er said gratefully. He was anxious to hear news of his family and Minister Wangsun.

"I am here not only to see you," said Minister Chu, "I am bringing you the emperor's edict. He wants you to return to Luoyang."

"Are you joking?" Li Er could hardly believe his ears.

"Joking?" said Minister Chu. "How many heads do you think I have playing jokes in the name of the Son of Heaven?"

Luoyang — where Li Er had studied and worked for so many years, where his wife and child were living — how could he forget it? But when the minister came with the emperor's edict summoning him back, it seemed like a message from another world.

It is Emperor Jing who is calling me back to Luoyang, Li Er thought. Has he forgotten about the bamboo slip "The emperor murdered his brother Ning Fu"? This referred, of course, to his father, Emperor Ling, as the murderer, but it also had something to do with him, because Ning Fu was murdered after he had acceded to the throne. True, I did not write the statement myself; still, in a way, I was a party to it. Besides, I resigned from my post without asking for his permission. Could it possibly be that the emperor did not, in fact, take offence with me and really wants me back in Luoyang?

Li Er had serious doubts about the whole matter.

"He is not calling you back for no reason at all," explained Minister Chu. "For one thing Minister Wangsun has spoken to the emperor on your behalf. For another, the royal house of Zhou has run into a series of troubles recently and its image is badly impaired. The Son of Heaven has decided to gather together outstanding personages from home and expatriates from abroad in an effort to enlist their support."

"What sort of trouble has the royal house run into?" Li Er asked.

"Something equally as serious as that which occurred in Lu some time ago," explained Minister Chu. "Earl Jiao, the Yuan based-minister, had imposed such cruel measures against the people that they rose up and drove him out of office, then put Jiao's brother Gui Xun in as magistrate. No matter how cruel Earl Jiao had been, to drive him away was an act of outright rebellion. Emperor Jing was in a towering rage about it, but he was helpless, which only made things worse. He had to acquiesce in the deed as a *fait accompli*.

"Scarcely had the uprising been settled when another bloody riot broke out in the town of Gan. As Duke Jian, the magistrate, had no sons, his brother Guo succeeded him as heir to his post and fief. This violated convention and was considered improper. For fear Duke Jian's other brothers and cousins would not accept him, Guo decided to eliminate them. Before he could take action, his opponents made a pre-emptive strike. They killed Guo and many of his subordinates, leaving the streets and markets of Gan strewn with corpses.

"These two bloody turmoils shocked not only the princes of the nearby states, but Emperor Jing as well. If the royal house itself has fallen into chaos, how can it keep order anywhere else?" Minister Chu paused, realising he had perhaps been indiscreet.

"I am speaking openly to you because we are old friends," he explained. "No matter what, do not hesitate, and do not harbour suspicions. Otherwise I can not return to Luoyang with my mission fulfilled."

"I will go back in response to Minister Wangsun's good will and the emperor's edict," said Li Er. "Luoyang may be in trouble, but is there a place which will always be free of trouble? Bad fortune is something in which good fortune resides, and good fortune is something in which bad fortune hides. Who knows why this is so? It's hard to tell. The upright can become crooked and the good can turn evil. People have long been puzzled about these things."

"Well put," said Minister Chu. "Penetrating views, of great originality, and to me, extremely enlightening!"

"Since you can view the situation of Luoyang in such perspective, I will go back with my mind at ease and report fulfillment of my task to the Son of Heaven. I look forward to seeing you in Luoyang.''

Minister Chu stood up to leave.

32

Li Er asked his servant Xu Jia to check the carriage in the shed for repairs and see if it needed oiling and fixing. If the ox was not strong enough to make the trip, it should be fed some good fodder and led outside for exercise.

Xu Jia had been with Li Er for many years. When Li Er brought him out from his hometown, he had no given name. Li Er said to him, "At home you can go about without a name, for in the countryside even husband and wife do not address each other by their names. They are nameless, so to speak. Man is one of the ten thousand creatures and the most intelligent one. Name is the mother of all things and each of them ought to have a name to distinguish itself from others. With the name as a guide you can get to know all things.''

The servant was overwhelmed by Li Er's mysterious yet interesting discourse.

"Sorry, I'm getting too far off the point,'' Li Er said. "In short, staying at home is one thing, but travelling around is another. Travelling around you meet many people. To get along with people, you need to have a name. Since you are the first and the only servant I have, let me name you Jia. It is the first of the ten names of the Heavenly Stems System. If I have more servants later, I will name them in the order of Yi (the second), Bing (the third)... In all probability, you are the first and the only servant I shall ever have.''

From then on the young man was called Xu Jia.

When told to check the carriage, he said to Li Er: "Sir, your participation in Gongye's funeral has stirred the whole city of Qufu. Gongye's family and his family officials have been talking about it these days. Because you helped with it, the famous young Kong Qiu offered to help. They all say this is a great posthumous honour bestowed on Gongye.''

"Previously, the Ji's were not on good terms with the Gongye's,'' continued Xu Jia, "but now Ji Pingzi has changed his attitude. I hear he is going to allow Gongye's position to be inherited by his son and recommend you to the Prince of Lu.''

"I asked you to see about the ox-cart,'' said Li Er. "What are you telling me all this for?'' Li Er looked at him squarely as if to say: you may wish to stay here; if so, you can stay, but as for me, I will not, under any circumstances, remain.

"I was just telling you what I have heard,'' Xu Jia explained. ''I'll do the job right away.'' When he got to the door he stopped. Turning around, he asked: "Are you going back to Luoyang, sir?''

Li Er did not answer. Xu Jia went out.

There was not much luggage. When the ox and cart were ready, Li Er was ready. The next morning they set out quietly, Xu Jia driving the ox-cart. Except for Gongye's family, Li Er did not say good-bye to anyone, not even to Kong Qiu.

Xu Jia, feeling somewhat lonely, complained to Li Er: "Kong Qiu is an honest young man and has always respected you as his teacher. You ought to have told him at least.''

"Yes, Kong Qiu is young,'' said Li Er, "but he is more habituated to proprieties than an adult. If he had known I was leaving, he would have arranged a farewell feast, come to see me off, accompanied me along the road for some distance, and so on. Telling one means telling many. Formalities are tiresome and boring. If Kong Qiu really respects me as his teacher, he will not hold it against me for not telling him, because we are both followers of Tao. Tao is light and insipid. When you look at it, it is invisible. When you listen to it, it is inaudible. But when you use it, it can never be used up. Lightness is a quality of Tao. Friendship is light as water and not bound up with ostentatious formalities.''

In the early morning the streets of Qufu were quiet. The cart rumbled on, and the jingling bells sounded far and wide. Li Er let down the curtain and sat back, his eyes closed. The long, uneventful journey provided time to meditate, and meditating was the greatest joy in his life.

They were now moving along the wide post road toward Luoyang. The high city wall loomed up ahead. It was the widest post road in the country, but the traffic on it was sparse. Their journey of almost one thousand *li* nearly over, the travellers were tired. As the ox plodded along, a horse with a young rider on its back galloped up. The ox proceeded at his customary slow pace, half asleep, oblivious of the horse.

Coming face to face with the ox startled the horse. It sprang up on its hind legs with a shrill neigh. Swirling around, it stamped its front legs down at the edge of the road and slipped with the momentum. The rider pulled in the reins, the horse reared again and raced off with a snort. The young man turned the horse around and rode back, his face red with anger. Li Er sat in his carriage, composed, waiting for the horseman to explode. When the rider saw it was an old scholar, solemn and self-possessed, he galloped off without a word. Li Er watched him from behind, his eyes full of admiration.

There had been few horsemen in the midland. Even the states along the borders had no cavalry. Only the nomadic tribes in the north and west used mounted troops. They had a big advantage over charioteers. Later the states continually harassed by the nomadic tribes, began to train their own cavalrymen. Though the midland had not started using horses as a military force, riding and archery had come into vogue among civilians. The young horseman whom Li Er met on the road was one of them.

Is it a good idea to train cavalrymen? I am not sure, Li Er thought. The states have been fighting among themselves for years. Their battle fields are covered with thorns and brambles. In the wake of wars, famines break out. He who assists a ruler with Tao does not tower over the world with armed forces. Intuitively Li Er appreciated the horsemanship of the young rider, but in fact he did not approve of the riding-and-archery fad that was thriving in the midland.

Zhen Gu was combing her hair by the window with a bronze mirror in front of her. Since Li Er left she had become casual about her hair and appearance in general. Life had not been very difficult for her. Li Er had left her some money and Minister Wangsun and Zheng Ji had often come to offer her help. But the loneliness was almost unbearable. When Li Er was at home, he sat at his desk all day, reading or meditating. Though he did not talk much, the house seemed to be filled with his voice and his activities. When he was gone, it was quiet and empty, like a tomb.

To occupy her time, she began to teach her son to read. Zheng Ji often invited her and her son to her house for a visit. The time was spent in talking and singing, which helped expel her loneliness. Zheng Ji's company would cheer her up, but when she was alone, her thoughts would always wander to where her husband was, what he was doing, when he would return, and so on. Her son Li Zong was an apt student. He could remember almost everything his mother taught him. But as he was already grown up, he found it impossible to sit still and remain indoors all day. When he asked to go out, his mother gave him permission. When she had been a small child, she had often gone out with her companions to pick wild herbs along the Zhen River. Li Zong began to make friends with boys his age from rich families and to develop an interest in riding and archery. One day, he returned home and said gaily, ''Mum, I have a present for you!''

''Why on earth are you bringing me a present?''

''It's your birthday today and I've got a birthday present

for you."

With a wistful smile Zhen Gu realised she had forgotten her own birthday. She unwrapped the package and found a bronze mirror.

"Your bronze mirror is getting old," said Li Zong. "When Father was at home, he used to polish it for you. Since he left, your mirror has become dim and corroded; you can hardly see yourself in it. Without a good mirror you seem to have lost interest in doing your hair and putting on make-up."

My dear child, Zhen Gu thought to herself, I have lost interest in my appearance, but not because the mirror is getting old. On the back of the new mirror there was a young armoured horseman with one hand holding the reins and the other a sword. It was of a unique design. She had never seen a mirror like that before. Li Zong explained that a friend of his had had it made to order for him, and with that he rushed out for his practice session again. Zhen Gu gazed at herself in the mirror. When she was young, she had an enviable white skin and sweet face. But now some thin wrinkles had formed on her forehead. For the first time, she realised with a jolt that she was getting old. Suddenly there was a knock at the gate. The mirror slipped to the floor with a clang. It was a familiar knock, which she had not heard for a long time.

Hurrying out to open the gate, she found her husband standing there quietly. He had changed somewhat, but not his peculiar charm. She embraced him and buried her face in his chest.

They came to the window, Zhen Gu still clinging to Li Er. "Am I getting old?"

"If you are getting old, I am getting decrepit," Li Er laughed. "To me, you are always a young girl!"

She held his hand to her forehead.

"Look, feel all the wrinkles I have."

"The wrinkles are nothing, and your white, delicate complexion is as beautiful as ever."

She looked her husband up and down affectionately. His grey

hair and beard had turned completely white, but he was still energetic and spirited. He was old but not declining.

"Where is our son?" Li Er asked.

"He is out for his riding session. Not long after you left, I began to teach him to read. He did very well in his lessons, and later he developed an interest in horsemanship. It wouldn't be right to keep him at home all day. When Minister Wangsun learned that he had taken to riding, he gave him a horse, a tall, spirited horse. Almost all the wealthy young men in Luoyang have horses of their own these days."

"Is he riding a brown horse? Wearing a short jacket, a pair of high boots and a headcloth? Carrying a big bow on his back and a long sword in his hand?"

"That sounds exactly like him," Zhen Gu said. "Have you seen him?"

Li Er told her about the young horseman he had met.

"That must have been our son Li Zong," Zhen Gu said. "Oh, can you imagine? Father and son did not even recognise each other!"

Li Er was amazed. Is he the son whom I have been so anxious to see? But he is completely different from what I had imagined!

Suddenly a few words rose in his mind: Weapons are instruments of evil and abhorred by people. He who pursues Tao dissociates himself from them, and the superior man does not use them. When he has to use them, he adopts an attitude of indifference.

Zhen Gu, seeing the change in his mood, explained apologetically: "Our son is not like you. You enjoy reading and meditating at home but he has a dynamic personality. He's lively and enjoys running around. Perhaps he takes more after me."

"It's good he takes after you," said Li Er. "What is the good of taking after me? Let him follow his own interests and do as he pleases. There is no point in forcing him to do what he does not enjoy doing. Let things take their own course, let people follow their own interests. This is called simple, this is called true. Being simple and true means taking the natural course. Heaven is subject to Tao and Tao is subject to its own way.''

What an understanding man her husband was! She nestled in his arms more closely.

Xu Jia unharnessed the ox and entered the courtyard. When he saw Li Er and his wife standing by the window, he stopped short. Turning around, he suddenly saw the unharnessed ox dashing out like mad toward the fields. He rushed out after the ox, shouting at him to stop and come back.

In no time, the ox reached a cow grazing in the field, and stopped short. They moved together, stroking each other's necks with their heads.

Xu Jia watched them from a distance, his jaw dropped open.

33

Li Er found Luoyang quiet, even more so than before. He recalled the first time he came. The desolate look or the metropolis as described in the poem ''Millet Grows Dense in Rows'' had made him feel indescribably sad. Zhou's illustrious past as a strong, prosperous empire was but a memory; now the dynasty was in a deplorable state of irreversible decline.

This time, returning to Luoyang, he was in a different frame of mind. He was clear-headed and detached. He was not anxious to seek an audience with the Son of Heaven or to visit the Archives. He wished only to stay at home and relax, for fatigue from travelling seemed to be closing in on him.

One day Xu Jia went to market as usual, but came back empty-handed.

''Where is the rice and where are the vegetables?'' Zhen Gu asked. ''I've been waiting for you to get back, so I could start cooking dinner."

Tossing the bag of coins on the table, Xu Jia said, "The peddlers in the market refuse to take the small coins."

"Why?" Zhen Gu asked. "What's wrong with them?"

"They say the Son of Heaven is going to mint coins of larger denominations. The small ones will soon go out of circulation."

Li Er was reading in his study when Zhen Gu came in frowning.

"What's the matter?" he asked.

She told him what was happening and said, "I don't wish to trouble you about such trivial matters, but I really don't know what to do. The savings you left behind are already used up and now there is nothing left except some small change. Where can we get large coins? I am afraid we may have to go hungry."

"Go hungry? It can't be that serious, surely," Li Er said with a smile, his mind still immersed in the book. He was not a bit worried, but at the same time, he had no idea how to cope with the crisis.

"Why don't you go and see the Son of Heaven instead of waiting to be summoned?" said Zhen Gu. "If you can find a position with a regular income, we won't have to worry about food, or about the haggling in the market."

Since the Son of Heaven has called me back to Luoyang, Li Er thought, he should arrange a visit with me. It was not I who asked to come back — why should I ask to be summoned? After a pause he said, "During my rounds of the states, I received various presents of gold, silver, jewels and what not from friends. I've put them all in the travelling bag, but never really made an itemised account of them." He went to a corner of the room and brought back a patched travelling bag of coarse cloth, covered with dust. "Open it up and see what there is and how long it can last us. If by the time we run out of resources and the Son of Heaven still has not granted me an audience, we can leave Luoyang again. Surely we can always make a living somewhere."

Untying the bag, Zhen Gu looked in. There were bronze coins, silver ingots and a few shiny gold bars lying at the bottom in a jumble. Her knitted brows unravelled. "You're always careless like this! Your bag is full of treasures but you just threw it there without saying a word about it. I could have dumped it all out as rubbish."

"Can it keep us going for some time?" Li Er asked.

"For some time? It's more money than we've had all our lives!"

Li Er was relieved. "In that case there is no need to see the Son of Heaven. There is no hurry about it really." As it turned out, the emperor wanted to see him. An edict arrived from the court. "There is gain in loss and loss in gain," Li Er said with a resigned smile, "there is no getting away from it. When you try to get close you are kept away; when you keep away you get close. You hit the target by fluke sometime."

When Li Er went to the palace in answer to the summons, he saw the emperor playing with a large, brand-new coin in his hands. The Son of Heaven has no need for money. What has he got the coin for? Li Er wondered.

True, the Son of Heaven had no need at all for money. Court officials took care of everything for him. Tailors made his garments, chefs cooked his food. He was served the best wine and drinks, the best fish and game. His hoards of gold and treasures were closely guarded.

The princes of the states and other high officials as well lived a life of luxury without handling money. Once Minister Zi Chan offered him some silver ingots in case he needed them. Li Er urged the minister to keep them, for he himself had enough to get along on. Zi Chan said with a laugh that he had no need for money. "Everyone needs money to buy food and clothes — how is it you don't need money?" Li Er asked.

Zi Chan's attendant explained that the minister never handled money. He had the steward take care of his salaries, the income from his fiefs and the rewards granted him by the court. He had a profuse supply of daily necessities: products from his fiefs, tributes from his subordinates, and bonuses from the treasury. What did he need money for?

If a virtuous minister like Zi Chan lives such a parasitic life, Li Er mused, it is not hard to imagine the kind of lives other officials live.

Emperor Jing asked Li Er: "Could Master Li Er guess how this coin weighs?"

What a topic to begin with! Li Er did not expect to be asked about anything like that. "Why would you ask me such a question?"

"As an experienced traveller," said the emperor, "you certainly appreciate importance of money. When travelling you need money for everything. You need money to stay at inns, money for food and clothes, money even to buy your way through the passes. Without it you can't go anywhere. You use money all the time, don't you? Especially small change? I suppose you must be familiar with the weight of different coins?"

Li Er took the piece in his hand. It was at least four or five times the size of the currency in circulation. "It weighs about twelve *zhu*, I would guess."

Emperor Jing was surprised. "When this coin was presented to me for approval, I had a hard time figuring out its weight. If the minister had not told me, I could never have guessed. They all say you are a dedicated scholar, a real bookworm, but you also seem to be knowledgeable about worldly matters like this."

Li Er had a mind to sting him with a jibe but he reconsidered: a sharp tongue in this case could not serve any useful purpose. He remained silent but beamed an equivocal smile.

"I propose to mint coins weighing twelve *zhu* or more," said Emperor Jing, "but the ministers have differing opinions. Some say it is not a good idea, others say it is. You are a learned scholar and have seen much of the world. I would like to hear what you think."

"It all depends," said Li Er. "If you mint larger coins such as this to be used in case of emergency, why not? Say, when the country is struck by natural calamities, provisions are in short supply and prices go up, you can put them in circulation to keep prices under control.

"However, if you invalidate the small coins and mint larger ones in order to show off, that would not be the proper thing to do; you would be inconveniencing the people. Though you give them time to change their small coins for the larger ones, if by the deadline the small coins are declared invalid and many people still have some in their possession, their coins will turn into worthless bronze. In that case the people will have a lot to lose, won't they?

"When the people are short of money, the treasury will be short of it too. When the Son of Heaven is indiscreet in spending money, the government will levy heavier taxes on the people. Then what happens is that the people will refuse to pay the heavy taxes and the government will force them to. In that case you will make yourself unpopular and the people will turn against you. You need to think it over carefully once more."

"There is another thing I would like to ask you opinion about," said the emperor. "As Luoyang is the metropolitan city of the realm, we should have a big bell to symbolise it. I am planning to cast a gigantic bell that can produce the high pitches of the twelve temperaments. The ministers hold different views about this also. Some say, as the Son of Heaven, I should have the biggest music bell to match the proprieties; others say the bells our ancient emperors cast were no more than seven feet in length and one *dan* (60 kilograms) in weight and a bell bigger than the ancient ones would violate the proprieties. What do you think, Master Li Er?"

"In fact, these two matters are about one thing," said Li Er.

"They are two different things, but why do you say they are about one thing?"

"Yes, they are two different things, but they have one point of departure. You are nostalgic about the good old days and you want to revive the once powerful and prosperous Zhou. In other words, you don't want to be the Son of Heaven in name only while ruling a small country with a sparse population in reality."

"Frankly speaking," said the emperor, "you are correct. But is there anything wrong in reviving the good old days?"

"It's perfectly justifiable," said Li Er. "Not only do you want to revitalise the Zhou Dynasty, the people who are loyal to you want this too. They even go lobbying in the name of restoring the Zhou proprieties and music, and of re-establishing your authority over the country. Even the strong states, when they conquer and annex the small ones, declare that they intend to yield them to the central government. This is called bullying the dukedoms in the name of the Son of Heaven."

"Since the idea is justifiable and acceptable, why can't I enhance the image of Zhou by minting larger coins and casting the big bell?"

"When I say it's perfectly justifiable, I am telling you how the common people look at it," said Li Er, "but I look at it differently."

"You have a different view about it from the common people?"

"For the past dozen years or so, I have visited a good number of states. These states used to be subordinate to Zhou but I know they have all become independent with a larger territory and a stronger army than the Zhou's and the princes have accumulated more wealth than the Son of Heaven.

"In their fight for hegemony they change their policies from day to day. One can be the senior minister today but he is put behind bars tomorrow. Soldiers are sent to the front, and peasants also, to kill or be killed. But what for? For nothing. In places like that there is no peace for the state, there is no security for the people and the prince can never set his mind at rest. If a state is in such a situation, what good does it do the people? People there become obsessed with selfish desires. The five colours blind their eyes, the five tones deafen their ears, the five flavours dull their palates, and hunting drives them wild. There the people crave whatever is hard to get, but things hard to get make people rapacious. When a country is governed with harshness and strictness, the country is bound to have errors or mistakes. When a country is governed with lenience and tolerance, the people will become simple and sincere.

"However, things are different here in Luoyang. This is like a small country with a small population. The government does not issue over-elaborate decrees, and the country is not plagued with constant wars. The emperors of Zhou have been content with the status quo. They remain weak and maintain tranquillity. They do not inflict meaningless strictures or attempt what is beyond their power. While the world is in turmoil, Luoyang remains tranquil and is free of trouble. Isn't it good for the country?

"The more prohibitions there are, the poorer the people will become; the more lethal weapons the people have, the more trouble the country will confront. If I take no action, the people will be transformed of their own accord; if I am tranquil, the people will be correct; if I leave them alone, they will prosper; if I have no desire, they will be simple and sincere. Thus ruling a large country resembles cooking small fish.

"Why do you always complain about the Son of Heaven's power weakening, the country's territory dwindling? Keep the country small and its people few. Even if there is an abundance of utensils, let them lie unused. Do not let the people risk their lives to migrate far. Though there are boats and carriages, make it unnecessary to ride in them. Though there are weapons, make it unnecessary to use them.

"In one word, let the people go back to the time when things were kept track of by knotting rope. Let the people have good food to eat, beautiful clothes to wear, comfortable houses to live in and gracious customs to enjoy. Though the people of neighbouring states are within sight and chickens and dogs within earshot, they live and die without visiting each other. Isn't it wonderful when the people live like this?

"At present Luoyang is pretty much the way as I've described. As the Son of Heaven, you should think of it as a good thing. You mustn't try to change it."

"This is a fantastic commentary," Emperor Jing said. "I have never heard anything like it! If you have nothing else to say, you can go back now and give me time to think it over."

After Li Er left, the attendant asked the emperor how he was going to use Li Er, because the ministers and the people outside the court were concerned. By calling Li Er back to Luoyang, the emperor said, he wanted to show the public that he valued learned and talented people. But this Li Er was too full of preposterous ideas. He was hardly fit for a government post of any kind.

"Let him go back to the Imperial Archives to take care of the books," the Son of Heaven said to his attendant. "That seems to be the only job he is interested in."

Back at home, Li Er regretted having talked so much. He thought to himself: He who knows others is clever; he who knows himself is enlightened. "I knew he would not listen to me. So why did I waste my breath saying so much? I know the kind of person I am. I am not fit for government. I cannot assist the Son of Heaven in any practical matter whatsoever. All I can offer is ideas. Why should I have taken it so seriously and gone into such detail?"

Weightiness is the foundation of lightness. Tranquillity is the commander of rashness. When one ignores the "commander", his actions go astray. But regrets are useless. He reminded himself. Man is a ridiculous creature. Sometimes he cannot restrain himself and when that happens he becomes light and rash.

34

Li Er went back to the Imperial Archives, keeping company with the classics as before.

There were complaints about the emperor. He had called Li Er back to Luoyang but had no intention of promoting him. Li Er, a man of virtue, had all the qualifications for a ministerial post. His seniority alone warranted a promotion. It was not fair to keep him as a minor archivist all his life.

When Li Er came within range of this buzzing, he pretended not to hear it. To him, the important thing in life is to do what one enjoys doing. If one enjoys what he is doing, even if his life is like that of a farmer, going to the fields at sunrise and coming back home at sunset, there is happiness in it. In his seventies, he still enjoyed a game of throwing wooden blocks out in the street, laughing and singing like a child as he played. He had no rank, no power, and he did not admire the emperor. He sang: However powerful the emperor may be, it has nothing to do with me. Unless you relish power for its own sake, it is like a yoke around your neck, whither you are a duke, a minister or the Son of Heaven.

In the Archives I can read and meditate and, through reading and meditating, I learn something daily. There I don't have to contend with anyone. It's a delightful place — to me, a paradise.

One day as Li Er was looking through some books, the doorkeeper came in: "A young man from a far-off place is here to see you. He says he is a disciple of yours."

A young man from a far-off place, a disciple of mine? Who could it be? He said to the doorkeeper: "Please tell him I am not in today and ask him to go back."

"This is exactly what I said to him, but he refuses to go, explaining that he has travelled several thousand *li* across several states just to visit you. He says he has come for help and must see you."

What can I do to help someone I hardly know? Li Er hesitated, then said, "All right. Let him in, please."

"I haven't seen you for ages, sir," the young man said as he entered, "but you have always been in my thoughts. You look as well as ever, sir." The caller was a tall young man, about a head taller than Li Er himself.

Hasn't seen me for ages? I look as well as ever? Who is he? Where have I seen him before? Li Er was puzzled.

"When Minister Gongye died," the young man continued, "both of us helped to officiate at the funeral. I learned a lot from you about funeral rituals and I still remember them clearly today."

Li Er now recalled how they first became acquainted. It was on the day of the solar eclipse when it turned completely dark, a rare astronomical phenomenon. Suddenly the dim image of the young Kong Qiu came back to his mind. But now he looked quite different, he was in his thirties, perhaps, with a sparse beard on his chin, wrinkles on his forehead, and lines at the corners of his eyes when he smiled.

"I ought to have come to see you immediately after I arrived in Luoyang," Kong Qiu apologised. "But, as so much to see here, my schedule was very tight."

"What have you seen in Luoyang since you came?" Li Er asked.

"I've visited the Altar in the southern suburb where the Son of Heaven offers sacrifices to Heaven at the winter solstice, and the Altar in the northern suburb where the Son of Heaven offers sacrifices to Land at the summer solstice. I inquired about sacrificial rituals on both visits. I've seen how the Son of Heaven receives foreign diplomats, attended the morning court session and visited the Hall of Distinction. I understand Duke Zhou once interpreted the Hall of Distinction as the place where the ranks of princes are distinguished. He formulated a complete set of rituals by which princes were received by the Son of Heaven.

"When Emperor Cheng was only fourteen years old, his uncle Duke Zhou assisted him in governing the country. He received princes for the emperor. He stood in the hall in army uniform, facing the south. The heads of states in the order of dukes, marquises, earls, viscounts and barons entered through different gates. The head of the Yi from the east stood waiting at the eastern gate, the head of the Man from the south stood waiting at the southern gate, the head of the Rong from the west stood waiting at the western gate and the head of the Di stood waiting at the northern gate. The reception was a great success and Duke Zhou's prestige rose among the states. Then he set about ritualising the proprieties and composing the music for various ceremonies. He formulated a system of standardised weights and measures, thus putting the empire in order and bringing the subordinate states under control.

"The doors and windows of the Hall are painted with portraits of Yao and Shun, and of Jie and Zhou. Yao and Shun were ancient sage kings; they are painted there as incarnations of virtue. Jie and Zhou were infamous despots; they are painted there as bad examples.

"To me these portraits have significant implications. By examining the past you can learn about the present. It's like a mirror in which you can see yourself. However, today's emperors, instead of studying why the ancient sage kings had succeeded and learning how to rule the country, they are interested only in why the ancient tyrants had failed and finding ways and means to make up. If they go on like this, how can they hope to catch up with the ancient sage kings?"

Li Er, listening in silence, had the impression this young man was rather talkative, in fact, quite a chatterbox.

Kong Qiu sensed a note of discouragement in his silence. He stopped, waiting for Li Er to interrupt.

Ignoring what Kong Qiu had said, Li Er asked: "Have you visited the Houji Temple?"

"Haven't had the time to."

"Of all the historical places in Luoyang, the Houji Temple is the one you should make a point of seeing, no matter what."

"Why?"

"Don't ask why. Go and see it. You may not find it interesting, but I tell you it is a place you mustn't miss."

The next day Kong Qiu went to see the Houji Temple. With him was Nangong Jingshu, the son of Meng Xizi, the second most powerful noble of Lu. When Meng Xizi was dying, he advised his son to learn proprieties from Kong Qiu. Accordingly, Nangong joined the first group of his disciples.

Kong Qiu had long planned on going to Luoyang, the best place for investigating proprieties and historical classics, and on paying his teacher, Li Er, a visit.

On the way to the temple, Nangong Jingshu asked his teacher: "Is this temple so important that we simply must not miss it? I wonder if Li Er was not exaggerating."

"I believe there is a point in what he says," Kong Qiu replied.

There was nothing impressive about the temple, neither its exterior, nor the sacrificial utensils inside it. Nangong was a bit disappointed. He had come all the way from Lu only to see a small temple like this? Such a temple would be one of dozens in Qufu. Kong Qiu also wondered if the temple was worth the trip at all, but he believed that Li Er was not the kind of person to give random advice or say something just off the top of his head.

Looking carefully, he saw a bronze statue in front of the steps on the right corner. It was of medium height, with nothing special about its design except that the mouth was tightly shut, which was unusual. Why was it cast with its mouth clamped shut like that?

As he glanced downward, his eyes fell upon a line of characters inscribed on the chest of the statue: A man of prudent speech.

He moved round and saw a long inscription on its back:

Careful, careful, careful!
Do not talk too much. Too much talk will ruin you. Do not be meddlesome. Meddlesomeness leads to disaster. When living in ease and comfort, avoid doing anything that causes remorse. Do not think it does not matter, it matters a lot in the long

run; do not think there is no harm in it, it will be very harmful in future; do not think it damages nothing; the damage will present itself; do not think no one is aware of it, God is omnipresent. A tiny flame, if not put out in time, will burn into a fierce blaze. A running trickle, if not stopped in time, will become a torrential river. If an extending thread is not cut in time, it will get entangled. If the shrublet is not weeded out in time, it must later be cut with a hatchet. Discretion is the source of good fortune. Indiscretion is the gate of bad fortune. The hard and domineering have no good end. The strong and competitive will meet their match. Thieves hate those from whom they steal. People resent those who lord it over them. The superior man knows that the country cannot be ruled with arrogance, so he adopts a humble attitude. He knows when there is profit to be made he must not get ahead of others; he stays behind. Gentleness, modesty and discretion are virtues that command respect. He who keeps to the weak and stays humble is invincible. I abide by all this while others go the opposite way. I won't change my mind though they think of me as inscrutable. I reserve my wisdom, never make a display of skill. Therefore, I am not vulnerable even though I stand high. Who can do this? Great rivers and seas are longer and wider than hundreds of streams because they are lower. Heaven's Way is dispassionate toward all men, but it helps good men. . .

Be careful!

Kong Qiu was reading the inscription when Nangong Jingshu came up. "Now I know," he said, "why Li Er said we must come and see this temple."

"Why?" Nangong still did not understand.

"He wants us to see this tight-lipped bronze statue."

"See this tight-lipped statue?"

"Remember, young man," said Kong Qiu, "these are really sincere and humane instructions. You cannot find a single word that is deceitful in it."

"Whose idea was it to erect this statue here?" asked Nangong. "Was it cast recently or in ancient times?"

"A good question," said Kong Qiu. "It reminds me of an old legend. Emperor Wu of Zhou once asked his teacher Lu Shang what teachings the ancient sage kings and emperors had given us. Lu Shang told him that the ancient Yellow Emperor, as the recognised ruler of the country, often felt uneasy. He kept reminding himself to be careful not to mislead the people. Later he had this tight-lipped bronze statue cast with the inscription as a warning to himself. I've heard the legend before but never had a chance to see what the bronze statue looked like. Now we've seen it and read the inscription. I feel today's visit was very rewarding."

"Was the inscription written by the Yellow Emperor himself?" queried Nangong Jingshu.

"There is no doubt about it," said Kong Qiu. "I believe many of Master Li Er's ideas are developed from the Yellow Emperor."

"How do you know?"

"I've had discussions with him," said Kong Qiu. "I feel some of his ideas are identical with those inscribed on the statue. The inscription says 'Discretion is the source of good fortune; indiscretion is the gate of bad fortune.' Li Er says 'Bad fortune is something in which good fortune lies; good fortune is something in which bad fortune hides.'

"The inscription says 'The hard and domineering have no good end; the strong and competitive will meet their match.'

"It resembles what Li Er says about man being soft and weak when alive, stiff and hard when dead. The stiff and hard are related with death, the soft and weak are related with life. Therefore, strong armies will be defeated and strong trees will be broken.

"The inscription says 'The superior man knows that the country cannot be ruled with arrogance, so he adopts a humble attitude; he knows when there is profit to make he mustn't get ahead of others; he stays behind.'

"Li Er says 'The sage, in order to rule the people, must speak in such a manner that he is lower than the people and, in order to lead the people, must stay behind them.'

"The inscription says 'Great rivers and seas are longer and wider than hundreds of streams because they are lower.'

"Li Er says 'Great rivers and seas can contain hundreds of streams because they are low and for this reason they can receive hundreds of streams.'

"The inscription says 'He who keeps to the weak and stays humble is invincible. I abide by all this while others go the opposite way.'

"Li Er says 'He knows the strength of the male but keeps to the weakness of the female. He knows glory but keeps to humility.' 'He puts himself in the back but is found to the fore. He stays apart, and he survives.'

"The inscription says 'I won't change my mind though they think of me as inscrutable. I reserve my wisdom, never display my skill.'

"Li Er says 'All men have enough and to spare, I alone seem to be short of everything.' 'Tune down the glare, be one with the dusty world.' 'While others are smart and bright, I alone seem to be muddle-headed. While others are all harsh and severe, I alone seem to be broad-minded and good-natured.'

"The inscription warns that one should 'not talk too much and not meddle.'

"Li Er often says, 'Act by taking no action. Do by doing nothing.'"

Kong Qiu's comparison seemed to have convinced Nangong Jingshu.

"Now I know, Master Li Er's learning has roots," Nangong said. "It was developed from the teachings of the Yellow Emperor."

"When Li Er told me to come and see this temple," said Kong Qiu frankly, "he wanted to show me something."

"What did he want to show you?" asked Nangong Jingshu.

"When I told him the other day what places I had seen in Luoyang and what I thought about them, I stretched my topic a bit. I talked about why the country had thrived in ancient times under the sage kings Yao and Shun and why it had collapsed under the tyrants Jie and Zhou. He listened in silence, not saying anything. From the way he looked I knew I had talked too much. Maybe he thought I had talked too much. I stopped at once. Then he said quietly to me, go and see the temple. Now isn't it clear what he intended for me to see here?"

"He thought you had talked too much?" said Nangong. "What's wrong with talking when you have a lot to say?"

"I think what is important is one's moral conduct," said Kong Qiu after a pause. "If one's moral conduct is upright, I don't believe it does him any harm to talk a lot."

"Kong Qiu is my teacher," Nangong thought, "and Master Li Er is Master Kong Qiu's teacher, but the two teachers are not always of the same mind."

35

Having minted the new coins and cast the giant bell despite Li Er's warning, Emperor Jing now set about selecting the heir to the throne, hoping to revitalise the House of Zhou.

Queen Mu had died ten years earlier and not much later, Crown Prince Shou also passed away. His death left the question of heirdom to the throne unsolved. Queen Mu had two other sons — one was Prince Meng, the other, Prince Gai. If the heir was to be one of the Queen's sons, Meng should have been designated. However, he was a mediocrity with no experience at all in managing affairs. Emperor Jing was not in favour of him.

If the heir was to be chosen with regard to age, Chao was the eldest. In addition, his talents were widely recognised. Obviously, he was entitled to the throne, but the fact that he was born to a concubine gave rise to objections. Emperor Jing favoured Prince Chao not only because his mother was a beauty (love the beautiful mother and love her son), but also because he needed a mature, intelligent successor to fulfill his dreams.

Both were qualified to be made heir to the throne. This set the emperor on the horns of a dilemma, because the ministers were divided into two factions, one of which favoured Prince Chao and the other Prince Meng. To make matters worse, the faction in favour of Prince Meng was stronger.

As emperor, he could mediate easily in trivial disputes among the ministers, but on the issue of heirdom to the throne which concerned their personal interests, neither side was willing to compromise, and both were more than willing to cross swords.

He could alleviate the imbroglio by acquiescing to Prince Meng, but this he would not do. He wanted someone on the throne who was capable of reviving the prestige and authority of the empire.

One day when Prince Chao's teacher Bin Qi was visiting him, the emperor asked if anything strange or unusual had happened outside the court.

"I came across something very strange today," said Bin Qi. "I went to the suburb on business this morning and there I saw a huge rooster destroying its own beautiful tail with its beak. I asked my attendant why it was destroying its own tail. He told me this was because it did not want to be slaughtered for the sacrifice. At sacrifices people offer roosters with perfect tail feathers to show their piety and reverence. Roosters with broken tails do not qualify for this ritual.

"From the behaviour of the rooster, I thought of scholars by way of contrast. Roosters destroy their feathers so that they will be spared at sacrifices. But scholars are different; they are ready to die for those who cherish them. If you cherish people who are close to you at heart, it's like raising horses; they can take you around when you travel. However, if you cherish people who are estranged from you, it's like raising tigers; sooner or later, they will kill you and eat you up."

Emperor Jing understood from the parable that Bin Qi was urging him to choose the one who was close to him at heart. But he made only a perfunctory comment on the rooster, as if he did not grasp the point of the story. He was necessarily cautious so as not to be overheard. It was a matter of general knowledge that Prince Meng had the two powerful dukes Dan Zi and Liu Zi behind him.

As early as the fourth month of the lunar year, the emperor issued an edict ordering the defence minister to prepare for the summer field hunt. According to the Zhou Proprieties, the defence minister was committed to organising a field hunt for each season of the year. Households joined in, each providing one or two able-bodied men equipped with weapons and chariots. They assembled at appointed locations, facing the flags of the towns and counties they came from. The mayors of towns and the magistrates of counties served as commanders under the defence minister, while the Son of Heaven acted as the Supreme Commander.

The hunt began with military exercises, such as practising "sit down", "stand up", "march" and "retreat", in close or open formation. The would-be soldiers were also trained to distinguish between drum and gong signals. The rattling of the drum signalled a charge while the striking of the gong meant retreat. Archery drill was given exceptionally close attention. Archery made up the greater part of the total grade. If one did not pass in archery, his total grade would be low no matter how well he performed at hunting or other activities. They practised combat drills. On uneven battle ground, foot soldiers were deployed in the front, charioteers following; on flat areas, charioteers went ahead, foot soldiers following.

At the end of the exercises, they burned wild weeds and rounded up wild game by beating drums. They cut off the left ears of the animals as a means of keeping count of their captives. When the fire had burned down and the hunters reached the other side of the hunting ground, drums were struck up and the soldiers hurrah'ed. That was the end of the hunt. Nets were gathered up and the game counted. Thirty mature, uninjured animals would be picked out and presented to the Son of Heaven. For the rest, some were slaughtered for sacrifices and the others distributed to the hunters as rewards.

Emperor Jing issued the edict commanding all the dukes and ministers of the court to participate in the summer hunt. Meanwhile he instructed his confidential followers to kill Dan Zi and Liu Zi as if by accident in the course of activities. Just as the hunters were about to march off toward the hunting ground in Mount Northern Mang in the suburb of Luoyang, the emperor had a sudden heart attack.

Earlier, when the emperor had decided to cast the giant bell, the court musician had predicted that he would die of a heart attack. He said only when the sounds of small instruments were not too thin and the sounds of large instruments not too loud, could there be harmony in the melody. When the sounds were too thin, they were inaudible; if they were too loud, they grated upon the ear and disturbed the heart. And a disturbed heart was susceptible to heart ailments. The giant bell produced sounds like thunder and had affected his heart adversely.

Besides, in preparing for the summer hunt and, specially, in the scheme against Dan Zi and Liu Zi, he had taxed his brains to the point of exhaustion. He had to take into account that the two dukes had formidable armed forces and that, in case of the slightest slip-up, the plot could easily fail and bring disaster on him as well as everyone else involved.

With the emperor ill and bed-ridden, the summer hunt was called off. He was taken by the imperial guards to recuperate at Minister Rong Qi's fief, where he died a few days later.

Taking advantage of Emperor Jing's death, Dan Zi and Liu Zi struck first. They killed Prince Chao's teacher Bin Qi, put

Prince Meng on the throne and then set about making preparations for Emperor Jing's funeral. Prince Chao did not acquiesce in these moves. He recalled the dismissed officials and court craftsmen, gathered together the nobles and ministers who were at odds with the two dukes, and with the support of the imperial clansmen, launched a counterattack against Dan Zi and Liu Zi.

True, the House of Zhou had long lost control over the dukes and princes of the states. The realm had dwindled to a small area of two or three hundred *li* surrounding Luoyang. Still, as Li Er put it, bad fortune is something in which good fortune lies. The House of Zhou was left with two hundred years of peace. Emperor Jing, however, had not appreciated the good fortune which the situation offered. He had been determined to revive Zhou's lost authority and splendour. This had brought endless turmoil to the court. Again Li Er had been proved right — good fortune is something in which bad fortune hides.

Li Er had not been in attendance at the Imperial Archives for some time. It was closed in case the invaluable classics should be destroyed during the turmoil. Most of the ministers ceased attending court sessions and carrying out their official duties. Dan Zi and Liu Zi, favouring Prince Meng and Prince Gai, had cultivated a strong faction of supporters. They declared Prince Meng lawful heir to the throne on the grounds that he was the legitimate son of the emperor and the queen.

The other eight princes, who were the sons of Emperor Jing's concubines, and a number of powerful court officials, headed by Prince Chao, formed another faction. They justified Prince Chao as lawful heir to the throne on the grounds that he was the eldest of all the princes. The two factions became engaged in continuous battles, in which Prince Meng sometimes got the upper hand, and at other times the situation was reversed. Countless people were killed, including the eight princes who had naturally joined up with Prince Chao.

Both sides suffered heavy losses and neither could defeat the other. Finally each occupied a part of the capital; Prince Chao, taking the west, was known as King of the West; Prince Meng, taking the east, was known as King of the East.

Dan Zi knew that his forces, even reinforced by Liu Zi, were not strong enough to expel Prince Chao from the capital. He went to Jin, begging for its interference, and during his absence, Liu Zi was defeated by Prince Chao. Soon Prince Meng died and his brother Prince Gai took the throne as Emperor Jing. Emperor Jing, escorted by Liu Zi, fled to Huadi where he was met and received by Jin's relief troops.

The Jin armies launched a crushing attack on Prince Chao forcing him to flee to Chu. The entourage took along with them a large quantity of priceless classics from the Archives. Li Er was shocked to hear the Archives had been broken into by Prince Chao's troops and a large number of classical works taken away. He wondered why Prince Chao should have wanted the books, since the inscribed bamboo strips were very heavy to carry away. He went to the Archives to see what had happened. The gate had been left ajar, its lock fallen to the ground, and bamboo strips were scattered about. Li Er became heavy of heart. Many inscribed bamboo strips which he had cherished as priceless treasures were now lying on the ground in a profusion of disorder. He picked some up, brushed off the dirt and went in, holding them in his arms. The interior of the Archives was a miserable shambles; most of the rooms had been turned upside down.

His heart sank, his head spun. He leaned against the wall and steadied himself. For the past several decades he had been working with the classics as if his life depended on it, and now he felt as if he had nothing to fall back on.

Suddenly he glared at the wall as if about to dash his head against it. With an effort, he composed himself, and smiled wanly. Why should I die for these external things? Are books that important? Not as compared with my life; and they all belong to to the court, at that. I am but a minor archivist here that can be dismissed at any moment. Why should I give up my life for them?

Excessive love results in dire consequences and abundant storing ends up in heavy losses. This is the way things are in the world.

Of gain and loss, which is more harmful? It depends. On the one hand I have gained from reading the collections in the Archives, on the other I have been confined in it like a caged bird. Now the Archives has been looted and the books frisked away. Though I have lost the pleasure and convenience of reading, I don't have to stay and work in it year in and year out. In this sense I have been set free.

Thinking along these lines gave Li Er a sense of relief. He walked out of the Archives and went straight home.

36

When Li Er returned home from the Archives, he found Zhen Gu waiting for him, anxious to console him.

He cherished the classical books with a passion few could understand, for he had worked on them the greater part of his life. It made little difference that they were not, strictly speaking, his very own. For example, one night, not long after Li Zong was born, a heavy rain set in. Water leaked through the roof down on to the sleeping child. Zhen Gu gave Li Er a push to wake him up. Sleepily he sat up and, moving the baby to one side, he rushed out.

"Where in heavens are you going?"

"There's a leak in the Archives. I have to go and see about the books..."

"Are you crazy? Leaving your child soaked in the rain and rushing to the Archives at midnight?"

"You can take care of him — he'll be all right; but the books might be damaged by the rain!"

Zhen Gu used to tease him: "Are the books your whole life? You love them more than your wife and son!" He just smiled good-naturedly, never taking offence.

Damage by rain now seemed trivial. The Archives had been looted and Zhen Gu could only guess what a heavy blow it must have been for him. Li Er entered the room without a word; Zhen Gu asked no questions. She kept a watchful eye on his moods, but perceived that he was heavy of heart.

"Everything all right at the Archives?" she finally asked tentatively.

"The place was raided by Prince Chao," said Li Er, "and the books have been taken away."

"You look as if nothing has happened," said Zhen Gu.

"What do you expect me to look like? If I cry all day will the books come back? The Archives are damaged, the books are gone. What do you expect me to do?

"Now I understand," Li Er went on to no one in particular. "This is the way things are in the world. Whatever treasure you have got, no matter how deeply you love it, you will lose it some day. As you collect it, you lose it. The more you collect, the more you lose. The previous kings and emperors collected countless treasures, but how many of them have they managed to keep? Excessive love results in dire consequences and abundant storing ends up in heavy losses."

"Since you can view the matter so philosophically," said Zhen Gu, "you have a long life ahead of you."

"I have been released from the Archives, you understand? You often tease me that the books are my life and I love them more than I love you and our son. In fact I've been like a bird in a cage there. Now the cage is broken and the bird is set free."

"What do you mean by that — the bird is set free?" asked Zhen Gu.

"From now on I don't have to sit in the Archives like a jailbird. I can go anywhere I like and look around."

"What? You're not going again?"

"A bird set free will never stay put in one place. But anyhow I am not going right away and I don't even have any idea where to go." True, he was not going right away, but his mind was beset with the idea of going.

Concerned with the whereabouts of the classical books of the Archives, Li Er kept track of Prince Chao and, indeed, kept receiving information about him. It was said Prince Chao had fled south. When he crossed the Yellow River, he dropped a sacred *gui* (a piece of jade with a square base and a pointed top that emperors and princes of states used at rituals) in the water, praying to the River God for protection. The next day the ferry boatman scooped it up from the river-bottom. Later Minister Wen Buning, who was pursuing Prince Chao, captured the boatman and discovered the *gui*.

Wen Buning attempted to sell it, but the moment he began to negotiate the terms it turned into rock, according to reports. He gave it back to the court and, in return, the Son of Heaven granted him the town of Dongzi as a reward.

Could the jade have turned into stone and back into jade again? Fantastic!

In fact the *gui* he returned to the court could have been made of ordinary jade which he claimed was the very *gui* dropped into the river by Prince Chao. Ostensibly, the muddle-headed Son of Heaven believed his story. Or he may have suspected that Wen Buning was lying but he accepted it as the genuine *gui* all the same, granted him the town of Dongzi and hoped to win his support, for the court was now under threat of internal strife.

True or not, the story provided evidence that Prince Chao had fled to the State of Chu. Not long after Prince Chao arrived there a proclamation appeared in Luoyang. Many believed it was written personally by Chao and distributed throughout the country by his messengers.

The proclamation read:

Emperor Wu overthrew the Shang Dynasty, Emperor Cheng

brought peace to the realm and Emperor Kang enabled the people to recover from the ravages of war. In order to strengthen the country's defence each of the three emperors had enfeoffed territories to brothers by the same mother. Both Emperors Cheng and Kang had promised to revitalise the empire in time of the country's decline and degeneration. Emperor Yi had been in poor health, constantly debilitated by various kinds of diseases, so the princes of the states prayed for his health. Emperor Li, whose cruelty the people found unendurable, was exiled to Zhi (Huo County of Shanxi Province today). In his absence, the princes of the states wielded the executive power of the court. Emperor Xuan, though, was talented enough to take the throne. The fatuous and muddle-headed Emperor You was soon dethroned. The princes of the states, therefore, set his son up as the emperor and moved the capital to Luoyang. Both Emperors Ling and Jing enjoyed good relations with the princes and reigned secure on the throne till their last day. Unfortunately, court affairs today are topsy-turvy. Dan Qi and Liu Di have turned the country upside down. They maintain that there is no unalterable rule of succession to the throne. They claim they have the mandate of Heaven to take over the court and they defy punitive action against them. Supported by a handful of vicious agents they manipulate the court at will. They insult the gods, break the law with impunity, undermine the authority of the court and lie about our ancestral emperors. The State of Jin, with no regard for righteousness, is backing up the nefarious Dan-Liu clique.

We are still wandering around in the wilderness, not knowing how or when to return to the court. If, my dear imperial kinsmen, you would follow the will of Heaven and turn your backs on the rebels, it would be one way of helping the sovereign out of this extremity. I am opening my heart to you and hope you will give thought to this.

Our ancestors taught us: "If the sovereign has no sons by the queen, crown the eldest son by a concubine. If there are two sons of the same age, crown the virtuous one. If both are virtuous, choose the heir by divination.'' But Dan and Liu, in defiance of these teachings, have bypassed the elder and put the younger one on the throne in pursuit of their personal ends. I sincerely hope you, my brothers and cousins, will think about it and make up your minds what is the wisest thing to do.

Li Er believed the proclamation attributable to Prince Chao; such a detailed history of the House of Zhou could not have been written by anyone outside the royal family. However, in Li Er's opinion, Prince Chao was simply inviting trouble for himself by fighting for the throne. Besides, he had estranged himself from Jin and, without Jin's support, he could not get anywhere.

Chu, which was strong enough to defy Jin, could not be forced by Jin to surrender Prince Chao. However, as Chu was far from Luoyang, it was not willing to mobilise its armies and resources to help Prince Chao in his struggle for the throne.

The invaluable information Li Er got from the proclamation confirmed that Prince Chao really had fled to Chu and had taken the classical books with him. However regrettable it seemed that the Archives were destroyed, most of the books taken away and the archivists out of a job, it could turn out advantageous for promoting cultural exchange between the north and south; the coming together of the two rich cultures was sure to promote Chinese civilisation.

Li Er considered going back to his hometown, which was now part of Chu, to keep track of the classical records and study the impact of this cultural integration. A fascinating idea! He became excited every time he thought of it. Outwardly he looked as calm as ever, but Zhen Gu, with her feminine intuition, detected anxiety and uneasiness in his deportment. He believed tranquillity could overcome restlessness. But man was not an apathetic vegetable; he could not maintain his usual composure when he had to make a choice which would influence his whole life.

At this juncture, Li Er received a message from his friend Yin Xi, whom he had not heard from for years.

At Hangu Pass across the vast distance, Yin Xi heard what had happened at the Imperial Archives. He invited Li Er to come there, where beyond the reach of Luoyang he could achieve the tranquillity he craved, he could read and write, or simply enjoy the spectacular landscape. He ended his letter on a hopeful note: Since he left Luoyang they had not had a chance to meet. The riot that had broken out in Luoyang was bad luck for Li Er, but it provided a chance for them to see each other again.

After reading the letter, Li Er observed: "So Yin Xi still remembers me."

"He often refers to you," said the messenger. "He didn't wish to disturb you when you were at the Archives; he knew you were too busy to leave your work. Now that the Archives are closed and you are out of a job, he sees this as a wonderful chance for you to come to the Pass for a visit."

"Tell Yin Xi I am grateful for the invitation. Give me one or two days to pack; I'll set out right away, and will be with him in no time!"

After the messenger left, Zhen Gu turned to Li Er: "Are you really heading for Hangu Pass to see Yin Xi?"

"What do you think?" Li Er countered.

"I have a feeling there's a lot on your mind these days. Since Yin Xi invites you, why not go and see him? The change might do you good. Otherwise you can get all pent up with worries."

The fair sex usually views departures through eyes blurred with tears. Li Er was wondering how to comfort her when she made it superfluous by agreeing with such promptness. His servant Xu Jia had the cart ready at the gate; the black ox was stamping the turf with his hoofs, anxious to set out on the road again.

When Li Er was about to leave, unbidden tears welled up in Zhen Gu's eyes. She knew the visit with Yin Xi was to be a short one, but Li Er had decided not to return to Luoyang.

Arriving at the Pass, he had an idea: the State of Qin is just over the border — why not go across and have a look? Before long it's bound to èmerge as a state to be reckoned with.

Since the time of Duke Mu, Qin had annexed twelve neighbouring states, driven back the Rong tribesmen from the west and launched a series of attacks on the State of Jin to the east. Jin was strong enough to check Qin's eastward movement, but it was disintegrating at the hands of three powerful ministers — Han, Zhao and Wei. When Jin fell apart, Qin was prepared to move toward the east and none of the states was strong enough to stop it. To Li Er, Qin was one of the most fascinating places to visit.

He promised Zhen Gu he would not be away for too long; then once he had settled down somewhere, he would send for her and their son, Li Zong. Li Zong had grown into a brave, handsome young man. He stood beside his mother, free of the slightest shade of sadness. A true man should go wherever he wanted to. He told his father he had been approached by several princes of states who wanted to employ him as an army commander but he had not made up his mind which offer to take. He told his father not to worry, he would take good care of his mother. In Li Er's eyes Li Zong was still a baby — how could he take over as an army commander? However, he did not say anything to discourage him.

"Take good care of your master on the road," Zhen Gu admonished Xu Jia. "He may be in excellent health, but remember he is getting on in years. Take it easy and don't race against time. He's always careless about food and clothing, so make sure that he eats properly and sleeps well; don't begrudge the money. Money is nothing to worry about. As you spend it you can make it. But health is different. Once it's gone, it's hard to recover."

In no mood for delay, Xu Jia still listened attentively, whip in hand, ready to smack the black ox on the rump to start him off.

They departed through the western gate. Last time they had turned eastward on their trip to Lu. The main post road had many branches with post houses at intervals, but there was no telling which branch marked the beginning of the road and which, the end. Following the road, one could travel east, west, north or south. In the absence of roads, the ground was level enough for walking or riding.

There are roads on earth and, likewise, there are paths in the sky along which wild geese and other migrant birds fly. The only difference is that the paths in the sky are invisible.

Isn't it like the thing that gives birth to Heaven and earth and the ten thousand creatures? It is everywhere and it goes everywhere. It seems formless but, in fact, it has the greatest form ever.

What shall I call it? I might as well call it "Tao".

Road is a carrier, taking men and objects from east to west, from north to south. When one has mastered Tao, he can go everywhere.

The thought set Li Er's mind at rest.

37

Xu Jia drove westward along the wide road, before long arriving at Mount Xiao. The further west they went, the narrower and the more dangerous the mountain paths became. As it was getting harder and harder for the two oxen to proceed, Xu Jia jumped down to walk alongside the cart, and Li Er got off too. The oxen pulled with difficulty. Sometimes Xu Jia and Li Er pushed from behind. Both men and beasts got out of breath and began perspiring all over. The mountain spread out in front of them like a fan. The path wound endlessly toward the west.

"Shall we leave the cart behind?" Li Er suggested.

"Leave it behind?" Xu Jia was surprised. "It would cost a lot to buy a new one."

"Instead of our riding in it as a convenience, we must ourselves push it from behind, as a burden. Whatever the cost, we must leave it behind."

Xu Jia could not bring himself to part with the conveyance; it had become dear to him like an inseparable companion.

Li Er tried to bring him round: "Suppose you have a tumour, and it keeps growing. If you don't remove it just because it is part of your body, it will kill you some day. If we had to push this wagon all the way, both men and beasts will be exhausted before we arrive at the Pass. In that case what's the use of keeping it? Abandon it! We can buy a new one when we get to Hangu."

Reluctantly Xu Jia unhitched the oxen and left the carriage off to one side. They each mounted an ox and continued their journey west, Li Er in the lead, Xu Jia following close behind. They travelled during the day and slept at night, passing one mountain after another. It was quiet in the mountains and they seldom spoke. Occasionally the oxen lifted their heads to emit a gruff low or two, but with no response from their own kind.

Once in a while they met a traveller going the other way. Xu Jia would jump off his ox and ask how much farther it was to the Hangu Pass. The answer they received was "another ten or twenty *li* or so". Two or three hours later when they asked the next traveller they met, the answer was the same: "Another ten or twenty *li* or so." It grew dark earlier in the valleys. They had to watch the time of day. If they missed a place in which to put up, they would have to spend the night out in the open, exposed to possible attack by wild animals. When the sun appeared near the mountain top, they knew they must make for the nearest village in all haste to find shelter for the night. The next morning they would ask the local people how far it was to the Hangu Pass. "Oh, ten or twenty *li* or so," a villager said. "It will take you about half a day to get there on the oxen," he added.

Doubtful about the answers, there was nothing for it but to find out for themselves just how far it was to the Hangu Pass.

They climbed a mountain and looked out upon a valley with precipitous cliffs on both sides. Before they started downhill, Li Er surveyed the way ahead, wondering which route to take. The ox he was riding suddenly began to bellow. To their surprise, a plaintive lowing in response reached them from far down in the valley. The beast dashed down the narrow path like mad with its master on its back holding on as best he could. Li Er, taken unawares, tried to steady himself, pulling hard on the reins and tightening his legs against the belly of the ox, but in vain. Hurled off, he hit the ground with a heavy thud. Xu Jia's ox, urged on with a few smart blows, refused to run. When they finally drew near, Li Er had risen to his feet. Luckily, he was pitched onto a soft grassy spot and was not injured except for a slight pain in the hip.

Lumbering up to the cow grazing on a plot of grass, the ox started necking her ardently. He then swirled round toward her behind. The cow threw up her tail in a simple gesture of acquiescence. The ox raised his front legs on the cow's back manoeuvred for a long time in a pitch of excitement, and then slipped off, looking helpless and distraught.

Xu Jia angrily picked up a tree branch from the ground: "Let me teach this beast a lesson!"

Li Er stopped him with a wave of his hand: "It's not all his fault; I am to blame too. I thought a castrated ox would have no desires — but I forgot there are exceptions. Even castrated oxen, if kept isolated for long, can get excited at the sight of cows and make trouble. It's difficult to keep free of desire, you see. You can remove the physical organ, but you can't eliminate the desire."

Li Er rubbed his hips to relieve the pain and dusted himself down. He got on his ox again ready to go on. Xu Jia who was gazing at a mountain ridge in the distance suddenly pointed and said, "Look up there, sir! Doesn't it look like a pass?"

Li Er turned in the direction Xu Jia pointed out: "That's the Hangu Pass."

Xu Jia fell into a fit of excitement while Li Er remained as calm as ever sitting solidly on his ox, which went lumbering along at its usual leisure pace. Xu Jia could only wonder at such incredible composure.

They had not gone much further ahead when they heard approaching sounds of horses' hooves and men's voices. Soon there came into view a four-horse chariot rounding a rocky ridge. This was followed by a group of soldiers. One of them demanded in a stentorian voice:

"Is that Master Li Er?"

"Yes," Xu Jia answered. "And who are you?"

The horses trotted over and one of the riders, dismounting, declared enthusiastically: "Brother Li Er! Brother Li Er! I've been looking forward to seeing you here and now you've come at last!"

Li Er slid down from his ox, exclaiming joyfully: "Yin Xi!"

Holding hands, they examined each other for time-inflicted changes and more persistent native qualities.

"Since the messenger returned from Luoyang," said Yin Xi, "I have been keeping a look-out from the tower of the Pass, toward the east. A moment ago a guard reported that he had sighted two riders on ox-back heading west toward the Pass. He thought one of them might be Li Er. I climbed up to the tower and watched them for a long time. The more I watched, the more one of them looked like you. I called for the chariot at once and hurried to meet you here!"

"Why didn't you take a carriage, brother? It's altogether too hard travelling such a long way on an ox."

Xu Jia explained that they had left their wagon behind.

"My ox-cart is not like your chariot," said Li Er with a wry smile. "Your chariot is light and strong. It can run in the mountains the same as on the plains."

Yin Xi helped Li Er into his chariot and they rode back to the Pass. Yin Xi's wife came out to welcome him. She looked around with wondering eyes: "You didn't come alone, surely...?"

"With my servant," answered Li Er.

"Zhen Gu did not come with you?"

"Well..."

"Do you mean to say you come here alone to visit him — your friend, but did not allow her to come here to visit me — her friend?"

Mrs Yin Xi was as out-spoken and sharp-tongued as ever. Li Er was taken aback by her directness.

"That's easy," Yin Xi said to rescue Li Er. "When brother Li Er settles in and gets accustomed to frontier life here at the Pass, I'll send a four-horse chariot to Luoyang to bring Zhen Gu here for you."

38

Li Er had a good look at the spectacular scenery around the Pass with Yin Xi drawing his attention to special points of interest. He stayed with Yin Xi for quite a few days. They had ample time to talk about what had happened to each other in the years since they parted. Eventually he began preparing to leave. Yin Xi thought it was probably because he was not accustomed to the simple way of life there.

Li Er explained: "A tranquil, simple life is just what I enjoy most. There is nothing here I am not accustomed to. But to tell you the truth, I am not planning to go back to Luoyang again. I decided to come to the west for two reasons: one was to see you, my friend, the other was to go further on westward to visit the State of Qin. I have been to the south, the north and the east, but the west is still unknown to me in many ways. Without a visit to the west I cannot say I know much about this vast territory we live in."

"If you have such a travelling plan," said Yin Xi, "I should not try to keep you here. I have benefitted enormously from our long friendship and the heart-to-heart talks we've had since you came. As always, your philosophical views and profound thoughts are enlightening and helpful. I gather you are not going to take an official position but plan to live the rest of your life in obscurity. If that is the case, unfortunately we shall not be able to see each other often. Where shall I seek to find you for advice? At any rate, I hope you can stay with me a few days longer and write about your ideas — especially the Tao you have been pursuing all these years. Though the terrain is bleak enough here at the Pass, it is rich in wood and bamboo. A good number of the guards at the station are skilled in carving. I can ask them to carve your writings on wooden or bamboo strips. These can be preserved and passed down for the edification of future generations. Isn't it a worthy project?"

"I cannot say how much it will edify future generations," said Li Er modestly. "But you and I have been good friends all our lives. How many friendships like you and I can we hope to have in this world?" The next day he shut himself up in a small shed at the Pass and began to work on his book. He picked up his burin and the first word he engraved was "Tao" — the word representing the foundation of all his thinking and the thing that had given birth to Heaven and earth, and the ten thousand creatures.

He began:

*

The Tao that is describable is not the eternal Tao; the name that is namable is not the eternal name. "Non-being" is the origin of Heaven and earth; "being" is the mother of the ten thousand creatures.

Therefore, from non-being, we realize the subtleties of Tao and, from being, distinguish between one thing and another. The two are of one origin, but with different names. They are both infinitely profound. They are the gateway to all mysteries.

*

When the world knows what is beauty, there comes the notion

of ugliness. When the world knows what is good, there comes the notion of evil.

Existence and non-existence arise against each other. As there is difficulty, there is ease; as there is long, there is short; as there is high, there is low; sound and voice are in harmony; front and back are in sequence.

Therefore, the Sage acts without taking action and teaches without using words. He lets all things emerge but does not interfere; he nurses all things but does not claim to possess them; he nurtures things but does not attribute it to his own ability; he achieves his mission but does not take credit for it. Because he does not take credit, his achievement does not vanish.

*

Not exalting worth keeps the people from rivalry. Not prizing what is hard to procure keeps the people from theft. Not to show them what they may covet is the way to keep their minds from disorder.

Therefore the Sage governs the people by simplifying their minds, filling their bellies, weakening their ambitions and toughening their bones. He always keeps them innocent of knowledge and free of desires so that the knowledgeable dare not act freely. Practice inaction, and there is nothing which cannot be done.

*

Tao is empty but, when used, it is inexhaustible. Deep, it seems to be the origin of all things. It withholds its sharpness, remains beyond tangles, softens its light and is one with the dusty world. It is profound. It is imperceptible but it is in substantial existence. I do not know what gave birth to it but I know it existed before the Divinity.

*

Heaven and earth show no favouritism; they regard all creatures as "straw dogs". The Sage shows no favouritism; he regards all people as "straw dogs".

The space between Heaven and earth is like a bellows. It is empty but inexhaustible. When set in motion, it produces more wind.

Much talk ends up in failure. It is better to keep the heart empty and the mind tranquil.

*

The very spirit of Tao does not die. It is called the mysterious female. The gate of the mysterious female is the root of Heaven and earth. It is formless and imperceptible but everlasting.

*

Heaven and earth are eternal. They do not exist for themselves; for this reason they are eternal.

Therefore the Sage always puts himself in the back but is found to the fore; he gives himself no consideration but he survives. Isn't it because he had no personal ends that his personal ends are fulfilled?

*

Superior virtue is like water that benefits all things but does not contend with them. It dwells in places — which people avoid. Therefore it is by nature close to Tao.

The superior man dwells where it is low, pursues what is profound, treats others with love, speaks with sincerity, administers with justice, he brings his merit into play and acts at the right time.

Because he does not contend, he does not err.

*

It is wiser to withhold in time than go to the full. An edge hammered to its finest cannot last long. A house filled with gold and jade cannot be kept safe. Pride in wealth and rank bring misfortune. Withdraw when the work is done. This is Heaven's Way.

*

Can you keep the unity of the soul and the body without separating them? Can you concentrate the vital energy, keep the breath and achieve gentleness like an infant without any desires? Can you cleanse and purify your profound insight without any flecks? Can you love the people and govern the state without personal knowledge? Can you recoil to take the feminine position in the course of Nature's opposition and change? Can you perceive all and comprehend all without taking any action?
  To let all things grow and increase,
  To beget all things, but not to take possession of them,
  To advance them, but not to take credit for doing so,
  To be leader but not master of them,
  This is the most profound virtue.

*

The hub is joined with thirty spokes but the utility of the cart depends on the hollow centre in which the axle turns. A vessel is molded of clay; but the utility of the vessel depends on its hollow interior. A house is built with doors and windows but it is in the empty spaces that man dwells. Therefore, while the existence of things provides convenience it is the non-existent which makes them serviceable.

*

The five colours blind the eyes, the five tones deafen the ears, the five flavours dull the palate, hunting drives one wild and things that are hard to acquire have a harmful influence.

Therefore, the Sage seeks to satisfy the belly, not the eyes, thus he takes the former and rejects the latter.

*

Take favour and disgrace as equally fearsome, value great trouble as one does one's own body.

What does it mean to take favour and disgrace as equally fearsome?

Favour is granted to one below; when gained it is fearsome, when lost it is also fearsome.

That is what it means to take favour and disgrace as equally fearsome.

What does it mean to value great trouble as one does one's own body?

I have great trouble because I have a body. If I did not have a body, what trouble would I have?

Therefore, he who values the state as he does his own body is fit to govern it; he who loves the whole world as his own body is fit to govern it.

*

Looking at it, you don't see it; it is called "yi" (invisible). Listening to it, you don't hear it; it is called "xi" (soundless). Touching it, you feel no impact; it is called "wei" (intangible). The three qualities of Tao cannot be apprehended; hence they may be blended into unity. Its upper part, though exposed to light, is not bright; its lower side, though shaded from light, is not obscure. Endless and boundless, it cannot be named. It returns again to formlessness. This is called shapeless shape and formless form. It is impalpable and imperceptible. Before it, you cannot see its face; behind it, you cannot see its back.

Grasp the Tao of old to govern the present. To know how

the universe began is called the Law of Tao.

*

In ancient times those who embraced Tao were subtle, profound and penetrating. They were so deep as to be incomprehensible. Because they are hard to comprehend, I will endeavour to describe them.

Shrinking, as if fording a stream in winter; cautious, as if confronted with danger from all sides; circumspect, like an unknown guest; self-effacing, like ice about to melt; true and simple like uncarved wood; vacant like a valley; opaque like muddy water.

Who can remain calm until the muddy water becomes clear? Who can maintain stability for long and allow activity to animate it?

He who masters Tao does not seek to go to the full and because he does not seek to go to the full he can achieve lasting balance.

*

Keep the heart utterly empty; keep the mind completely tranquil.

While the ten thousand things thrive, I find them going back where they come from.

All things go back to their roots. Going back to one's roots is called tranquility; tranquillity is called returning to the origin. Returning to one's origin is called the Constant. Knowing the Constant is called wisdom. Not knowing the Constant makes one impetuous and impetuosity brings trouble.

To know the Constant is to be all-embracing. To be all-embracing is to be fair. To be fair is to be approached by the world. To be approached by the world means taking the natural course. Taking the natural course is in line with Tao. To be in line with Tao is to be constant and free from danger all one's life.

*

Under the best government the people are not aware of the ruler; under next to the best, the people befriend and praise him; under still the next, the people fear him; under the worst government, the people despise him. Lack of faithfulness results in being distrusted. How leisurely the best ruler is! He seldom gives orders. When something is done with success, the people say "This is the way things ought to be done."

*

When the great Tao is abandoned, benevolence and righteousness appear. Intelligence and knowledge give rise to hypocrisy. When family harmony is upset, there is filial piety. When the country is in trouble there are loyal ministers.

*

Abandon intelligence, discard wisdom, and it is a hundred times better for the people. Abandon benevolence, discard righteousness, and filial piety and humanity will return to the people. Abandon craftiness, discard profit-making, and there will be no theft or robbery. As the three are ornamental and therefore inadequate for the rule of the country, let there be something positive for the people to follow: be plain and simple, be free from selfish desires.

*

Abandon learning and there is nothing to worry about. How much difference is there between yes and no? How much difference is there between good and evil? What others dread, I must avoid. This is the way it has been since the beginning of history and it has not come to an end.

All men are as merry as if at a sacrificial feast or climbing a tower on a spring day. I alone am light of mind with no desires, like a sucking infant that has not begun to smile, like a weary wanderer without a home.

All men have enough and more to spare; I alone seem to be short of everything. I am a silly old man whose mind is slow and dull. While all are smart and bright, I alone seem to be muddle-headed. While all are harsh and severe, I alone seem to be broad-minded and good-natured like the vast ocean, like the drifting wind. While all men have something to aspire to, I seem to be stupid with nothing to seek. I choose to differ from others, valuing the nursing-mother — Tao.

*

The character of Great Virtue is consistent with Tao.

Tao as an existence is impalpable and imperceptible. Impalpable and imperceptible, yet it has form. Imperceptible and impalpable, yet it is substantial. Though deep and subtle, it has vital force. The vital force is real and reliable.

Since ancient times, its name has never vanished, by which I come to know the origin of all things. How do I know the origin of all things? Through Tao.

*

Endure wrongs and your are safe; bend, and you can straighten, stay hollow and you can be filled, be exhausted and you can be renewed, take less and you have more, take too much and you are confused.

Therefore, the Sage takes the One (Tao) as the standard to measure the world. He who does not rely on his own eyes sees clearly; he who does not claim to be in the right is distinguished; he who does not boast of himself succeeds; he who is not conceited can lead.

Because he does not contend, none can defeat him. Is the old saying "Endure wrongs and you are safe" not true? It is indeed a practical doctrine to follow.

*

Nature's Way is one of few words.

Therefore strong winds do not last for a whole morning, and rainstorms do not last for a whole day. What is behind weather manifestations? Heaven and earth. Not even Heaven and earth can make them last long, to say nothing of man. He who pursues Tao is identifiable with Tao. He who pursues virtue is identifiable with virtue. He who loses Tao and virtue is identifiable with the loss of Tao and virtue. He who is identified with Tao, Tao is with him. He who is identified with virtue, virtue is with him. He who loses Tao and virtue, Tao and virtue are pleased to turn away from him.

Unfaithfulness results in being distrusted.

*

He who stands on tiptoe does not stand firm; he who takes long strides does not go far; he who relies on his own eyes cannot see clearly; he who claims to be in the right is not distinguished; he who boasts of himself does not succeed; he who is conceited cannot lead.

From Tao's point of view, these traits are like left-over food or tumours on the body — objects of universal dislike. One who has Tao will not adopt them.

*

There was something, undefined yet complete, which existed before Heaven and Earth.

It is soundless and formless, independent and unchanging. It goes cyclically and ceaselessly. It must be regarded as the Mother of the Universe. I do not know its name, but to designate it I call it Tao. To describe it, I call it Great. Being great it goes in cycles; going in cycles it extends far and wide; extending far and wide it comes back to its origin.

Therefore Tao is great; Heaven is great; the Earth is great; and so is Man. In the Universe there are four powers, of which Man is one.

Man takes his law from the Earth; the Earth takes its law from Heaven; Heaven takes its law from Tao, but the law of Tao is its own spontaneity.

*

The heavy is the foundation of the light. Tranquillity is the commander of rashness.

Therefore the Sage, while travelling, does not part from his baggage in the carriage. Though his life is full of comforts, he does not indulge in them. Why does the ruler with ten thousand chariots govern the country with lightness?

With lightness he loses the foundation. With hastiness he loses the commander.

*

A seasoned traveller leaves no tracks or foot-steps behind; a good speaker makes no errors of speech; an accurate calculator needs no counting tools; a skillful closer needs no bolts or bars, while what he shuts cannot be opened; he who knows how to bind can do so without a rope, a tie so tight that it cannot be undone.

Therefore the Sage is good at saving men and abandons none; he is good at saving things and abandons nothing. This is called "hidden wisdom".

The good man is the teacher of the bad; the bad is an example the good man guards against. He who does not respect the ''teacher'' or he who does not value the ''example'', is muddle-headed though he may think highly of himself. This way of handling matters is, in essence, a mystery.

*

He knows the strength of the male but keeps to the weakness of the female, to be the ravine of the world. Being the ravine of the world, he has eternal virtue; therefore, he returns to the simplicity of infancy.

He knows the brilliance of the white but keeps to the obscurity of the black to be the model of the world. Being the model of the world he does not depart from eternal virtue and therefore he returns to the infinite Tao. He knows glory but keeps to humility to be the valley of the world. Being the valley of the world he is filled with eternal virtue and therefore he returns to the state of ''uncarved wood''.

When uncarved wood is wrought, it becomes ten thousand things. The Sage employs it and becomes the ruler. Therefore, sound institutions are inseparably linked.

*

If one wants to govern the country by taking action, I think he cannot succeed. The country is sacred and it cannot be governed by taking action. To govern it by taking action, he is sure to ruin it. To dominate with force he will lose it.

Of the creatures in the world, some go in front, others follow; some blow hot, others blow cold; some are strong, others are weak; some are safe, others are in danger.

Therefore the Sage does away with the absolute, the extravagant and the excessive.

*

He who assists the ruler with Tao does not assert mastery

over the kingdom by force. The use of force will backfire. Where armies are deployed thorns and brambles grow. In the wake of wars famines break out.

When a skillful commander achieves his goal, he withholds; he does not swagger about with a show of force. When he achieves his goal he does not brag about it. When he achieves his goal he does not boast. He has done it because he had no alternative. When he achieves his goal he must not attempt to dominate the world.

All things begin to turn old after they reach their peak. Domination with force violates Tao. He who violates Tao will soon perish.

*

Weapons are ominous instruments and abhorred by men. Therefore, he who pursues Tao keeps away from them.

The superior man, in peaceful days, honours the left and, during wars, honours the right. Weapons are ominous instruments and the superior man does not use them. When he has no alternative but to use them, he adopts an attitude of indifference. When he wins, he is not transported with joy. If he is transported with joy, it means he takes pleasure in killing. He who takes pleasure in killing will not succeed in the world.

With good fortune the left is regarded as the place of honour. With bad fortune the right is regarded as the place of honour. The assistant general stands on the left and the principal general stands on the right. That is to say, at war, the rituals of funerals are observed. As large numbers of soldiers are slain at war, wars are fought with grief and victories are celebrated with funeral ceremonies.

*

Tao is eternally nameless and simple. Though it is subtle and invisible, no one can dictate to it. If kings and princes can keep to it, all will submit to them of their own accord. When (the *yang* of) Heaven and (the *yin* of) earth join together, sweet dew falls and it falls evenly though it is not ordered to do so.

When all things thrive, they begin to have names. Once things have names, one should know when to stop. Knowing when to stop is to avoid danger.

Tao is to the world what the sea is to the rivers.

*

He who knows others is clever; he who knows himself is enlightened; he who overcomes others is strong; he so overcomes himself is mightier still. He is rich who knows when he has enough; he who perseveres in his pursuit has will; he who keeps to his root endures; he who dies but does not perish enjoys true longevity.

*

The Great Tao is all-pervading. It may be found on the left hand and on the right. All creatures depend on it for life and it does not refuse them. When it achieves success, it takes no credit. It clothes and nourishes all things but does not act as master. We may call it Small. All things turn to it, yet it does not act as master. We may call it Great. Because it does not regard itself as great, it achieves greatness.

*

Whoever adheres to the Great Tao, the people turn to him. They will come and suffer no harm, but find rest, peace and tranquillity.

Music and fine foods attract passers-by. Tao, when expressed in words, is light and tasteless. When you look at it, it is not visible. When you listen to it, it is not audible. But when you use it, it cannot be used up.

*

If you would shrink it, you must first expand it. If you would weaken it, you must first strengthen it. If you would overthrow it, you must first raise it up. If you would take, you must first give. This is called the dawn of intelligence. The soft and weak overcome the hard and strong. Fish should not be taken from the deep and the sharp weapons of the state must not be shown to the public.

*

Tao is eternally inactive, and yet it leaves nothing undone. If kings and princes could but hold fast to it, all things would work out their own transformation. If, in the course of transformation, they still desire to act, I would have them restrained by the simplicity of the Nameless Tao. The simplicity of Tao can keep them free of desire. Absence of desire can bring about tranquillity. Thus the world will rectify itself.

*

The man of greater virtue is not conscious of his fine quality, and therefore he has virtue. The man of lesser virtue is constantly aware that he is a man of virtue and therefore he has no virtue.

The man of greater virtue lets the world take its own course and acts without striving. The man of lesser virtue takes action and acts with willfulness.

The man of superior humanity takes action and acts with no designs. The man of superior righteousness takes action and acts with designs.

The man of superior propriety takes actions but when his actions receive no response, he stretches out his arms to extract a response.

When Tao is lost there comes virtue, when virtue is lost there comes humanity, when humanity is lost there comes righteousness, when righteousness is lost there comes propriety.

Propriety is lack of loyalty and faithfulness; it is the beginning of trouble.

Prophecy is a garish embellishment of Tao, the first step toward ignorance. A true man should base himself on the substantial and reject the shallow, be simple but not pretentious. Therefore he should pursue the former and discard the latter.

*

Since ancient times, when the One (Tao) is achieved, Heaven becomes clear, earth becomes tranquil, spirits become divine, valleys become full, the ten thousand creatures thrive, kings and princes put their countries in order.

By the same logic, if Heaven were not clear it would break, if earth were not tranquil it would sink, if spirits were not divine they would perish, if valleys were not full they would dry up, if the ten thousand creatures did not thrive they would become extinct, if kings and princes did not maintain their nobility they would be overturned.

Therefore, the noble is built on the humble and the high rests on the low. For this reason kings and princes refer to themselves as the "lonely", the "orphaned" or "of small account". This illustrates that humility is the base on which nobility is built, doesn't it? Therefore the pursuit of too much honour ends up in no honour. The ruler should be like the imperishable stone rather than the elegant jade.

*

Tao goes in cycles and functions with weakness. All creatures are born of "being", and "being" of "non-being".

*

When the superior scholar hears of Tao, he diligently practises it. When the average scholar hears of Tao, he sometimes retains it, sometimes abandons it. When the inferior scholar hears of Tao, he laughs loudly at it. If he did not ridicule it, it would not be worthy of the name of Tao. Therefore, since ancient times, it had been said:

The brilliant Tao seems dim; the forward-going Tao seems backward-going; the even Tao seems uneven; the highest virtue is like a low valley; purest white seems tarnished; wide-ranging virtue seems insufficient; strong virtue seems fragile; simplicity and purity seem changeable; Tao is a great square with no angles; a great vessel which takes long to complete; a great sound which cannot be heard; a great image with no form; Tao is obscure and nameless. Yet it is Tao and Tao alone that provides for the ten thousand creatures from beginning to end and makes them complete.

*

Tao gives birth to the One, the One gives birth to the Two, the Two give birth to three, the three give birth to the ten thousand creatures. The ten thousand creatures have *yin* and *yang* as their components. The joining together of *yin* and *yang* brings harmony.

Men abhor being parentless, spouseless and without kindness, but kings and princes use such terms in referring to themselves. It is often true that there is gain in loss and loss in gain. This is what has been taught and I'll teach it to others: Violent men come to no good end. I'll make it the first and foremost of my teaching.

*

The softest things in the world can go through the hardest. A formless force can enter where there is no crevice. I therefore realise the advantage of inaction. Few people in the world are capable of teaching with no words or realise the advantage of taking no action.

*

Between fame and life, which is dearer? Between life and wealth, which is more important? Between gain and loss, which is more harmful?

Therefore, excessive love of fame results in dire consequences and abundant storing of wealth ends up in heavy losses.

To be content is not to be humiliated; to know when to stop is to avert danger. Thus one can endure.

*

The most perfect seems to be imperfect, but its usefulness is unimpaired. The fullest seems empty, but its usefulness is inexhaustible. The straightest seems curved. The most ingenious seems awkward. The most eloquent seems to stutter. A fast walk can overcome cold and tranquillity can overcome heat. By being tranquil and taking no action one can become the ruler of the country.

*

When the country is governed in keeping with Tao, war horses are turned back to farming. When the country is not governed in keeping with Tao, pregnant mares are taken to war and give birth by the battle field.

No disaster is greater than discontent, no evil is greater than excessive desires. Therefore, he who knows what contentment is may always rest content.

*

Without going out of doors, one may know the whole world; without looking out of the window, one may see the Way of Heaven. The farther he travels, the less he may know. Therefore the Sage knows the world without having to travel in it, he understands the world without having to see it; he achieves his purpose without having to take action.

*

The pursuit of book learning increases knowledge. The practice of Tao brings about daily loss. Decrease desires again and again until one arrives at inaction.

Without taking action, all things can be done. Without taking action he rules the country. If he takes too much action, he cannot rule the country.

*

The Sage has no fixed ideas of his own. He follows the ideas of the people. To those who are kind, I am kind; to those who are unkind, I am kind too, so that kindness prevails. Those who are honest, I trust, and those who are dishonest, I trust too, so that honesty prevails. In governing the country, the Sage restrains himself and simplifies the minds of the people. The people have their own interests to pursue. The responsibility of the Sage is to deal with them as innocent infants.

*

Between birth and death, those who are long-lived make up three tenths, those who are short-lived make up three tenths. Those who could be long-lived but seek death themselves also make up three tenths. Why? Because in cherishing life too much, they use excessive, indiscriminate methods in running their lives. I hear he who knows how to properly take care of his life will not meet rhinos or tigers on land and not be wounded in battle. Rhinos cannot thrust their horns at him, tigers cannot sink their claws in him, and sharp swords cannot insert their blades. Why? Because he takes care to distance himself from them, and is beyond their reach.

*

Tao gives birth to the ten thousand creatures, virtue nurtures them, substance gives form to them and circumstances complete them. Therefore, the ten thousand creatures revere Tao and value virtue.

Tao is revered and virtue is valued because Tao and virtue do not interfere; they let the ten thousand creatures take their own course.

Tao gives birth to them, virtue nurtures them; they develop and complete them; they nourish and protect them. Tao gives birth to things but does not try to possess them. Tao animates them but does not attribute it to its own doing. Tao raises them but does not claim mastery over them. This is the most profound virtue.

*

The universe has a beginning. The beginning is the mother of all things. Having embraced the mother, you get to know all things. When you know all things and, at the same time, keep to the mother, all your life you will meet no danger.

Close the openings of desires, shut the doors of cravings and you have nothing to worry about. Unclose the openings of desires, seek to realise your cravings and you will be beyond cure all your life.

Being observant about minute things is called wisdom. Being

able to keep to weakness is called strength. Using the light of Tao to illuminate your wisdom brings no misfortune to yourself. This is called following the constant Tao.

*

However slight my knowledge, I will take the wide road, ever careful not to turn off.

The road is even, but people are apt to follow bypaths. The court palaces are lavishly decorated, the fields are choked with weeds and the granaries are empty. Their wearing of gay, embroidered robes, their swash-buckling surfeit of fine food and wealth stored up in abundance may be called flaunting robbery! This is assuredly not Tao.

*

He who is firmly established cannot be uprooted. He who holds fast cannot slip. Following him, his offspring will keep up the ancestral sacrifice. The individual, through cultivation, attains genuine virtue. When his family is cultivated, he has virtue to spare. When his village is cultivated, his virtue is extended. When the country is cultivated, there is virtue in abundance. When the world is cultivated, his virtue is universal.

Therefore, as a cultivated individual, view other persons through your own person, other families through your own family, other villages through your own village, other countries through your own country, and the world from the cultivation of the world. How do I know the state of the world? Through this method.

*

The man of virtue can be compared to an infant. Poisonous creatures do not sting him, fierce beasts do not harm him, birds of prey do not attack him. His bones are soft, his sinews are pliant but his grip is firm. Though he is ignorant about the sexual union between male and female, his organs are complete — he is full of vital power. Though he cries all day, he does not cry himself hoarse — he is in a harmonious state of mind.

To know harmony is called the constant. To know the constant is called enlightenment. To live one's life to excess is inviting trouble. Vitality when aroused by unrestrained desires indulges in excesses. Thus driven to reach its prime, it starts to decline. This is against Tao. Anything that goes against Tao meets an early death.

*

Those who know do not speak; those who speak do not know.

Block the outlet of desires, shut the gates, temper the sharpness, disentangle the ideas, shake the glare, be one with the dusty world. This is called identifying with Tao. Such a person is impervious to favour and disgrace, to benefits and injuries, to honour and contempt. Therefore, he is highly esteemed by the world.

*

Govern the country with honesty, conduct battles by surprise tactics, and rule the people by leaving them alone. How do I know this is true? Through the following:

The more prohibitions there are, the poorer the people will be; the more lethal weapons the people have, the more trouble the country will face. The more crafty the people are, the more wicked happenings will take place; the more stringent penal laws are promulgated, the more thieves and bandits there will be.

Therefore, a Sage said, "If I take no action, the people will be transformed of their own accord; if I am tranquil, the people will be correct; if I leave them alone, they will prosper; if I have no desires they will be simple and sincere."

*

When the country is governed with lenience and tolerance, the people will be simple and sincere; when the country is governed with harshness and strictness, the people will be sly and cunning.

Bad fortune is that in which good fortune lies; good fortune is that in which bad fortune hides. Who knows why this is so? There is no standard to judge. The upright can become crooked, the good can become the evil. People have long been puzzled about it.

Therefore, the Sage is square with edges but does not hurt, sharp but does not pierce, straightforward but not unbridled, gives forth light but does not shine.

*

In governing men and serving Heaven, nothing is better than thrift.

Being frugal is to make timely preparations; making timely preparations is to cultivate virtue. If one keeps cultivating virtue, he can overcome anything. If he has power beyond measure, he is capable of governing the country. When he understands the mother of government, he can rule for long. This is called "deep-rooted and long-lived".

*

Ruling a large country resembles cooking small fish. When the large country is ruled with Tao, ghosts do not make trouble. Not that ghosts do not make trouble, but that the trouble they make is harmless to men. Not that the trouble they make is harmless to men, but that sages are harmless to men. Since both ghosts and sages are harmless to men, virtue returns to men.

*

A large country should be like the low sea that receives all rivers, as taking the part of the female. The female, willing to occupy a lowly position, overcomes the male through quietude.

When the large country adopts a modest attitude toward small states, it will win their trust. When small states show deference toward the large country, they will, in turn, win its trust. Sometimes the large country, by taking a modest attitude, wins the trust of small states; sometimes small states, by taking a humble attitude, win the trust of the large country. What the large country wants is simply to establish control over small states and what small states want is only to have close relations with the large country. Since both the large country and small states obtain what they want, the large country should adopt a modest attitude.

*

Tao is the sanctuary of all things. Good people treasure it and bad people find refuge in it.

Fine words win respect. Fine deeds raise one's status. Evil persons have no reason to reject Tao. Therefore, when the Son of Heaven is enthroned and the three dukes installed, Tao is a better gift than jade and elegant carriages.

Why was Tao valued by the ancients? Did they not say whoever seeks will find it, whoever has done wrong is pardoned by it? This is why Tao is valued by all.

*

Act by taking no action. Do without doing. Find taste in the tasteless.

No matter how much wrong is done to you, repay it with kindness. When coping with what is difficult, start from what is easy. When dealing with what is great, start from what is small. In dealing with the difficult one has to begin with the easy. In dealing with the great one has to begin with the small. The Sage never seeks for the great, thus he achieves greatness.

He who dispenses ready promises must lack credibility. He who underestimates a task will meet with many difficulties. The Sage takes difficulties into full account; therefore in the long run, he has no difficulties.

*

What is at rest is easy to maintain. What has not taken shape is easy to make plans for. What is fragile is easily broken. What is minute is easy to disperse. Make proper arrangements in advance. Put things in order before confusion arises.

A tree large as a man's embrace grows from tiny sprout. A nine-storey tower is begun with a basketful of earth. A journey of one thousand *li* begins with the first step.

Action courts failure; grasping means losing. Therefore as the Sage takes no action, he does not fail; as he grasps nothing, he loses nothing.

It is often the case that people fail when on the verge of success. If they took as much care toward the end as at the beginning, they would not fail. Therefore, the Sage's desire is not to desire. He does not treasure things that are difficult to obtain. He learns not to learn in order to revert to a condition which mankind in general has lost. He leaves all things to take their natural course and does not interfere.

*

In the old days he who practised Tao kept the people simple instead of educating them.

The people are hard to rule only because they know too much. When the country is governed by wisdom, it is a misfortune for the country. When the country is not governed by wisdom, the country is fortunate.

To know the difference between the two is to understand the principle of government. Constant awareness of the principle is called profound virtue, which is deep-going and far-reaching. With all things together it returns to simplicity and then becomes harmonious with the natural course.

*

Great rivers and seas can contain hundreds of streams because they are low and it is for this reason that they can receive hundreds of streams.

Therefore the Sage, in order to rule the people, must speak in such a manner that places him lower than the people, and in order to guide the people, must stay behind them. Though the Sage is higher than the people, they do not feel any burden. Though he is ahead of them, they do not feel threatened. Therefore, they are happy to exalt him and do not abhor him. Because he does not contend, none can contend with him.

*

People all say my Tao is great and it does not resemble anything else. Because it is great, it does not resemble anything else. If it did, it would be small.

I have three treasures that I keep, one is love, one is frugality, and the other is humility, which keeps me from putting myself ahead of others.

With love, one can be brave; with frugality, one can be rich in resources; with "not putting oneself ahead of others", one can be head of the world.

If one abandons love and seeks to be brave, abandons frugality and seeks to be rich in resources, abandons the rear and seeks to be ahead, he is doomed.

With love one can be victorious in attack and firm in defence. When Heaven intends to help a person, it protects him with love.

*

A good general does not show off his strength. A good fighter does not fall into a rage. A good strategist does not meet the enemy head-on. He who is good in bringing out the best in men maintains a modest and humble attitude. This is the "virtue of not competing". This is "bringing the strength of men into play". This is "taking the natural course". It has been regarded as the highest standard since ancient times.

*

A master of the art of war is very correct in saying:

"I dare not take the offensive, but prefer to take the defensive; I dare not advance an inch, but prefer to retreat a foot."

This is called: Disposing no lines of troops, raising no arms, confronting no enemy, and grasping no weapons. There is no disaster greater than underestimating the enemy, underestimating the enemy nearly makes me lose my "three precious things".

Therefore the side in grief conquers in case of the balance of the forces of two sides.

*

My words are easy to grasp and easy to practise, but none in the world can understand or practise them.

What I say is based on a doctrine. What I do is in line with a principle. As they are ignorant of this, they do not understand me.

Those who understand me are few. Those who follow my doctrine are hard to find. Therefore, the Sage is like one who wears sackcloth while he carries his jade in his bosom.

*

It is the best to know when one does not know. It is a disease to assume one knows when one does not know. The Sage is free from the disease because he regards it as a disease. It is because he regards it as a disease that he is free of it.

*

When the people refuse to be intimidated by threat, great calamities will arise. Do not oppress them so hard as to reduce their dwellings and strip them of their livelihood. Only when the ruler does not oppress them, will they not abhor him. Therefore, the Sage knows his own worth but does not show off. He loves himself but does not exalt himself. So take the former and reject the latter.

*

If you are brave in taking action, you will die; if you are brave in not taking action, you will live. Of the two forms of bravery, one is advantageous and the other harmful. Who knows why Heaven abhors one of them?

Heaven's Way is to win without contending, to respond without words, to come without being summoned. It is unhurried but skilled in planning. The net of Heaven is wide spread. Though its meshes is wide, nothing slips through.

*

Since the people are not afraid of death, why frighten them with death? If you want them to fear death, I can have the troublemakers arrested and executed, then see who would dare to make trouble again.

Execution is always the responsibility of the executioner. He who executes for the executioner is like one who chops wood for the carpenter. Who chops wood for the carpenter scarcely ever misses cutting his own fingers.

*

The people are starving because the ruler taxes them too heavily; this is why they are starving.

The people are difficult to rule because the ruler takes action; this is why they are difficult to rule. The people make light of death because the ruler sets too much store by his life. This is why the people make light of death (to fight against him).

He who does not set too much store by his life is superior to the one who does.

*

When alive, man is soft and weak; when dead, stiff and hard. Plants and trees are soft and supple when alive, but dry and withered when dead. So the stiff and hard are related with death and the soft and weak with life. Therefore, strong armies will be defeated and tall trees will be broken.

The hard and strong is below; the soft and weak is above.

*

Heaven's Way is like bending a bow. When it is held high, lower it; when it is held low, raise it; when it is overbent, loosen it; when it is underbent, bent it further.

Heaven's Way is to take from those who have too much and give it to those who have too little. Yet man's way is different. He takes away from those who have too little and gives it to those who have too much. What man is there who can take from his own super abundance and give it to mankind? Only the man of Tao can do so. Therefore, the Sage benefits the world, but he does not claim credit. He achieves but does not seek reward. He does not show off his worthiness.

*

Nothing in the world is softer and weaker than water, yet in overcoming hard things nothing else is more competent than water, for nothing can substitute for it.

The weak can overcome the strong, the soft can overcome the hard. This is a fact all the world understands but none can practise.

Therefore the Sage says he who withstands shame for the country is worthy of being its lord. He who bears the misfortunes of the country is worthy of being its king. True words seem paradoxical.

*

When rancor is appeased, remnants of resentment remain; it is not a good solution. Therefore the Sage who holds the left-hand half of the contract does not dun the debtor for payment. The man of virtue is like the holder of the left-hand half of the contract. The man who is without virtue is like a tax-collector. Heaven's Way has no favouritism, yet it always helps the good man.

*

Keep the country small and its inhabitants few. Though there is an abundance of various implements, let them lie unused. Do not let the people risk their lives to migrate. Though there are boats and carriages, make it unnecessary to ride in them. Though there are weapons, make it unnecessary to use them.

Let the people go back to the ancient times when records were kept by tying knots in a rope.

Let them have good food to eat, beautiful clothes to wear, comfortable houses to live in and gracious customs to enjoy. Though the people of neighbouring states are within sight, chickens and dogs within earshot, they live and die without visiting each other.

*

True words are not high-sounding; high-sounding words are not true.

A good man never justifies himself by arguing; he who justifies himself by arguing is not a good man.

Those who know (the Tao) are not widely knowledgeable; the widely knowledgeable do not know it.

The Sage does not hoard for himself. The more he offers, the more he has; the more he gives, the more he possesses. Heaven's Way is to benefit but not harm; the Sage's way is to do but not contend.

39

When Li Er had engraved the last pictograph of the five-thousand-word *Dao De Jing*, he was exhausted. He felt as if he had come down with a serious disease. He put his graver aside with an air of detachment, crawled onto his bed to relax and closed his eyes.

Knowing his master was tired out, Xu Jia came and asked tentatively: "Wouldn't you like something to eat?"

Li Er shook his head.

"Shall I bring you some water to drink?"

Li Er shook his head again.

Xu Jia waited by the bed in silence.

A few moments later Li Er stirred a little, his eyes still closed, and mumbled in a low voice:

"I don't need your help in here right now. You can go and leave me alone for a while. Lock the door from the outside and don't let anyone in for the next three days."

Xu Jia went out and locked the door from the outside.

The mountains and valleys around had now turned green. He had no idea how long Li Er had taken to write the book. He had been in constant attendance preparing food and water, getting gravers and bamboo strips from the storehouse of the Pass to keep pace with his writing and, in general, trying to "keep body and soul together" on behalf of his master while he himself went about his tasks in a state of bewilderment. Attending Li Er day and night while he was on the book had kept him busier than he had ever been in his whole life.

Now off duty for the next three days, he felt like taking a walk in the mountains.

Alone outside in the wilderness, he felt gloriously free. He just let himself go. He ran around, yelling skyward, swinging his arms, picking wild flowers, climbing rocks, jumping down again... He felt rested; his fatigue was gone like a cloud blown away by a gust of wind.

Suddenly he seemed to hear someone, obviously a girl's voice, calling:

"Old man, old naughty fellow..."

There was no one in sight. Could it be birds? Mynas perhaps? As the climate turned milder in the north, they left their homes in the south and migrated to the Yellow River. Marvelous birds, they were capable of mimicking human speech.

Xu Jia was about to turn toward the trees to look for the singing myna when he heard more sounds coming from a cluster of blossoming shrubs on the side of a hill. Turning, he found himself face to face with a smiling young girl. She was out gathering wild vegetables.

"Old man, old naughty fellow," she taunted.

"Who's this old man, the old naughty fellow?" Xu Jia asked.

"You are," laughed the girl. "Who else is around here but you?"

Old man? Xu Jia felt wronged. Why does she call me an old man?

"The people here all say your master is a fantastic person," said the girl. "His mother became pregnant after eating a magic plum and carried him for a term of eighty-one years. When he was born he had grey hair and looked like an old man. Since then he has been called Lao Zi the Old Boy. No one knows exactly how old he is. He is probably two or three hundred years old. I hear he has been working on a book behind closed doors, writing about the secret of longevity for the world to read. Since your master is so old, you can't be too young yourself. You've been driving for him a good many years, remember. Why shouldn't I call you 'old man'?"

Xu Jia burst out laughing and the girl became nonplussed.

"What are you laughing at?"

"At this ridiculous story! It travels fast and far. It was here at the Hangu Pass before we arrived!"

"Ridiculous story? You mean it's not true? Don't try to fool me..."

"Why should I try to fool you? I know my master better than anyone else in the world. He is a mortal like you and me. There must be some old men just like him in your village! Since his hair has turned white, shining with silvery threads, he is sometimes mistaken for someone several hundred years old.

"My master is a learned scholar. He has his own way of looking at things different from that of others. He comes out with what people call 'strange paradoxes'. Sometimes he talks about things as if he were out of his mind. He sounds plum crazy, but he is really only telling the truth. That's what gives people the impression that he sounds like an immortal.

"In fact he is not an immortal and he is not all that ancient. To tell you the truth, I am not so very old either, at least not old enough to be called 'old man'. I am only forty-eight, and in my prime. In your village people my age must be the pillars of the community, isn't that so?''

"You say you are only forty-eight?'' the girl queried, sizing him up in amazement. "You certainly look it. But here the villagers your age look much older because they toil in the fields year in and year out.''

"Well then, all right! I hope you'll stop calling me 'old man',''said Xu Jia.

"What have you to lose by being called 'old man'?'' said the girl. "In this place women even call their husbands 'old man'...''

She broke off, her face flushing crimson. Picking up her basket, she turned to go.

Xu Jia stood there like a log, staring at the girl with bewildered eyes.

"'Old man'...''

Three colourful butterflies fluttered up and down, refusing to fly away. Three bees whirled around his ears; their buzzing echoed in his heart with a disturbing effect. Someone was singing on the side of the hill across the valley:

> A roe lies in the field,
> Wrapped in couchgrass green
> A maid in her early teens
> Is wooed but does not yield.
> ......

Spring was the time to sing love songs of course, Xu Jia thought, but the words should be changed:

> A man in his early teens
> Attracted by a maid,
> ......

No wonder my master often says desire for love is a ghost. It was said that before Heaven and earth took shape, the universe was filled with a vague formless mass of vital elements. There was no day and no night; there was no being and no form. Then the elements split up into *yin* and *yang*, which drew and repelled each other at the same time. Sometimes they moved apart and at other times they came together. Finally the clear and limpid came away from the murky and muddy. The clear and limpid ascended and became Heaven; the murky and muddy descended and became earth.

Having created the ten thousand creatures Heaven and earth discovered that man, the last creature they created, had more vitality — he was more intelligent and more powerful than the other creatures. If man was not kept under control, he would upset the balance of the world and destroy it. Something had to be done about him.

So they created a lust, the lust for love, and put it inside man. The lust for love was a "ghost". It had crept into the flesh and blood of man and it would live or die with man. Man could check the ghost and keep it from making trouble, but he could not drive it out of his body.

However, men capable of checking the "ghost" are very rare. There may be, if any, one or two in a thousand years. The one who is capable of it is the Sage and guide for mankind.

Most people cannot help being lured by this ghost. They are ordinary men. Ordinary men are higher and stronger than other creatures only by a small margin and they rely on the other creatures for existence and growth.

Those who are under complete control of the ghost are incarnations of ghosts, but there have been very few of them. There may be, if any, one or two in a hundred years.

Too many sages can destroy the world; too many ghosts can also destroy the world. When there are too many sages, let them go up to Heaven. When there are too many ghosts, let them go down to hell. The majority of human beings left in the world are the ordinary people.

......

Xu Jia has heard stories of this kind from the country folks when he was small, but they were coarse and fragmentary. Later he had heard such stories from Li Er and they were more refined and complete. From his experience with Li Er over the years he came to know Li Er was the one who could keep the ghost under control. He was one of the few that came in a millennium. He was the Sage to guide men.

His master had told him about keeping free from desires, keeping the heart empty and the mind tranquil. He might not be able to live up to it, but he believed, through self-cultivation, he could resist the lure of the "ghost" and be a man different from the ordinary. So thinking, he took his eyes off the departing girl and strode back toward the Pass with confidence.

The next morning his master was still asleep and Xu Jia had nothing particular to do. He sat in his room to meditate, his eyes closed, but he could not sit still and could not concentrate. He stood up and wandered off absent-mindedly. He came to the same spot on the side of the hill and again found himself face to face with the same girl of the day before, the same smile on her face.

"I say, old man," the girl said, "why are you fooling around here? You should be back there waiting on your master!"

He knew she was teasing him, but he wanted to be serious.

"My master has finished his book and he's now asleep. For the time being there's nothing for me to do, so it's a good chance to come out for a stroll."

"Around the Pass, there are plenty of places for you to go strolling in, so why do you pick out a place where a girl is out gathering wild vegetables? You're not afraid of gossip, it seems!"

"But I didn't especially choose to come to this particular place..."

"Who cares whether you chose to come here or not," the

girl said with a giggle.

"You mean you don't mind my coming here?" Xu Jia asked tentatively.

The girl went on picking vegetables and giggling.

Delighted, Xu Jia laughed too.

"Look, I'm free today, let me help you," Xu Jia offered.

"Can you tell what's edible from all the rest? Does your master eat things like this?"

"Not very often; once in a while maybe. He says plants or animals raised by man are usually weak; the wild ones are stronger. They're good for the health. When I was small, I used to pick wild vegetables practically every day like you. I even know the names of some of them."

They chatted as they went on picking, and found so much to talk about that they forgot the time. Suddenly the girl noticed the sun was setting:

"Oh! I must go now. Look how late it is!"

"Me too," said Xu Jia.

The girl looked straight at Xu Jia with her large dark eyes.

"Old man, I really enjoy being with you — more than with the girls of my village."

"Me, too," said Xu Jia. "It's more fun being with you than with my master. You're such good company!"

"Are you coming tomorrow?" the girl asked.

"Are you?"

"I come here every day."

"If you come, I'll be sure to come."

40

After sleeping three days and three nights, Li Er woke up rested and refreshed.

"Xu Jia, how long have I been sleeping?"

"Three days and three nights. Today is the fourth day."

"I feel as if I just had a short nap," said Li Er. "Have you been waiting for me to wake up all this time?"

"Well…"

Li Er, stretching, turned to look out the window.

"What lovely spring weather. Why don't you go out and take a walk around?"

"I have, as a matter of fact, and…"

"And what?" Li Er waited for him to go on.

"And…"

Li Er's expectant eyes made him feel ill at ease. He hesitated, at a loss what to say.

Li Er reflected a moment and nodded: "Oh, I see. Now I know."

What does he know? Xu Jia wondered, feeling even more uncomfortable. Has he suddenly become omniscient after such a long sleep?

Knowing Li Er was awake, Yin Xi dropped in to see him. "How are you, brother?"

"You've come just in time," said Li Er. "I've finished the writing you wanted me to do."

"Have you really? That was fast work!" Yin Xi was amazed to see so many strips piled high on the table.

Li Er gathered up a big pile and handed them to Yin Xi:

"This is Book One."

Yin Xi picked up the first strip. Inscribed on it were the words:

The *Tao* that is describable is not the eternal Tao; the name that is namable is not the eternal name…

"You might call it *The Book of Dao*," Li Er suggested.

"Good, very good," Yin Xi said with a nod.

Li Er brought another pile of strips. "This is Book Two."

Yin Xi picked up the first strip. Inscribed on it were the words:

The man of greater virtue is not conscious of his fine quality and therefore he has virtue. The man of lesser virtue is constantly aware that he is a man of virtue and therefore he has no virtue...

"You might call it *The Book of De*," said Li Er.

"Good! Excellent!" exclaimed Yin Xi with a nod. "Couldn't we put the two books together and call it *The Book of Dao and De*?"

"I think we might," Li Er agreed. "It's a natural combination of the two titles."

"You've been working your brains day and night," said Yin Xi. "You must be exhausted! Why not take a good rest and relax for a few days? We're not very busy these days and I'd have plenty of time to be with you."

"Relax for a few days? I've slept three days and three nights; I'm well rested. I plan to leave tomorrow."

"Why rush off like this? Stay for a few more days at least!"

"I must go. Originally I had planned to stay with you and Madam Yin Xi for only two or three days, but now two or three months have gone by and I'm still here!"

Yin Xi knew Li Er had made up his mind. When he said he was leaving, he meant it. Urging him to stay on would be useless.

Turning over the piles of strips, Yin Xi said admiringly, "This is marvellous! It's the most valuable book in the world, and its value will increase with time! I'll keep it at the Pass for the time being and later make it known to the world. But how can I pay you for all your painstaking labour? I can't just accept the book for nothing, brother."

"If you want to pay me, in fact there happens to be something to pay for; I need a rather large sum of money to clear a debt."

"Tell me how much you need," said Yin Xi.

Pointing to Xu Jia, Li Er said, "You can give the money to him. I owe him wages for several decades of service."

"Give him the money?" Yin Xi was confused. "You owe

him wages for several decades? Are you serious, Li Er?''

"I mean it. He has been with me since he was a young man and now he's middle-aged. I must not keep him until he becomes an old man. It's high time he had his own family. When I set out for the west, Xu Jia shall stay behind. He'll stay here to establish his own family and for that reason he needs mony.''

"How can I ask for money from you?'' said Xu Jia. "You've been so kind to me over all these years that I can never repay your kindness.''

"True, you have not asked for the money," said Li Er, "but I ought to give it to you.''

"No, tomorrow I'll go with you to take care of you on the road... You need someone...''

"Say no more about it," Li Er interrupted. "We'll discuss it later.''

He turned to Yin Xi. "Do you think my book is worth the money I owe him?''

"Why certainly!'' said Yin Xi. "Your book cannot be measured in terms of money; it's invaluable! It's worth much, much more than whatever you may owe him for services.''

"Then give him the amount I owe him and keep the rest with you if there is any left.''

Yin Xi went out, leaving Xu Jia alone in the room with Li Er. He dared not look Li Er in the face; he was feeling vaguely guilty.

"During the three days you were asleep,'' he mumbled, "I seemed to be possessed by ghosts; or else Heaven was testing me to see how sincere I was in 'keeping the heart empty and the mind tranquil' ...''

"Heaven sent a pretty young angel with rouged lips and white teeth to test your...''

"You know all about it?'' Xu Jia was surprised.

"Yes, I do,'' Li Er said with a nod.

Xu Jia had heard rumours that his master had the magical

powers of an immortal, capable of telling about the past and predicting the future. He began to wonder if the girl was his master's magic creation to use as a foil to test his sincerity by bringing them together.

He went down on his knees and began to plead:

"You are correct when you say 'lust for love is a ghost'. Over all these years I have benefitted from your instructions and teachings, but I have failed to resist the lure of the ghost," he confessed. "I am awfully sorry about that and I am determined to correct myself. I will abide by the doctrines of Tao and be your disciple for the rest of my life. Please let me go with you tomorrow."

"Please get up and listen to me," said Li Er. "I have indeed said 'lust for love is a ghost' and I have also said that not everyone can drive the ghost out of him and become a sage. It's no sin unless you indulge in the lust. By the same token, it does not mean he who is not a sage is a ghost. Between the sage and the ghost there are millions of ordinary people and it is these ordinary people who sustain the world. Stay behind and establish your family here. Take things as they come and you will have your share of luck."

Xu Jia wanted to continue his plea, but Li Er went on: "We have fixed it all up with Yin Xi, commander of the Pass. We cannot break out agreement with him, you know."

The more understanding his master was, the more guilty he felt. "But who will drive for you tomorrow?"

"The road through the Qinling Mountains is so narrow and bumpy, I'm not even planning to use carriage. I will ride the ox, and travel light."

"But who will take care of your food and lodging? What if you fall ill?"

"Old as I am," said Li Er, "I am still in fairly good shape. I should be able to take care of myself. Besides, aren't you turning fifty yourself? A man at fifty is an old man. I cannot have an old man looking after another old man."

Sensitive to the two words "old man", Xu Jia said hastily, "I still have a couple of years to go before I become an old man."

"A couple of years is but the wink of an eye," said Li Er. "When I need help, I'll find a younger person to look after me."

With that Li Er put an end to the argument.

The road outside the west gate of the Hangu Pass was lined with people to see him off.

"It seems we cannot keep you from going," Yin Xi said affectionately, holding his hand. "If you don't wish to go back to Luoyang, you probably want to find a quiet place where you can read for the rest of your life. I think this is the very place for that purpose. There is no need for you to go any further."

"For that purpose I cannot find a better place," agreed Li Er. "With you taking care of me, life will be easy and comfortable here. But when I set out from Luoyang I had already put the State of Qin on my itinerary. Qin covers a large area from the Drifting Sand to Mount Kunwu where the ancient Yellow Emperor defeated Chiyou. I have never been there. When I was working in the Archives, I did not have the time to travel. Since I now have the time and I am in good health, why should I give up half way?

"The trip between the Drifting Sand and the Ruoshui River is risky. The sand drifts about with the winds and the river trickles through the sand in a tiny stream. The endless Gobi desert is a barren waste with no plants and no trace of man whatsoever. Many people have learned of this place through hearsay but few have set foot on it. If I can go there and see it for myself, it will be a fascinating experience."

"I'm already inspired by your picturesque description," said Yin Xi. "If I were not tied down here by my defence duties, I would like to go with you myself. Anyway, wherever you go, you will return here and I expect you to drop in on me on your way back."

"Thank you for your kind invitation," said Li Er, "but I'll see how things go and leave it to luck."

"See how things go and leave it to luck" — a remark that settled everything. What else could Yin Xi say?

Xu Jia had seen that the ox was rested and well fed for the trip. He stood by the ox, waiting. More than once, Yin Xi had offered to provide a carriage and a servant, but Li Er would not hear of it. The ox, his long-time companion, was good enough to carry him around. He took the reins from Xu Jia who helped him mount. "Good-byes" mingled with "take cares" were exchanged all round, and he was on his way.

The gate of the Pass was thrown wide open to a road leading westward into the far distance. The Yellow River, not far to the north, was within hearing as its torrents thundered down the valley.

Li Er rode on and on until he became a vague, receding patch of gray in the dark green mountains.

Yin Xi stood by the gate, staring into the distance...

This free and unrestrained man from the south, though born with a head of white hair, never seems to get old — in his seventies he is still strong and full of life.

Will he get lost in the Drifting Sand?

Will he settle in Qin, there to get old and die by the Yellow River?

Will he return to his hometown in Chu?

No matter where he goes, no matter what happens to him, he has left his spirit behind at the Pass. His spirit will become one with the trees and rocks. As the Pass is ageless, his spirit will never die.

图书在版编目(CIP)数据

老子: 英文/ 杨书案著; 刘士聪译. – 北京: 中国文学出版社, 1997.1

ISBN 7－5071－0352－8

I. 老... II. ① 杨... ② 刘... III. 传记小说: 长篇小说 – 中国 – 当代 – 英文 IV. I247.53

中国版本图书馆 CIP 数据核字(96) 第 04692 号

老 子

杨书案

熊猫丛书

*

中国文学出版社出版

(中国北京百万庄路 24 号)

中国国际图书贸易总公司发行

(中国北京车公庄西路 35 号)

北京邮政信箱第 399 号　　邮政编码 100044

1997年 第 1 版(英)

ISBN 7－5071－0352－8

03800

10－E－3143 P